Sustaining budget deficits in open economies

The US economy has in recent years been characterized by growing budget and current account deficits, and by increasing amounts of foreign capital inflows. For the UK, too, the budget deficit remains a central weakness in the economy.

With these problems in mind, the author presents a consistent economic framework for analysing the effects and implications of large bond-financed deficits. He uses an open economy–rational expectations model to explore the extent to which government can simply 'roll over' debt by issuing more bonds without any help from the monetary authority. He examines the impact of foreign capital on the sustainability of domestic budget deficits, the behaviour of exchange rates, and the possible effects of fiscal and monetary policies. This model is examined in the context of the major economic orthodoxies and their competing stances, and also of American monetary history from Truman to Reagan, including the crash of 1987.

Dealing with both domestic and foreign sectors, the book is an important contribution to the understanding of a major problem in macroeconomics.

Farrokh K. Langdana is Assistant Professor in the Department of Economics/Finance at the Graduate School of Management, Rutgers University, New Jersey.

Sustaining budget deficits in open economies

Farrokh K. Langdana

Routledge
London and New York

First published 1990 by Routledge
11 New Fetter Lane, London EC4P 4EE

Simultaneously published in the USA and Canada by Routledge
a division of Routledge, Chapman and Hall, Inc.
29 West 35th Street, New York, NY 10001

Typeset by Leaper & Gard Ltd, Bristol, England
Printed in Great Britain

British Library Cataloguing in Publication Data

Langdana, Farrokh K. *1958–*
Sustaining budget deficits in open economies.
1. United States. Deficits
I. Title
339.5′23′0973

ISBN 0–415–03735–2

Library of Congress Cataloging in Publication Data
Langdana, Farrokh K.
Sustaining budget deficits in open economies / Farrokh K. Langdana.
p. cm.
Bibliography: p.
ISBN 0–415–03735–2
1. Budget deficits–United States. 2. Balance of trade–United States. 3. Fiscal policy–United States. 4. Government securities–United States. 5. United States–Economic conditions–1981–
I. Title
HJ2052.L36 1989 89–6296
339.5′23′0973–dc20 CIP

To
Zarrin and Keki
and
Mary and Christopher

Any bonds today?
Bonds of Freedom, that's what I'm selling,
Any bonds today?
Scrape up the most you can, here comes
the freedom man,
Asking you to buy a share of freedom today.

The words and music were a gift from Irving Berlin to Treasury Secretary Henry J. Morgenthau. The song was later used as the Official Theme Song of the National Defense Savings Program.

Contents

Preface

This is not a book portending dire apocalyptical happenings in the world economy; nor is it a 'How to Make it Through the Next Great Depression' kind of book. It is, on the other hand, a book that provides the reader with an economically consistent framework within which the cause and effects of budget deficits and trade deficits can be understood. Macroeconomics today is in a state of flux, with economists clinging doggedly to two or three major schools of thought. This, unfortunately, has been a major source of confusion for policy makers, the general public, and, of course, the news media, who find themselves flitting between these different schools of thought instead of analysing policies within a particular framework.

Therefore, in this book I have attempted to provide the reader with brief intuitive reviews of these different economic frameworks, as well as an analysis of the history of the US budget and trade deficits from the Truman to the Reagan administrations. Whenever I have come across analyses of certain fiscal and monetary policies that are still hotly debated, I have attempted to include and discuss all the conflicting arguments.

My main goal in writing this book is to provide a framework within which questions pertaining to the sustainability of the twin deficits, the behaviour of exchange rates, and the possible effects of fiscal and monetary policies can be competently analysed. I have, however, refrained from making any economic forecasts.

Economic forecasts extending over, say, three months, are meaningful only when all the fiscal and monetary policies remain unchanged. When these policies change, as they frequently do, individuals use their past experience and respond to these actual or anticipated changes in a manner that might actually negate the purpose of these policy changes!

This is what separates macroeconomics from engineering. In the former, policy experiments are performed within an environment of rational agents with expectations, and certain specific policies that might have been successful in the past might fail dismally when repeated a few years down the road. On the other hand, in civil engineering for example, a dam successfully built with inanimate concrete and steel under conditions *XYZ* would certainly be successful when replicated under the same conditions in the future.

It is for this reason that I feel that the incorporation of individuals' expectations is indispensable to the understanding, and analysis, of the behaviour of prices, interest rates, exchange rates, output, and the budget and trade deficits. Hence, considerable attention has been paid to the concept of rational expectations.

Acknowledgements

In writing this book, I have benefited from the useful comments and suggestions of a large number of people. To begin with, I am grateful to the faculty of the Virginia Polytechnic Institute and State University, where the bulk of my research (chapters 11–13) was done. I am especially grateful to my chairmen, Allan Mandelstamm and Douglas McTaggart, and to Daniel Orr, Barbara Craig, and Richard Cothren. I also received a huge amount of technical and strategic advice from Jaques Cremer, Cathy Eckel, Jim Friedman, Mark Lowenstein, Herve Moulin, Nilanjan Sen, Gary Shelley, Bill Smith, Bart Toub, Garcia Wills, and James Wilson.

I would also like to thank Warren Weber (Federal Reserve Bank of Minneapolis), Michael Cox (Federal Reserve Bank of Dallas), and of course Douglas McTaggart (Virginia Tech), as it is largely because of them that I decided to become a 'macro-type'.

My colleagues at the Graduate School of Management at Rutgers University have been extremely helpful. I am especially grateful to Dean David Blake, Ivan Brick, my chairman Michael Crew, Larry Fisher, Michael Frierman, Jack Lucken, Giles Mellon, the late George Morrison, Charles Upton, and David Whitcomb. I am also thankful to Farok Contractor, for first suggesting that I write a book, and to the Research Resources Committee at Rutgerts–GSM for its financial assistance.

I am also in debt to the participants of the meetings of the Southern, Eastern, and Western Economics Association in Washington DC, Boston, and Los Angeles, respectively, as well as to the participants of the Economics/Finance workshop at Rutgers, for their comments.

Richard Burdekin has been a tremendous help in my research, particularly in the extension of case I incorporating the real rate, and for that I am grateful. Thanks also go to Mark Desautels of the Congressional Budget Office for permission to use data and publications such as the *Economic Outlook* and the *Economic Update.*

An important debt is to Mary Langdana, whose questioning mind and sound economic intuition have helped me achieve my objective of writing a book that would present a consistent and useful economic framework incorporating some of the newer, and more technical, macroeconomic concepts.

Several generations of undergraduate and graduate students have provided me with their insights, opinions, and comments, and these acknowledgements would be seriously incomplete if I did not thank them.

My tireless editor, Andrew Lockett of Routledge, has provided me with suggestions and solutions that have contributed tremendously to the final format of this book, and I thank him for them.

I am also very grateful to Cietta George for her valuable typing, formatting, and printing assistance.

Chapter one

Introduction

The stock-market crash of October 1987, coupled with the change in the policy regime in the United States, has caused a wave of renewed and vigorous attention to be devoted to its large budget and current account deficits. Prognostications of the sustainability of these deficits range from the mildly gloomy to the extremely calamitous, with some policy makers firmly believing in the inevitability of a tax increase.

This book, therefore, attempts to dispel some of this gloom by providing a consistent framework for the analysis of the issue of the sustainability of bond-financed deficits. The economy under consideration is one characterized by the large current account deficit and capital inflows of the kind presently experienced by the United States. Sustainability is viewed in the context of the fiscal authority (Treasury/Congress) to incur a continually increasing stream of deficits by issuing new debt to retire the principal plus interest on that of the previous period. A 'sustainable' deficit-financing policy is defined as one in which an upper limit of debt financing, characterized by adverse effects on the price level, nominal exchange rates, and real wealth, is not attained, and the possibility of future unanticipated monetization to wipe out the debt in real terms is non-existent.

The issues involved

The present state of the US economy is one of burgeoning domestic and current account deficits, increasing amounts of foreign capital inflows, and an exchange rate that has only recently come off its 1985 record-high. This scenario makes the sustainability issue timely and pertinent. The time plots of domestic and current account deficits, nominal exchange rates and interest rates, and the price level for the period 1974–87 are presented in later chapters and towards the end of the book.

The rapidly growing net inflow of capital from abroad, mirroring the extraordinary deterioration of the US current account balance, has played a significant role in equilibrating overall savings and investments in the United States. Partly responsible for this inflow are the unprecedented large and persistent domestic budget deficits during the 1980s. The current size of the domestic budget deficit is of the order of $149 billion, or about 3.4 per cent of the gross national product (GNP). The 1986 record-high of 5.4 per cent of the GNP was exceeded only in the Second World War when the deficit was as large as 28 per cent of GNP. This situation has raised a host of issues, some of which are:

1. Can the government continue on a path of large fiscal deficits without accommodation from the monetary authority, or, how long can the government 'roll over' its debt by issuing more bonds and without any help from the monetary authority?
2. How does the inflow of capital affect the sustainability of domestic budget deficits, or, how is the 'rolling over' policy affected in a milieu of large capital inflows?
3. How should fiscal and monetary policy be conducted in the above situation, and what are the effects of these policies on key macroeconomic variables such as the price level, nominal and real interest rates and exchange rates, and the individual's real wealth holdings?
4. And, most importantly, is there an *upper limit* on the amount of debt that the government can 'roll over' by issuing new debt? In other words, how sustainable is the US domestic budget deficit in the presence of capital inflows and under the current policies of rolling over a substantial portion of the existing debt by issuing new government bonds?

General overview

Before discussing these issues of sustainability, it is imperative that we have a good understanding of how these deficits are measured, how they came to assume such tremendous proportions lately, and why the current budget deficits are quite different in magnitude *and nature* from those experienced in the past. This is accomplished in chapter 2 where we will learn how to interpret the various budget deficit figures that appear with increasing frequency in a wide variety of publications. Chapter 3 is a review chapter which begins with a brief discussion of the phenomenon of business cycles, and ends with a description of the stabilization policies enacted by policy makers in different regimes. This chapter includes a review of the classical and Keynesian frameworks which are essential for a full understanding of the macroeconomic events since 1980.

Chapter 4 presents an overview of the specific fiscal and monetary stabilization policies with which past administrations, from Truman to Reagan, have attempted (with varying degrees of success) to 'fine-tune' the economy by targeting domestic output, employment, and inflation rates.

We will then study why these stabilization policies mysteriously broke down in the late 1970s, resulting in the phenomenon of 'stagflation' and the advent of the rational expectations approach to economic theory and policy making. This is done in chapter 5. Chapter 6 is devoted to the understanding of the concept of rational expectations and to dispelling some myths commonly associated with it.

I then introduce the so-called 'supply-side revolution' by explaining how macroeconomic events of the late 1970s led to a policy emphasis on the supply side. A discussion and review of supply-side economics as well as the role and size of efficient government is presented in chapter 7.

This is followed by an evaluation of 'Reaganomics' in chapter 8. Its goals are compared with its economic record. We will try and determine if it was truly an economic revolution that caused an unprecedented peacetime recovery in the United States, or if it was an 'incomplete revolution' that has left the country saddled with these immense budget and trade deficits that, according to some, only spell disaster for the future? Furthermore, if it is not economically sound, as some of its critics claim, then why has it (the tax cut in particular) been mimicked so widely in the industrialized countries? A summary of the accomplishments and/or the failures of Reaganomics from some of its staunchest supporters and its harshest critics is also presented in chapter 8.

The critics of Reaganomics contend that the economic recovery of the 1980s can be explained perfectly well within a standard Keynesian framework. According to them, there was no 'supply-side revolution', but a plain and simple Keynesian fiscal expansion stimulated by increased government spending. These views are presented and evaluated in chapter 9.

Chapter 10 provides an overview of the extremely important and unique link between domestic budget deficits and trade deficits. This crucial macroeconomic identity is still widely misunderstood and not nearly emphasized enough in macroeconomic policy making. We will understand why domestic macropolicies *cannot* be made without explicitly considering the foreign sector.

Domestic policies and international trade policies are *not* mutually exclusive – more so now than ever before – and it is a common (and at times, convenient) mistake for policy makers to consider only part of the equation to satisfy a certain specific segment of their electorate.

This chapter also includes a brief history of the huge capital inflows experienced by the United States and the effects of these inflows on domestic interest rates.

The theoretical models for cases I and II are presented in chapter 12. In case I, domestic money creation is held fixed and any increases in government expenditures are financed by issuing government bonds. The Federal Reserve adopted a 'tight money' policy in the early 1980s and the results obtained in this case closely resemble the behaviour of prices, interest rates, and exchange rates during that period. Furthermore, an extension of this case incorporating the long-term real interest rate effects on the output supply has been included here, too. It turns out that, in the long term, bond-financed deficits might indeed be sustainable under certain restrictive circumstances, namely the relationship of the real interest rate and wealth elasticities of output relative to certain threshold values.

Case II closely resembles post-1983 Federal Reserve policy. Here domestic money creation is endogenous (unlike case I) with government debt being monetized in every time period, and bond-financed deficits are found to be 'strongly non-sustainable', with 'strong non-sustainability' defined in chapter 11. A description of the solution technique is presented in chapter 12.

The results of case I are interpreted in chapter 13 along with those incorporating the long-run real interest rate effects on output supply.

We will discuss in chapter 14 the effects and economics of central bank intervention (to manipulate the strength of the dollar) on the sustainability of the deficits. The G-5 and G-7 accords of policy co-ordination between the major industrialized countries to 'manage' the relative strengths of their currencies is also included here.

There is a strong and growing sentiment in the United States at present that argues against policy co-ordination of the kind discussed above. In fact, some leading economists argue that the bickering among the G-7 members was partly responsible for the crash on 19 October 1987 (which will be discussed in detail in chapter 16). In this chapter I present some explanations for the failure of policy co-ordination and argue that international exchange rate agreements are, at best, successful only in the short term.

The results for the sustainability of bond-financed deficits for case II, in the context of current US fiscal and monetary policy, are analysed in chapter 15.

Finally, economics aside, the large and growing amount of government debt outstanding has exerted a tremendous psychological toll on the market-place. The October 1987 crash is a case in point, with analysts immediately pointing to the large domestic and current account deficits as the primary culprits. While it is extremely improbable that the crash will eventually manifest itself in the form of a full-fledged depression reminiscent of the 1930s, there is a certain underlying wariness that the storm is not really over. Most of this uneasiness stems from the absence of a unified and consistent framework within which the affects of the twin deficits can be analysed. Ignorance breeds fear, and fear in turn breeds drastic fiscal and monetary policy changes.

It is precisely these changes that I hope to avert by providing the reader with an economically consistent framework for discussing policy implications in an environment characterized by the large twin deficits.

I have attempted to write this book on essentially two parallel and mutually independent planes of economic interest. One plane caters for individuals with a basic level of economic knowledge and stresses the general economic intuition underlying all my results, constantly accompanied by brief summaries and reviews of the relevant economic theories in use. The other plane, constituting the research chapters 11, 12, and 13, is more technical in nature and caters primarily for the research economist – the kind that has a morbid interest in linear stochastic difference equations (the kind that I plead guilty to being).

On either plane, I hope you enjoy this book.

Chapter two

Interpreting budget deficits

The unprecedented US budget deficits have drawn sufficient attention to the issue of the ability of the government to finance these deficits continuously by borrowing ever-increasing amounts from domestic and foreign residents by issuing government bonds. What might be particularly worrisome is that, since 1977, the US government has been issuing debt (borrowing) in the current time period to pay back the principal and interest due on the debt it issued in previous periods. In other words, it has been simply 'rolling over' increasingly large chunks of government bonds. Adding to this concern is the belief intrinsic to most individuals that there is something inherently wrong with deficits and that, eventually, they would have to be reduced to zero.

Before we attempt to dispel some of the myths and remove some of the confusion, let us start with a discussion of the measures of the budget deficit and the correct interpretation of these measures.

Measuring deficits: some definitions

The budget deficit is the amount by which the government's expenditures exceed its receipts during some specified time period, usually one year. The national debt, also called the public debt, is the total value of the government's indebtedness which has resulted from previous deficits. In 1987, the budget deficit was of the order of \$221 billion and the national debt was a staggering \$2.1 trillion (1×10^{12}).

If G denotes all the government purchases of goods and services, Tr the transfer payments, for example unemployment compensation and social security benefits, and T the tax revenues, then the deficit is

$$\text{deficit} = G + Tr - T$$

This deficit has to be financed either by borrowing from domestic and foreign residents (selling bonds) or by monetization, both of which we will discuss later.

The most important sources of tax revenue for the government are income taxes, corporate taxes, and payroll taxes. As all these tax revenues are functions of the national income, they consequently decrease when GNP falls, or when the economy goes into recession. On the other hand, transfer payments such as unemployment benefits increase in recessions, thereby causing budget deficits to rise in periods of economic sluggishness, even in the absence of any change in fiscal policy. Because of this independence of the magnitude of the deficit to changes in policy, many economists feel that less attention should be paid to the actual deficit and more to what is known as the high-employment or the standardized-employment deficit (also full-employment deficit, structural deficit). This is a hypothetical construct that replaces both the actual government spending and tax revenues in the actual budget by estimates of what government spending and tax revenues *would be*, given current tax rates and spending provisions, if the economy were operating at full employment. A 6 per cent unemployment rate is assumed to be the full-employment mark.[1]

The high-employment deficit, therefore, is unaffected by the state of the economy, since it ignores the actual expenditures and tax revenues and instead focuses on what they would be at full employment. This measure of deficit changes only when specific policies change, and for this reason economists believe that it is a better indicator of fiscal policy than the actual deficit, as the aggregate business cycle effects have now been sifted out.[2]

This definition of the high-employment, or standardized-employment, deficit enables us to understand why the Reagan deficits are different from the preceding ones not only in magnitude, but also in nature as table 2.1 and figure 2.1 show.

We can now understand just how important the distinction between the actual deficits and the high-employment deficits has been in recent years. In 1980 through 1982, the high-employment deficits were much smaller relative to the actual budget deficits. However, since 1983 a very different trend has emerged in the measures of the full-employment deficits – they grow progressively larger, and with the economy hovering at around full employment for 1986 and 1987, they are of the order of $180–200 billion.[3]

In other words, changes in high-employment deficits, which are endemic to a particular administration's fiscal policies, have assumed dramatic and unprecedented proportions for most of the

Table 2.1 High employment deficits

Fiscal year	*Official deficit ($ billion)*	*Adjustment to high employment (A)*	*High-employment deficit*
1980	−60	+9	−51
1981	−58	+11	−47
1982	−111	+60	−51
1983	−195	+89	−106
1984	−175	+44	−131
1985	−212	+40	−172
1986	−221	+34	−187
1987	−149	+32	−117

Source: Congressional Budget Office *Outlook*, February 1988

Reagan administration. What caused these deficits? What are the effects? Will the country always be in the shadow of the Reagan deficit legacy? Before proceeding with these rather disturbing issues, let us put the measurement and the interpretation of the deficits in perspective by studying the inflation-adjusted deficit.

The inflation-adjusted deficit is the actual deficit adjusted for the inflation component of the interest payments. When the US government (or any borrower for that matter) pays interest on the government bonds outstanding in an inflationary environment, more dollars must be returned to the lender in recognition of the fact that inflation has eroded the purchasing power of the currency. These interest payments, made to restore the lenders' purchasing power, exaggerate interest expenses and distort the government expenditure figures. To sift out this additional government expenditure due to inflation, we subtract the inflation premium from the interest paid on the national debt, thereby counting only the real interest payments, a technique which provides us with a more accurate measure of the deficits.

Table 2.2 shows that, in recent years, reported (actual) budget deficits would have been reduced significantly (by $45 billion, according to some estimates) by making the inflation adjustment to the interest payments. However the trend of sharply increasing deficits post 1982 manifests itself again, indicating once more that even after adjusting for inflation, the Reagan deficits are in a class of their own.

Putting our two major deficit-measuring adjustments together, we get some interesting results. From table 2.3 we can see that it was *only since* 1983 that large and growing high-employment inflation-adjusted deficits have been experienced! The years 1980–

Figure 2.1 The standardized employment deficit

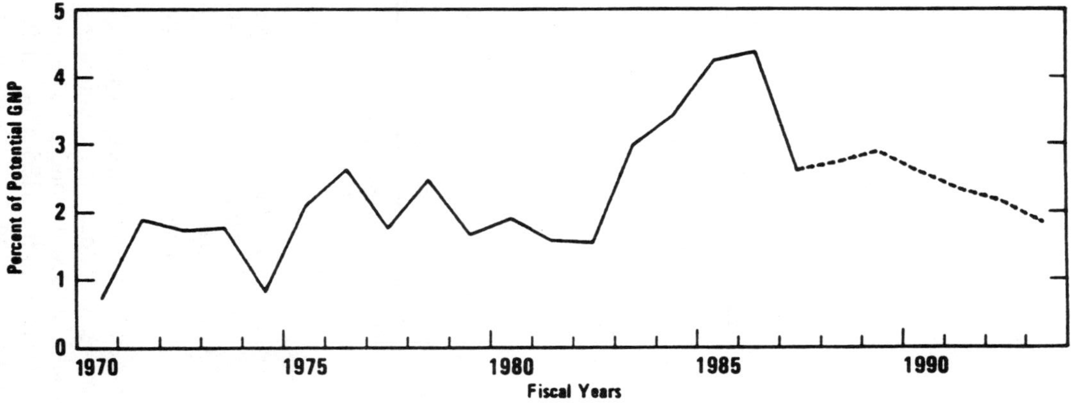

Sources: Congressional Budget Office; Department of Commerce, Bureau of Economic Analysis
Note: This measure of the deficit substantially overstates the degree of restrictiveness in fiscal year 1987 and understates the restraint between fiscal years 1987 and 1989.

Table 2.2 Inflation adjusted deficits

Fiscal year	*Official deficit* (*$ billion*)	*Inflation adjustment for interest expense (B)*	*Inflation-adjusted deficit*
1980	−60	+44	−12
1981	−58	+55	−3
1982	−111	+38	−73
1983	−195	+34	−161
1984	−175	+54	−121
1985	−212	+56	−156
1986	−221	+51	−170
1987	−149	+44	−105

Source: Congressional Budget Office *Outlook*, February 1988, and 1988 Annual Report

Table 2.3 High employment and inflation adjusted deficits

Fiscal year	*(1) Official deficit ($ billion)*	*(2) (A)**	*(3) (B)**	*(4) Adjusted deficit (−) or surplus (+)*
1980	−60	+9	+48	−3
1981	−58	+11	+55	+8
1982	−111	+60	+38	−13
1983	−195	+89	+34	−72
1984	−175	+44	+54	−77
1985	−212	+40	+56	−116
1986	−221	+34	+51	−136
1987	−149	+32	+44	−73

Source: Congressional Budget Office *Outlook*, February 1988
Notes: *Column (A) from table 2.1; column (B) from table 2.2.

2 were not years in which the federal government incurred comparably large budget deficits in spite of the prevailing recession, and 1981 was actually a year in which the budget balance, adjusted for inflation and high employment, was in surplus.

It should be noted here that it does not mean that the negative values in column (4) are values for the amounts of additional tax revenues that would balance the budget. The numbers only mean that in 1984, for instance, of the $175 billion deficit in column (1), about $44 billion was attributed to the fact that the economy was operating at a level of unemployment well above the full-employment benchmark of 6 per cent, and about $54 billion was an accounting adjustment for inflation.

The adjusted deficit values, therefore, assist us in putting the deficits in perspective and enable us to attribute changes in deficits to specific policy regimes.

Another important form of measurement of the budget deficit is the primary deficit. The total budget deficit can be divided into two components: the primary or non-interest deficit, and the interest payments on the public debt, that is

total deficit = primary deficit + interest payments

The primary deficit therefore represents all government outlays, except interest payments, less all government revenue. This definition will have huge significance when we discuss the role of the interest payments on outstanding government bonds. The overall budget might be in deficit *even* if the primary deficit is in surplus (or when we have a primary surplus). This is because in every time period the government makes a significant amount of interest payments on past debt. After mandatory spending, interest payments constitute the second largest chunk of US government expenditures. Thus we can see that the overall budget will be in deficit unless the interest payments on the existing debt are more than matched by a primary surplus.[4] According to Dornbusch and Fischer, this forms the core of the mechanics of deficit financing.[5] They write: 'If there is a primary deficit in the budget, then the total budget deficit will keep growing as the debt grows because of the deficit, and interest payments rise because the debt is growing.'

The analogy to the individual runs along the same lines. If individual A spends more than he or she earns, borrowing to make up the difference, then this individual will need to borrow more and more each year just to make the interest payments on the additional debt. We will discuss the Dornbusch model of sustainability in greater detail in chapter 11.

Now that we have a good understanding of how deficits are measured and how they are to be interpreted, let us examine how and why these deficits were incurred in the first place. What are the fiscal and monetary implications of deficits? Are deficits deliberately caused, or are they gross errors of oversight on the part of successive administrations? And why are the current US deficits different in magnitude and nature from their predecessors? These questions will be answered in the following chapters.

Chapter three

Stabilization policies

Business cycles

Throughout the ages, national economies have experienced repeated fluctuations about trend in output, employment, prices, and interest rates, known as business cycles. Many explanations have been offered for these fluctuations in economic activity. They range from sudden supply-side disturbances, or shocks, caused by changes in technology or adverse weather conditions, to unanticipated changes in the money supply.

Early business cycle theories assumed that the fluctuations in output and prices about trend were caused by the internal dynamics of a market economy. Sustained economic growth was thought to place severe strains upon the economy. For example, after a prolonged economic recovery, the continually increasing aggregate demand might cause wages and input costs to rise faster than selling prices. This, according to the early theories, would lead to a cutback in business investment and employment as firms, particularly those that had overinvested earlier, started to experience shrinking profits. This link between real and nominal variables, coming in the wake of a sustained period of recovery, was thought to cause recessions.

During the era of the gold standard and fixed exchange rates, it was widely believed that business cycles were transmitted across national boundaries by detrimental fiscal and monetary policies of countries that were trading partners. Most of the early theories were in the gold standard era, and hence financial factors such as bank panics, shortages of liquidity, and fluctuations in interest rates were thought to be primarily responsible for economic downturns.

While economists are by no means unanimous in their analyses of business cycles, the trend today is towards a demand-side money-induced explanation of these cycles in economic activity.[1]

Today, business cycles are defined quite technically in terms of economic time series. Movements about trend in the gross national product of any country can be represented quite easily by a low-order stochastic difference equation.[2] It should be noted that these movements in output do not exhibit uniformity of either period or amplitude. Business cycles could range from a duration of a few months to over a decade.

While fluctuations in economic activity are not periodic in nature, there are, however, fairly *well-defined co-movements* among time series of different macroeconomic variables. A detailed and extensive study of a variety of economic time series for the US inter-war period was done by Mitchell (1951) and for earlier British series by Gayer *et al.* (1953).[3]

Some of the principal co-movements are the following:[4]

1. Output movements across generally classified sectors of the economy are unidirectional. In other words, the rates of growth of output in different sectors roughly increase and decrease together, thus resulting in the familiar stylized peaks and troughs of economic activity found in most economics textbooks. In Mitchell's terminology these rates of growth are said to exhibit high conformity, while today they are said to have high coherence.
2. Time series of the production of producer and consumer durables exhibit much greater amplitude than those of the production of non-durables. This is not surprising because durables constitute consumer savings, and since consumption is a function of permanent income, fluctuations in income over business cycles should therefore be reflected by fluctuations in savings.
3. Prices are procyclical, or, the rate of growth of prices increases with that of GNP, and vice versa.
4. Monetary aggregates and velocity measures are procyclical too.
5. Agricultural cycles exhibit very low conformity with that of GNP.
6. International trade does not display any strong co-movement with that of GNP.

Points 3–6 have had a very strong impact on the direction of macroeconomic research over the last two decades. With prices and money being procyclic, and with international trade and agriculture not conforming (or conforming very weakly) to changes in GNP, it became evident that there was a monetary explanation for business cycles. Gone was the emphasis on the international transmission of business cycles and the effects of the agricultural cycles on economic activity. The cyclical fluctuations in economic activity were accepted as inspired by the demand side and not the supply side.

In perhaps some of the most widely cited macroeconomic papers in the US since 1973, Robert E. Lucas in 'Some international evidence of output–inflation trade-offs' and 'Understanding business cycles' describes how hedging behaviour on the part of individuals who are unable to differentiate between relative and general price changes due to imperfect information results in the co-movements of prices and output.[5]

For our purposes here, it suffices to say that increases or decreases in GNP from the long-run trend rate of growth are motivated by aggregate demand-side effects stemming from fiscal and monetary policies. Moreover, from Mitchell's findings, we know that the behaviour of the aggregate time series described above is not confined to any particular country or to any point in time. In Lucas's words, 'with respect to the qualitative behavior of co-movements among series, *business cycles are alike*'.[6] This very important conclusion suggests the possibility of one unified explanation for business cycles, be they in the UK or the US or in any other capitalist economy.

Now that we have some understanding of business cycles, and the fact that demand-side policies are responsible for the fluctuations in output and prices, let us see what exactly these demand-side policies are. How do these policies affect budget deficits? How exactly were these policies implemented by past administrations and with what degree of success?

Our next task is to study these demand-side stabilization policies.

What are stabilization policies?

One of the few things that macroeconomists can be made to agree upon is what an ideal macroeconomic performance would look like. First, a zero unemployment rate (not including voluntary unemployment such as normal labour turnover) would be ideal. In this case the unemployment rate would coincide with the 'natural' unemployment rate. This would imply that output would be ideally and continuously maintained at this full-employment equilibrium value. Second, an inflation rate of zero, or in any case, some low steady-state rate, would be ideal too. The nominal or market rate of interest would then be equal to the real rate.

Stating these goals in slightly more realistic terms, the objectives can be explained in terms of minimizing the deviations of: (i) unemployment from its natural rate, (ii) output from its full-employment rate, (iii) inflation from a zero inflation rate, and (iv) market interest rates from real interest rates.[7]

The objective of macroeconomic policy, then, is to *minimize the variability* of unemployment and output about their natural rates, and inflation about some low, possibly zero, value. Policies that do so are called stabilization policies, since they 'stabilize', or try and dampen out, the fluctuations of prices, output, and employment over the business cycle, as shown in figure 3.1.

In this book, 'stabilization policies' will be used interchangeably with 'activist' or 'discretionary' fiscal and monetary policies.

Stabilization in classical and Keynesian frameworks: a review

The classical framework

In the pre-Keynesian or classical era, the business cycle was seen as entirely uncontrollable. Deviations of actual output and employ-

Figure 3.1

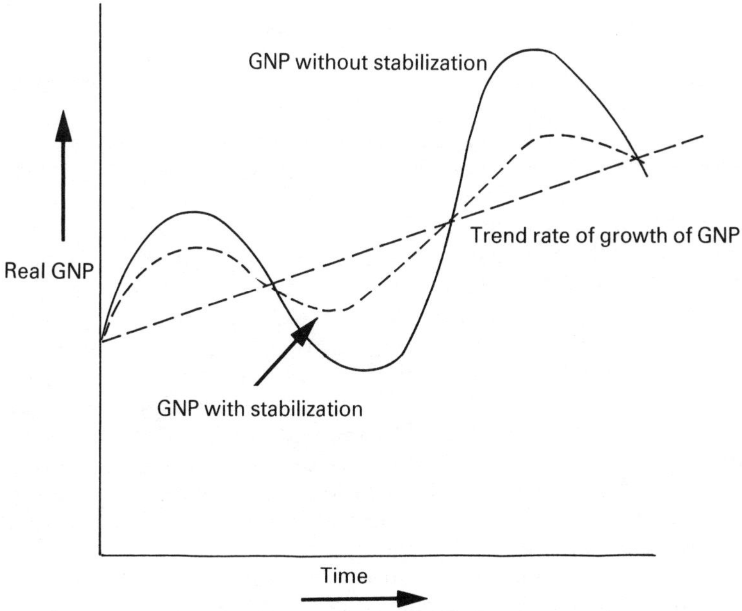

ment from their natural steady-state values were viewed as exogenous phenomena.[8] There were no policy implications for the stimulation of economies towards recovery, and involuntary unemployment was assumed not to exist. There was no specific policy role for the governing body to manipulate domestic prices and interest rates and reduce the gap between the actual and the full-employment output, usually referred to as the GNP gap.

From the diagram of the aggregate demand–aggregate supply (AD/AS) sector of a standard textbook classical economy (figure 3.2), we can see why the classical economists felt that output and hence unemployment were neutral with respect to stabilization policies. This economy is characterized by a vertical classical aggregate supply curve (which stems from the classical nominal wage–price flexibility assumption) and initial equilibrium price and output levels of p_0 and y_0, respectively. Let the output corresponding to full employment (6 per cent unemployment) be y_f in figure 3.2(b). The actual current output in this economy, y_0, corresponds to a higher unemployment rate of 10 per cent. Is there any role for discretionary fiscal and monetary policies to enable the economy to attain the output corresponding to y_f? The answer is that there is none, for the following reasons.

To close this GNP gap ($y_f - y_0$), both the fiscal and monetary policies would have to be stimulative. A stimulative fiscal policy is one that constitutes either an increase in government spending or a cut in taxes, or some combination of both. In any case, any of these three options would tend to shift the aggregate demand curve to the right, from AD_0 to AD_S. This stands to reason, as the aggregate demand is derived by synthesizing the goods and the asset, or money, markets. The demand for goods in the goods market is composed of consumption demand, investment demand, foreign demand, and government demand. As this last component increases with increased government spending due to the enactment of a stimulative fiscal policy, the aggregate demand increases too, and hence AD_0 shifts to the right to AD_S.

What does this policy-induced shift in the aggregate demand do to the equilibrium output? Nothing. As the aggregate demand shifts to AD_S, the new equilibrium output *remains* at y_0 and all we get is a higher price level, p_1. Discretionary fiscal policy, therefore, has *no real effect*, only a nominal one in terms of increased inflation. A cut in taxes would produce almost the same result, depending on whether the tax cut was in the form of a lump-sum tax or a marginal tax rate change.

Would discretionary monetary policy have the same result of output neutrality? Once again, in this economy under consider-

Figure 3.2

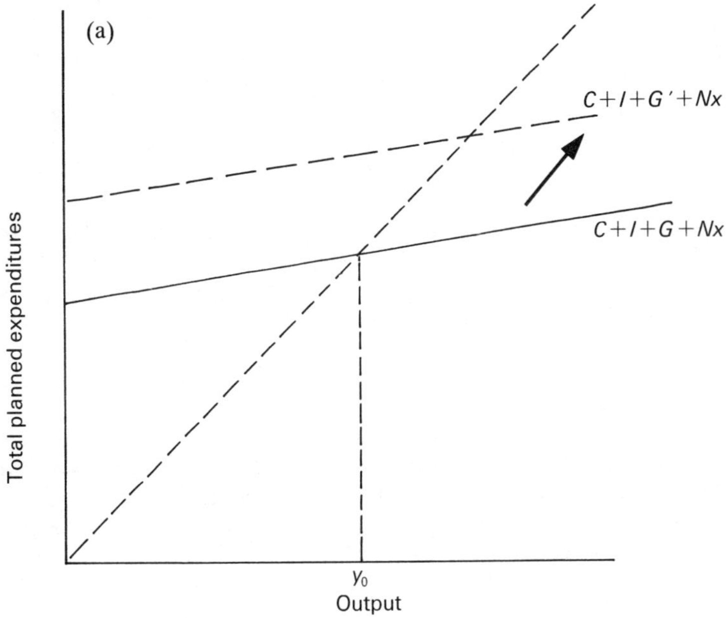

(a)
C+I+G′+Nx
C+I+G+Nx
Total planned expenditures
y0
Output

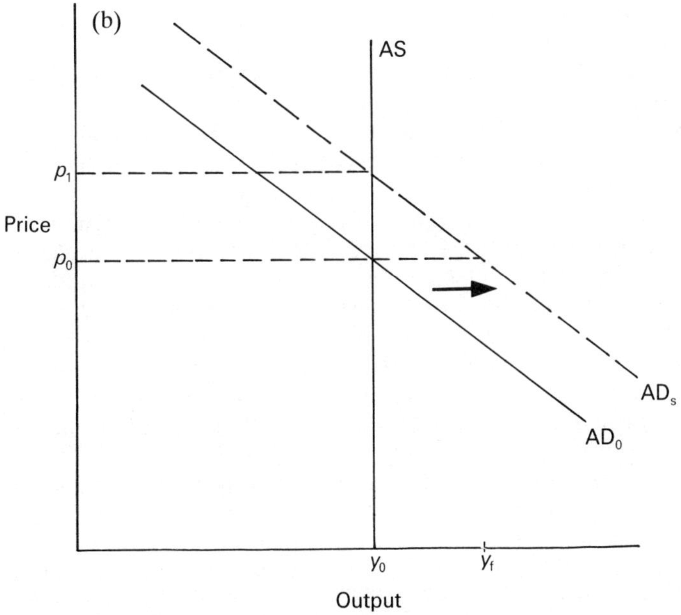

(b)
AS
p1
Price
p0
ADs
AD0
y0
yf
Output

ation, it would have to be an expansionary or stimulative monetary policy – one where the Federal Reserve indulges in open market operations by buying government bonds and increasing the reserves available to banks, and thereby eventually increasing the money supply. Here, as in the case of stimulative fiscal policy, an increase in the money supply again leads to a shift to the right in the aggregate demand curve from AD_0 to AD_S as shown in figure 3.3(b). The increase in the money supply leads to the temporary lowering of nominal interest rates and eventually to an increased investment demand, resulting in the shift to the right in the aggregate demand.

This discretionary monetary policy, however, fails to increase the equilibrium GNP from y_0 to y_f. Once again, discretionary stabilization policies have failed to produce any real effects. Output is still neutral, and the only result of both the policies discussed above is increased inflation from p_0 to p_1.

It is hardly surprising then that the pre-Keynesian era was characterized by policy irrelevance. Recessions were viewed as exogenous disturbances, or uncontrollable phenomena like storms and droughts. The vertical nature of the classical aggregate supply curve precluded discretionary fiscal and monetary policies from having any real effects on output and employment. The economy in this example remains at y_0 output and 10 per cent unemployment. While the goods and asset markets are in equilibrium, it is, however, *an* equilibrium, one that corresponds to 10 per cent unemployment, y_0 output, and a price level of p_0. It was Keynes who pointed out that, while equilibrium was indeed attained in the respective goods and asset markets, it was *not the optimal* equilibrium point as far as unemployment was concerned.[9] As we shall see, there are actually an infinite number of equilibrium points, each associated with different levels of output and employment.

In fact Keynes performed a very simple, and yet very important, policy experiment. He opened the windows of his study, and looking out he saw the lines of hungry and disconsolate souls – the unemployed thousands of the Great Depression. And almost immediately, the classical tenet of the absence of involuntary unemployment disappeared as quickly as the lines of the unemployed formed as the recession of 1929–30 deteriorated into the Great Depression.

While working on *The General Theory*, Keynes wrote to his friend George Bernard Shaw: 'I believe myself to be writing a book on economic theory which will largely revolutionize . . . the way the world thinks about economic problems.' And revolutionize it he did.

Figure 3.3

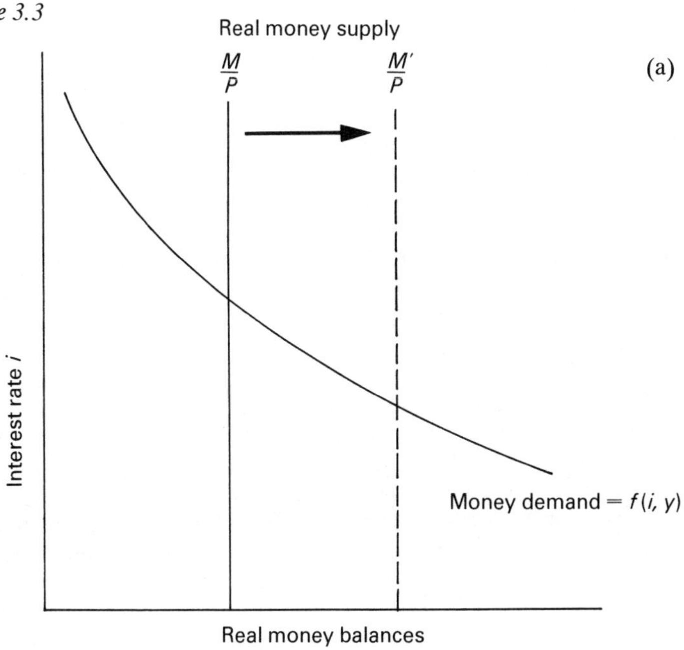

Real money supply
M/P
M′/P
(a)
Interest rate i
Money demand = f (i, y)
Real money balances

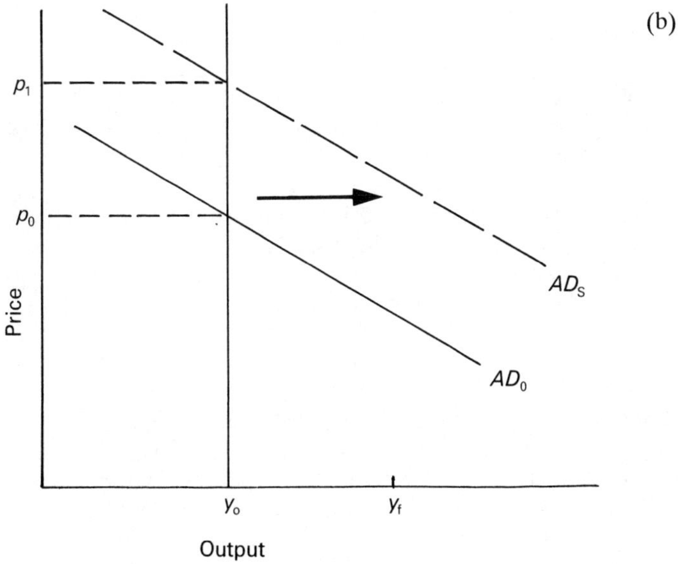

(b)
p1
p0
Price
ADS
AD0
y0
yf
Output

The Keynesian framework

The Keynesian revolution began in the middle 1930s, but it was only in the 1950s and the 1960s that it achieved its maximum influence. The Employment Act of 1946 assigned to the Federal Government the official responsibility of achieving and maintaining a high level of employment. According to the Act: 'The Congress declares that it is the continuing policy and responsibility of the Federal Government to use all practicable means . . . to promote maximum employment, production and purchasing power.'[10]

With this licence, the government actively pursued discretionary stabilization policies, and the period 1952–68 was practically Camelot for the macroeconomist. Gone were the days when fiscal and monetary policies were neutral with respect to real variables. Now, the business cycle was seen as entirely controllable. It was widely believed that macroeconomic stabilization policies could either invigorate recessionary economies by increasing output and employment, or, on the other hand, 'cool down' overheated economies when the danger of escalating inflation was imminent. In either case, these policies were quite successful as we will see later in chapter 4.

In figures 3.4 and 3.5, we have substituted the vertical classical aggregate supply curve with the familiar positively sloped segment of the Keynesian curve. We can see that, contrary to the classical case, the inflexibility of the nominal wages and prices which leads to this form of aggregate supply (AS) curve results in both fiscal and monetary policies having effects on real variables.

In figure 3.4, an increase in government spending causes the shift to the right in the aggregate demand from AD_0 to AD_S (as discussed earlier). This, in turn, results in an *increase* in the equilibrium output from y_0 to the full-employment target, y_f. Increases in government spending, therefore, are accompanied by *increases in output and increases in inflation* – in this case from p_0 to p_1. This is the output–inflation trade-off or the unemployment–inflation trade-off, known as the Phillips curve, that macroeconomists exploited with some success in the 1950s and 1960s.

In figure 3.5, an expansionary monetary policy results in the attainment of full-employment output, and in figure 3.5c we have co-ordinated and stimulative fiscal and monetary policies obtaining y_f output without the rise in interest experienced in figure 3.4. The possible effects of crowding out, inflation tax, debt neutrality, and currency fluctuations stemming from budget deficits will be discussed later in chapter 10.

Figure 3.4

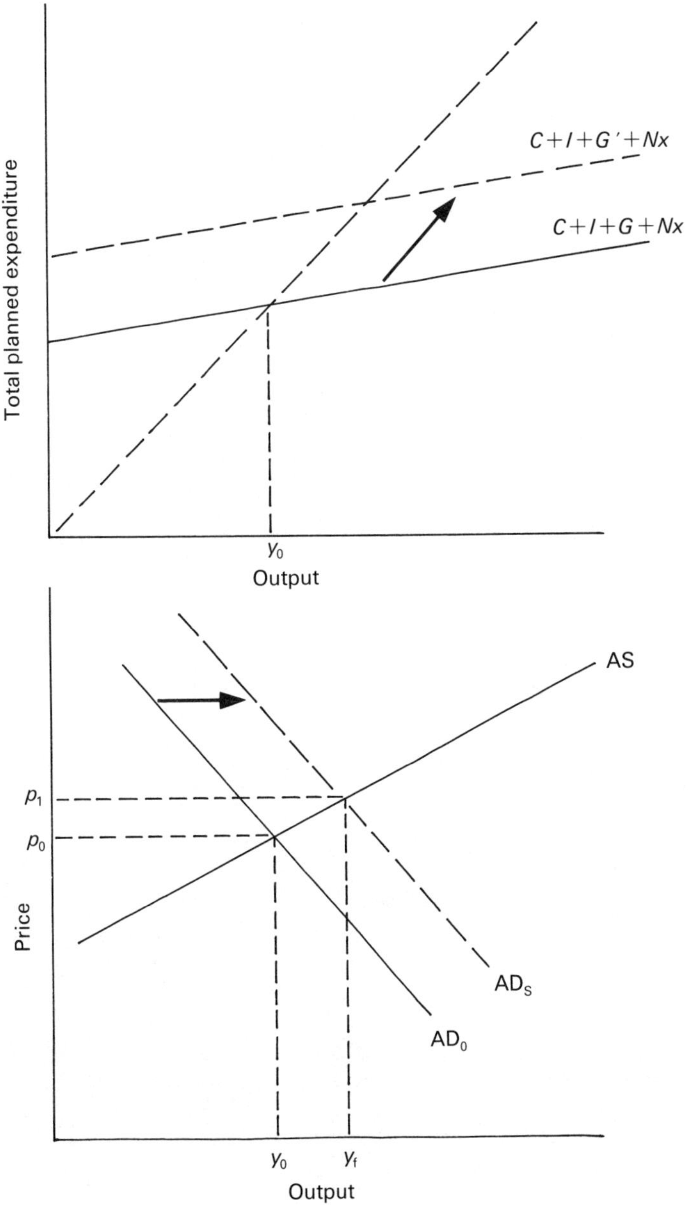

C+I+G′+Nx
C+I+G+Nx
Total planned expenditure
y_0
Output
AS
p_1
p_0
Price
AD_S
AD_0
y_0
y_f
Output

Figure 3.5

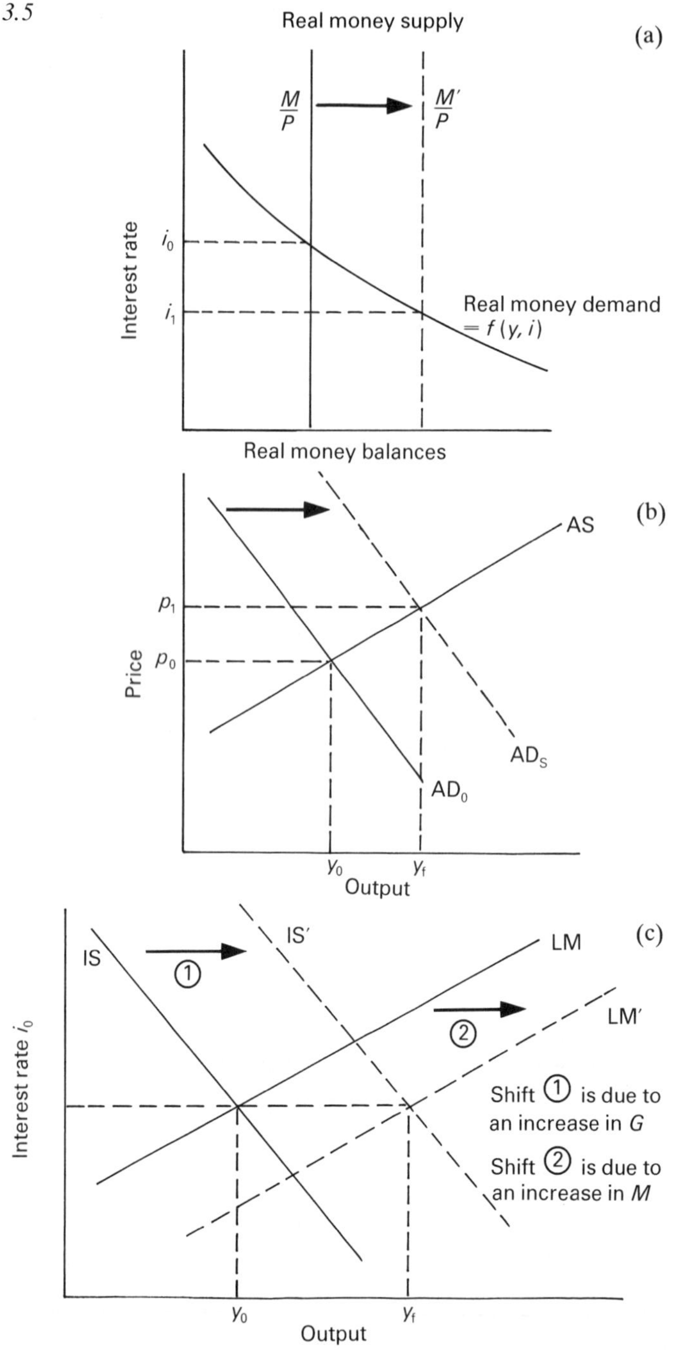

Real money supply
(a)
M/P
M′/P
Interest rate
i0
i1
Real money demand = f (y, i)
Real money balances
(b)
AS
Price
p1
p0
ADS
AD0
y0
yf
Output
(c)
IS
IS′
LM
LM′
①
②
Interest rate i0
Shift ① is due to an increase in G
Shift ② is due to an increase in M
y0
yf
Output

What is the implication of these stabilization policies for deficits?

In recessions, with tax revenues being lower than the trend rate of growth due to the slump in national income, would not an increase in government spending result in *even larger* budget deficits? The answer is that it would. Keynesian policy makers believed that budget deficits would eventually be balanced over the business cycle. There would be deficits in recessions, and the ensuing recovery sparked by increases in government spending would eventually lead to larger tax revenues. This, accompanied by a phasing-out of the increased government spending, would lead to a budget surplus in the recovery phase, thereby ensuring a balanced budget over the business cycle.

This, needless to say, did not work exactly as planned. Deficits tended to grow larger over successive business cycles. This can be attributed to four main causes. First, the budget surpluses in the recovery phases of the cycles almost never matched the deficits incurred during the recessionary phases. Second, government spending increases instituted to drag the economy out of recession worked with varying degrees of success, but were very difficult to 'phase out' once the economy was well on its way to recovery. Thus the residual amount of government spending increased over trend and was carried over into the next business cycle. Third, interest payments on government bonds issued to finance the deficit kept mounting. We will discuss this in detail in a later chapter, but for now let us remember the definition of the primary deficit that we studied earlier. Tax revenues would have not only to equal government expenditures on goods and services, but also to match expenditures on interest payments on past debt. Large deficits therefore tended to linger on over successive business cycles by virtue of the continuous interest payments on the debt that had been issued to finance them.

Later, we will see how the policy of issuing more debt to meet the current interest payments, or the policy of 'rolling over' the debt, has led to the compounding of these interest payments, and finally to the astronomical debt figures of today.

Perhaps the fourth major reason why successive deficits have grown larger is that in the mid 1970s the stabilization policies that had worked with considerable success in the past broke down. Increases in government spending which had very conveniently resulted in increases in output and employment now only resulted in more inflation. This completely confused policy makers. Monetary expansion produced the same annoying result – even more inflation with no accompanying increase in output. The output–inflation trade-off was, unfortunately, no more.

As desperate policy makers relentlessly pursued the stabilization policies of the past, they only served to aggravate the budget deficits further. Increases in government spending were now not offset by any accompanying increases in tax revenues. Stagflation had set in, and by some accounts the days of discretionary fiscal and monetary policies were over. In the next three chapters we will examine these issues in some detail.

Now let us compare the performance of past US administrations. We will trace the history of government expenditures and budget deficits from Truman to early Reagan and see how, why, and by how much the present deficits are different from those of the past. The middle and final years of the Reagan administration will be discussed along with supply-side economics in chapter 7.

Chapter four

A brief history of government expenditures and deficits from Truman to Reagan

While monetary policy is controlled by the Federal Reserve, fiscal policy, which comprises of changes in federal spending or tax rates, is directly influenced by the current political regime. Therefore, past administrations armed with these policy instruments pursued the goals of the Employment Act of 1946 with a vengeance.

Recessionary economies were revived by large doses of increases in government spending, and in some cases, tax cuts. The short escalations of government spending stemming from the Korean and Vietnam wars did nothing to stem the increasing tide of federal expenditures. Inflationary, or 'overheated', economies were cooled down by decreases in the rate of growth of the money supply as cuts in government spending and/or increases in tax rates proved to be too difficult to implement. Therefore, government spending grew steadily – in sharp bursts during recessionary periods and wars when expansionary fiscal policies were enacted, and gradually in others.

Let us now look at the performance of past US administrations from Truman to early Reagan. Figure 4.1 and table 4.1 summarize the main features of fiscal policy since 1949. Federal government spending and the federal budget surplus are expressed as fractions of GNP (dashed lines). Tax receipts are not included here, but they can be easily computed since the deficits represent the difference between spending and revenues. From this simple diagram, some fairly striking patterns in fiscal policy become apparent.[1]

We see that the level of federal spending expressed as a percentage of GNP has demonstrated a persistent increase during this period. Simultaneously, the surplus has also persistently decreased. As Parkin puts it, 'there is a clear upward trend to the spending and a downward trend to the surplus . . .'.[2] Federal spending as a fraction of GNP has risen faster than taxes, so that the surplus (as a fraction of GNP) has declined. Indeed, by the 1970s the surplus

Figure 4.1

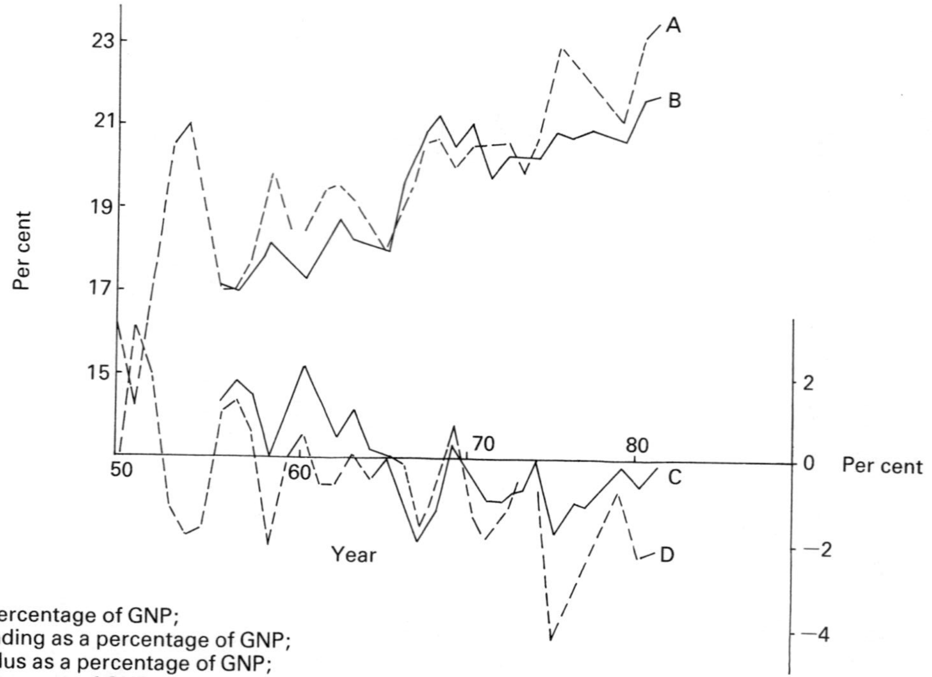

A, Actual government spending as a percentage of GNP;
B, high-employment government spending as a percentage of GNP;
C, high-employment government surplus as a percentage of GNP;
D, actual government surplus as a percentage of GNP.

Sources: Congressional Budget Office *Outlook* 1982; Survey of Current Business 1982.

Table 4.1 Macroeconomic performance of past administrations

Regime	*Inflation*	*Unemployment*	*Money supply growth*	*Federal spending (% GNP)*	*Surplus deficit (% GNP)*
Truman 1949–52					
Year 1	−1.0	5.9	−1.0	16.0	−1.0
Year last	2.2	3.0	4.9	20.4	−1.1
Average	2.1	4.4	2.7	17.0	+0.8
Eisenhower 1952–60					
Year 1	0.8	2.9	2.5	21.0	−1.9
Year last	1.6	5.5	−0.1	18.4	+0.6
Average	1.4	4.9	1.6	18.6	+1.0
Kennedy–Johnson 1961–8					
Year 1	1.0	6.7	2.0	19.4	−0.7
Year last	4.2	3.6	6.8	20.7	−0.7
Average	2.0	4.9	3.8	19.3	−0.5
Nixon–Ford 1969–76					
Year 1	5.4	3.5	5.8	20.0	+0.9
Year last	5.8	7.7	5.5	22.4	−3.1
Average	5.7	5.8	5.6	21.0	−1.6
Carter 1977–80					
Year 1	6.5	7.0	7.4	22.0	−2.4
Year last	13.5	7.1	6.1	22.9	−2.4
Average	9.7	7.5	7.2	21.0	−1.7
Reagan 1981–8					
Year 1	9.9	7.6	6.9	23.5	−2.1
Year 4	3.3	7.0	13.8	24.0	−5.4
Year 7 approx.	2.8	6.2	4.3	22.8	−3.4

Sources: Congressional Budget Office *Outlook*, 1987–8; Economic Report of the President, 1985–7; Federal Reserve Bank of St Louis, International Economic Conditions, August 1988

became a deficit as evidenced by the negative values in figure 4.1. The sharp decrease in federal spending, which is really the dominant fiscal change in the 1950s, was due to the curtailment of military spending after the Korean war.

Another observation that can be made is that the government spending and deficit cycles have an average duration of approximately five years with the cycles either measured from peak to peak or trough to trough. Does this imply some causal relationship between business cycles and fluctuations in deficits?

There is a relationship between the two as we have discussed earlier. As the economy slips into recession, spending rises as a result of increased expenditures on welfare programmes. Simultaneously, tax revenues fall as the declining national income results in lower tax payments. This is why there is a tendency for deficits to be countercyclical, that is for government spending to rise and the surplus to fall as national output falls or goes into recession. Similarly, in a period of economic recovery, deficits decrease with lower expenditures on fewer welfare programmes and higher tax revenues stemming from higher taxes paid on larger incomes. Thus deficits are found to have some residual cyclical movement (we studied cyclical deficits earlier) running counter to those of real economic activity, namely GNP.

But how do we distinguish cyclical deficits from those deliberately incurred by specific administrations? In other words, how do we sift out these residual business cycle effects on deficits in order to determine changes in spending and deficits that can be directly attributed to a particular administration? We do this by computing our high-employment deficits and levels of government spending as a fraction of GNP, and these are displayed by the full lines in figure 4.1.[3] The difference between the full and the dashed lines can be thought of as spending and deficit changes that are an automatic response to the economy and not caused by policy changes. Thus the full lines are the indicators of the effects of activist fiscal policy decisions made by the administrations of the past.

Three general observations become apparent. First, cycles in fiscal policy are less pronounced than the cycles in the actual levels of government spending and the budget surplus/deficit. Second, and perhaps more strikingly apparent, is that both the full and dashed lines are very similar from a long-term trend perspective. Once again, we have a trend increase in spending and a trend decrease in the surplus, implying that, business cycle effects aside, there was a marked and persistent increase in government spending and deficits resulting from the continuous enactment of activist stabilization policies. It should also be noted that this persistent trend decrease in the full-employment surplus is nevertheless dominated by a sharper decrease beginning in 1983 during the Reagan administration (table 4.1). (This was discussed earlier in chapter 1.) Third, this upward trend in federal spending based on the high-employment figures is seen to be particularly strong during the 1960s and is almost absent in the 1970s when spending was held at between 20.5 and 21.4 per cent of GNP. This accomplishment, however, was short lived as our graphs quite literally take a turn for the worst in the 1980s, and the explanation is once again relegated to the 'Reaganomics' chapter.

From table 4.1 we can see that during the Truman administration (1949 to 1952) inflation began to accelerate. Unemployment fell and money supply growth and federal spending (as a fraction of GNP) grew sharply, mainly due to the Korean war. The deficit, however, remained stable at around 1 per cent of GNP.

During the two terms of the Eisenhower administration, from 1952 to 1960, inflation was contained at 1.7 per cent and unemployment averaged below 5 per cent. The budget deficit again remained at 1 per cent of GNP. Towards the end of this period, unemployment at 5.5 per cent was generally regarded as being unsatisfactorily high.

Keynesian stabilization policies reached their zenith during the Kennedy administration, which publicly and explicitly endorsed discretionary fiscal and monetary policies. This was the period when the economy was 'fine-tuned' to attain the full-employment GNP. While unemployment was high for that era (6.7 per cent), the inflation rate was well behaved (1 per cent).

Lyndon Johnson became President following Kennedy's assassination in November 1963, and was in office till 1968. The Great Society programme got under way with substantial increases in government spending and monetary growth. The war in Vietnam further increased federal expenditures. In terms of inflation and employment, the Kennedy–Johnson policy performance was almost identical to that of Eisenhower. Unfortunately, different trends had started to emerge. By the end of the Kennedy–Johnson period, while unemployment had been reduced from 6.7 per cent in year 1 to 3.6 per cent in the last year, inflation had quadrupled and federal government spending had begun its slow and insidious climb by increasing more than one percentage point of GNP between the two regimes.

The Nixon and Ford administrations that came next managed to hold inflation at around 5.7 per cent, but unemployment doubled and federal government spending increased from 20 per cent of GNP in 1969 to 22.4 per cent by 1976. The deficit now increased from the 0.5 per cent of GNP of the Kennedy–Johnson era to a staggering 3.1 per cent of GNP by 1976.

Increases in discretionary stimulative fiscal policy were now not met by the accompanying GNP increases of the past and the larger tax revenues associated with them, but were met instead by a further increase in the inflation rate. Consequently, as government spending increased in a futile attempt at stabilization, so did deficits and so did inflation. Government spending rose further to almost 23 per cent of GNP in the Carter administration. The deficit managed to remain steady at about 2.5 per cent of GNP, before reaching the now familiar and unprecedented levels experienced during the Reagan administration.

In narrow macroeconomic terms (according to Parkin), in comparing inflation and unemployment rates, the Eisenhower administration performed best in the post-war years. All administrations since then have presided over rising inflation and rising unemployment.[4] This might indicate a gradual erosion of the output–inflation trade-off resulting from the continuous manipulation of the aggregate demand stabilization policies.[5] Perhaps the most important conclusion for our purposes is that, regardless of the political regime, both government spending and budget deficits have followed an upward trend – from the Truman administration in 1949 to the Reagan administration in 1988.

Our next task is to study the phenomenon of stagflation that rendered the Keynesian policies of the 1950s and 1960s ineffective. We will first understand *how* and *why* stagflation took place and we will then be in a position to appreciate *why* macroeconomists chose policy instruments based on the supply side. This discussion will eventually provide us with a framework within which the effects of these policies on budget deficits can be analysed.

Crucial to the understanding of the breakdown of discretionary stabilization policies is the concept of rational expectations. This is a fairly recent school of macroeconomic thought and the theory was formulated in the 1970s as an alternative to the then-failing Keynesian model. It is also known as the new classical macroeconomics as the aggregate supply curve in this framework resembles that of the classical model.

The next chapter continues with an explanation of stagflation followed by a discussion of rational expectations, which eventually leads to the dynamics of deficit financing.

Chapter five

Rational expectations and the demise of discretionary stabilization policies

In the terms of explaining the procyclical co-movements of GNP and prices, the Keynesian model had indeed performed better than the classical one. Output and prices tended to move together in the Keynesian framework, while output stayed at its 'natural', or full-employment, state in the classical model. The 1970s, however, proved to be the undoing of the Keynesian framework.

Let us begin with the effects of standard Keynesian stabilization policies within a modified Phelps model of imperfect information.[1] We will now incorporate the expectations formation process of individuals, and we will see how models that explicitly incorporate these expectations produce policy results quite different from those of the past.

Fiscal and monetary policies never are, and never have been, exercised in a vacuum. The final results of equilibrium output, employment, and inflation are results derived from the interaction of individuals, producers, consumers, and policy makers who remember the effects of past policies, incorporate the changes of the present, and anticipate effects of future policies. We will begin with a discussion of the Phelps model and then move on to define rational expectations quite rigorously.

In the system presented in figure 5.1, the economy is initially at a GNP of y_0 and a price level of p_0, as shown in 5.1(d). The economy's production function is presented in 5.1(a) and the labour market in 5.1(c). Equilibrium exists in the labour market at n_0 employment and a real wage of w_0/p_0, where w_0 is the initial nominal wage.

Let y_0 be some recessionary low value of GNP corresponding to a low level of unemployment n_0. The objective then is to stabilize the economy, or to dampen this negative recessionary deviation in the business cycle by enacting expansionary or stimulative stabilization policies. Let the goals of full employment and output be n_f and y_f, respectively.

Figure 5.1

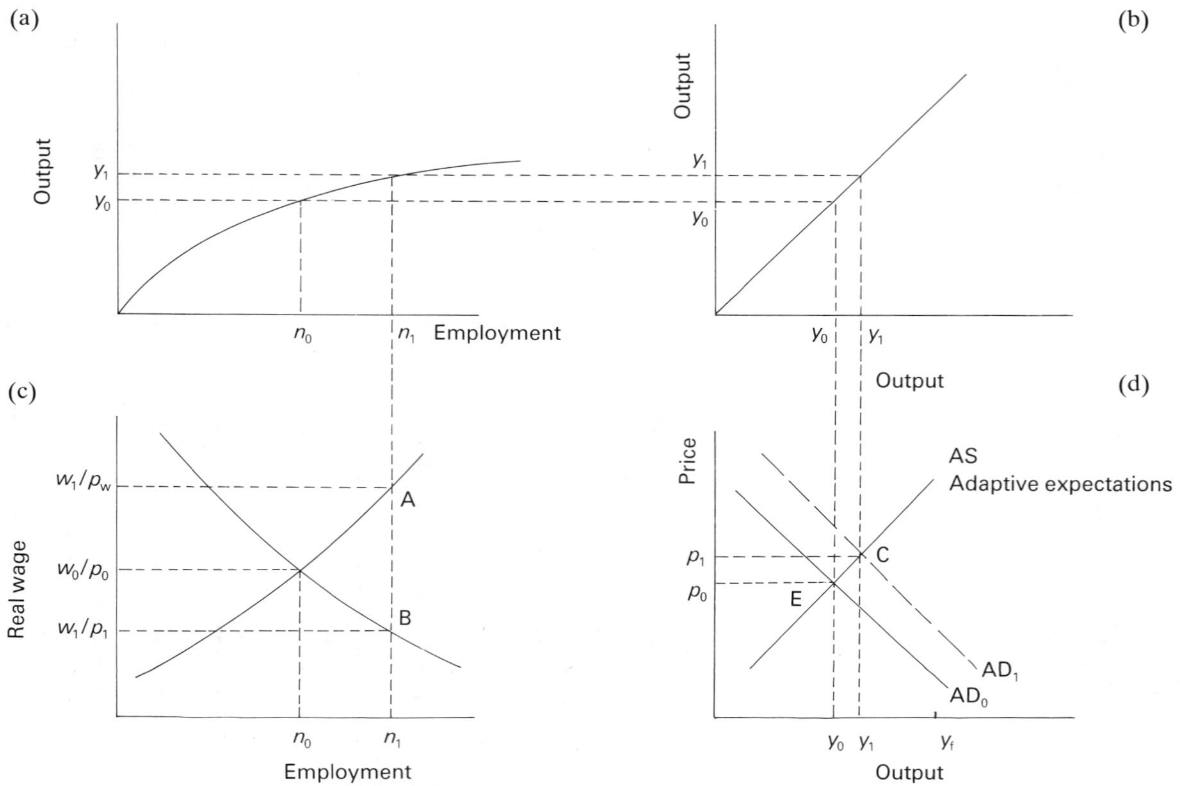
(a)
(b)
(c)
(d)
Output
Employment
y_1
y_0
n_0
n_1
Real wage
w_1/p_w
w_0/p_0
w_1/p_1
A
B
Price
p_1
p_0
C
E
AS
Adaptive expectations
AD_1
AD_0
y_f

The stabilization policies, which could be either in the form of increased federal expenditures and tax cuts or a monetary expansion, lead to an increase in the price level from p_0 to p_1. Now this is where imperfect information, or in this case asymmetric information, comes into play for the first time in our analysis. In this economy the demanders of labour (producers) are assumed to have more information about current prices than the suppliers of labour (workers). This assumption does not imply that workers are inherently ill-informed, but it recognizes the fact that since producers are constantly exposed to more prices (input prices, raw material prices, their output prices, and those of the competition, etc.) they stand a better chance of knowing the current price level. So once the stabilization policies have gone into effect, the producers know that the price level has increased from p_0 to p_1, but workers, however, are *still uncertain* of the new price level and, unlike their employers, do not know exactly how much inflation has resulted from this latest bout of fiscal and monetary stabilization.

In the meantime, their (the workers') nominal wages have adjusted upwards too – from w_0 to w_1. But these nominal wages have not increased by as much as the price level. In other words, since increases in the nominal wage are more than matched by increases in inflation, the resulting real wage is now *lower* than it was initially. The final real wage, w_1/p_1 (point B in figure 5.1(c)) is less than the real wage before stabilization, w_0/p_0, because the percentage increase in price is larger than the percentage increase in nominal wages.[2]

Now this is where the asymmetric information structure becomes crucial in driving the model. Workers in this economy now think that they are better off. They have 'seen' their nominal wages go up from w_0 to w_1 but they do not know that the price level has gone up, and that too by a lot more. They think that the price has only marginally increased from p_1 to p_w, instead of from p_0 to p_1. Consequently, they are inadvertently fooled into thinking that they are at point A in the labour market – at a point of higher real wages – but they are *actually* at point B, and at a *lower* real wage, which the producers or demanders of labour discern correctly. Therefore, since suppliers of labour (workers) are willing to supply more labour at what they mistakenly believe to be a higher real wage, and since demanders of labour (producers) are willing to demand more, since they know that they are actually paying a lower real wage, equilibrium employment increases.

More workers are employed as employment increases from n_0 to n_1, as shown in figure 5.1(c). Output increases from y_0 to y_1

(figure 5.1.l(d)) as we move from point E to point C and derive what is known as the adaptive expectations aggregate supply curve.[3]

Once again, we obtain the familiar output–inflation trade-off, but there is one *very crucial* difference between this aggregate supply curve and that of the Keynesian model. The positive slope of the AS curve in the Keynesian model, and the resulting ability of AD stabilization policies to have real effects, resulted from a downward inflexibility in nominal wages. In the case discussed in the above figure, however, the trade-off stems from something quite different, namely the asymmetric expectations on the part of suppliers and demanders of labour that result in the former being 'fooled' into thinking that they are getting higher real wages, and hence supplying more labour.

By now, we are probably wondering if this is indeed a perpetual trade-off? Or are workers only momentarily 'fooled' into thinking that they are better off? Would they not eventually catch on and realize that their real wages had actually deteriorated? The answer to all the above is, yes, they would. Simply put, you can't fool all the people all the time. As the stabilization policies were pursued with unprecedented vigour, the trade-off finally eroded away into output neutrality. Stagflation had set in. Figure 5.2 portrays this grim picture.

In our earlier example of the economy in figure 5.1, stabilization policies had succeeded in increasing output and employment. But as these policies were relentlessly pursued with each successive recession, individuals (workers, in this model) eventually realized that the accompanying increase in their nominal wages was not sufficiently matched by the increase in the general price level. As a consequence, they were worse off in terms of the real purchasing power of their wages. So they updated their information sets and revised their expectations to incorporate this new additional piece of information.

Let the economy in figure 5.2 be in a recessionary stage, with output y_0 and employment n_0. Let us also assume that this 'photograph' of the economy (in figure 5.2) is separated from that in figure 5.1 by a succession of business cycles, say, a time period of 8–12 years. In other words, individuals are now well aware of the price and wage effects of discretionary stabilization policies from past experience.

Therefore, in figure 5.2, when the administration or the Federal Reserve repeatedly implements the same expansionary stabilization policies that it had in the past, workers, anticipating a loss in their purchasing power, now contract for *higher* nominal

Figure 5.2

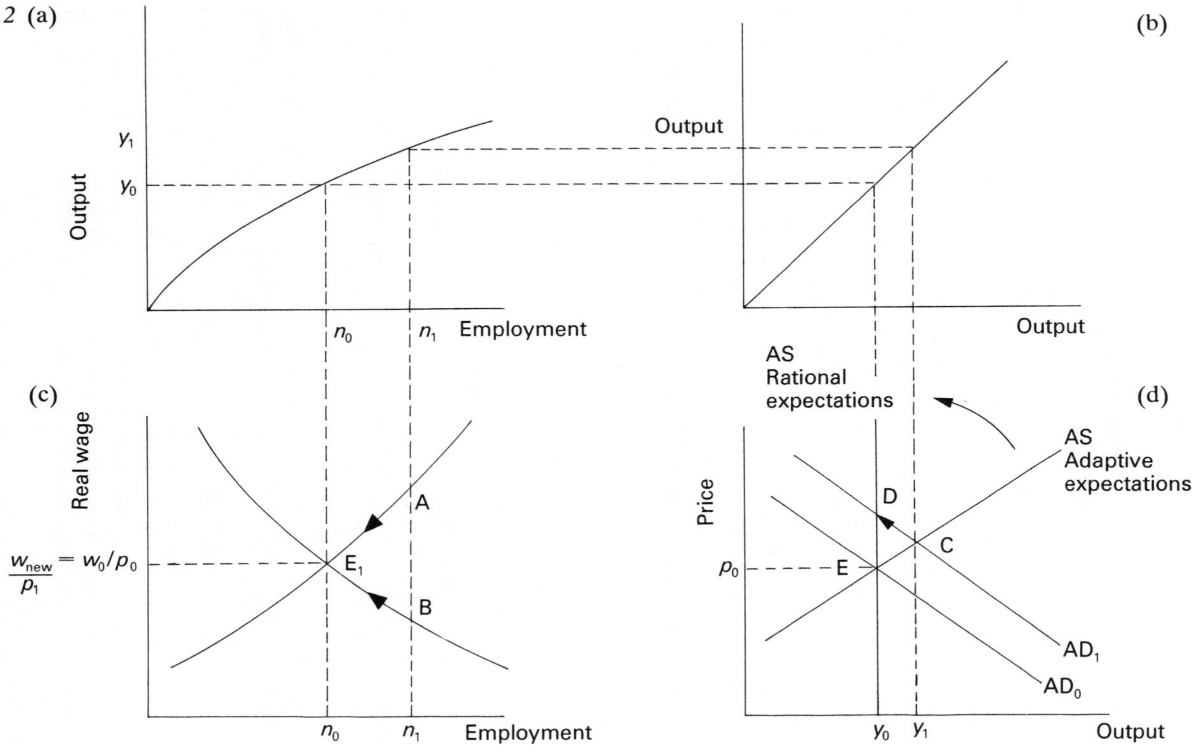
(a)
Output
y_1
y_0
n_0
n_1
Employment
(b)
Output
Output
(c)
Real wage
$\frac{w_{new}}{p_1} = w_0/p_0$
A
E_1
B
n_0
n_1
Employment
AS
Rational
expectations
(d)
Price
AS
Adaptive
expectations
D
C
p_0
E
AD_1
AD_0
y_0
y_1
Output

wage increases based on their past inflationary experience. In doing so, they plan to have the percentage increase in their nominal wages *equal* the percentage increase in prices, thus leaving their real wages unchanged.

By insulating themselves from inflation in this manner, there is no more confusion about the real wage on the part of suppliers and demanders of labour. Workers are no longer fooled, and the asymmetric information points A and B gradually converge on the full information point E_1 in the labour market, resulting in equilibrium employment of n_0 and equilibrium output of y_0. The new equilibrium real wage is equal to what it was before the stabilization policies were enacted, or $w_{new}/p_1 = w_0/p_0$.

In the AD/AS diagram, we can see that the adaptive expectations aggregate supply curve gradually rotates counterclockwise as the asymmetric information between workers and producers becomes less pronounced with workers contracting for larger nominal wage increases and thus causing points A and B to move towards E_1 in the labour market. Finally, when E_1 is attained, the AS curve once again becomes vertical, reminiscent of the classical model, and is known as the rational expectations aggregate supply curve.[4]

Therefore, stabilization policies in this case result only in an equal percentage increase in prices and nominal wages, with no change in real variables. No more workers will be employed and consequently there will be no increase in output. In the AD/AS diagram in figure 5.3, we see that when the powers that be stubbornly persist in demand-side stabilization policies, all we get is the classical result of output neutrality and increased inflation. This is why rational expectations macroeconomics is also referred to as the new classical macroeconomics.

The modified Phelps model that we have just discussed actually belongs to a group of models (other examples being Taylor, King, Jo Anna Gray) called the new Keynesian models.[5] These are models that provide us with an output–inflation trade-off that is driven by inflexibilities due to some form of imperfect information, usually related to the formation of contracts in the labour market.

These models, however, differ from the mainstream Keynesian models in *one extremely important* aspect. In the Keynesian models, the presence of a convenient output–inflation trade-off led to its continuous exploitation by discretionary demand-side stabilization policies. Economies could be either stimulated or cooled down by appropriate time-worn policy prescriptions of shifting the aggregate demand either to the right or to the left.

In the class of the new Keynesian models, the trade-off exists

Figure 5.3

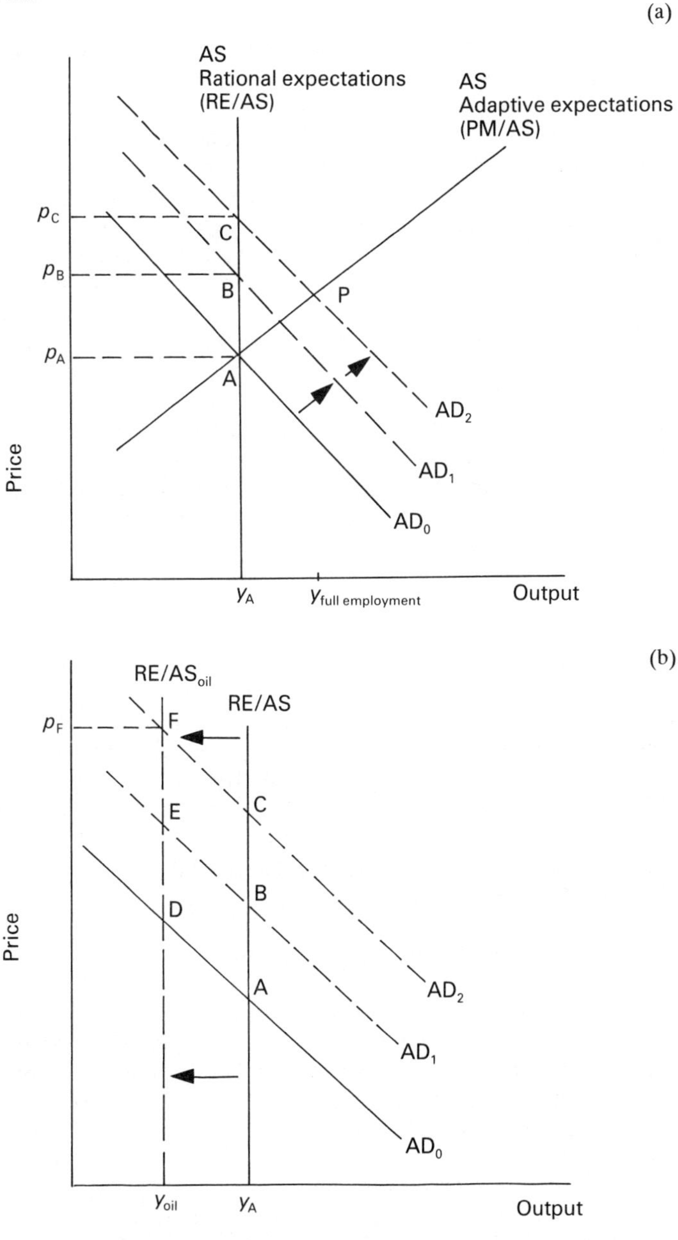
(a)
AS
Rational expectations
(RE/AS)
AS
Adaptive expectations
(PM/AS)
p_C
p_B
p_A
C
B
A
P
AD_2
AD_1
AD_0
Price
y_A
$y_{full\ employment}$
Output
(b)
RE/AS_{oil}
RE/AS
p_F
F
E
D
C
B
A
AD_2
AD_1
AD_0
Price
y_{oil}
y_A
Output

but it is *not exploitable* by repeated discretionary policies. These models are driven by the asymmetric information sets of suppliers and demanders of labour. Any explicit and repeated attempts at stabilization only serve to narrow this information discrepancy between producers and workers, as workers constantly update their information sets with the inflationary experience they gain from each successive bout of discretionary policy. Eventually the information asymmetry ceases to exist, and with it the output–inflation trade-off.

These models belong to the newer generation of macroeconomic models that recognize that policy is not made in a vacuum but in an environment characterized by the interactions of individuals who constantly guess, expect, and anticipate future policy actions by using all the information at their disposal in an efficient manner. Therein lies the strength of this new class of macromodels, for it is only by the explicit incorporation of expectations that we can understand the one event that delivered the *coup de grâce* to the mainstream Keynesian policies – stagflation.

Before we begin our discussion of stagflation, let us define adaptive and rational expectations more rigorously.

For our purposes, adaptive expectations can best be explained by

$$p_t^e - p_t^e = K(p_{t-1} - p_{t-1}^e)$$

Where p_t^e is the forecast of this period's price level. The superscript 'e' denotes that it is an expected price, while the subscript 't' denotes that it is price pertaining to the current period. p_{t-1}^e is therefore the forecast (or expected value) of last period's price, with the forecast made in the beginning of period $t-1$. K is some proportionality constant and p_{t-1} is the actual price in period $t-1$. This expression can be rewritten as

$$p_t^e = p_{t-1}^e + K(p_{t-1} - p_{t-1}^e)$$

The expression in parentheses is the difference between the actual price that existed in period $t-1$ and the expected value of what that price would be. In other words, this difference is nothing but the forecast error of the price in time $t-1$.

So we have:

$$p_t^e = p_{t-1}^e = K(\text{forecast error})$$

This says that the expected value of the current period's price (note that this expectation is formed during period t), p^e_t, is equal to the expectation value of last period's price, p^e_{t-1}, plus some function of the forecast error that was made in forming p_{t-1}.

This is a very simple description of the expectations formation structure in an adaptive expectation economy. Individuals simply extrapolate their past expected values by adding on some function of their forecast errors. In doing so, they *ignore any additional information* that they might have obtained during the current period. Therefore, they might systematically underpredict or over-predict the current price level.

Individuals in a rational expectations economy, on the other hand, use all the information, including that obtained in the current period, in an efficient manner. Though still controversial, the rational expectations approach has a great deal of economic appeal because it assumes that people are indeed rational, do not waste information, and behave in the most efficient and economical manner that they can. Their forecasts are free of systematic errors as they constantly attempt to revise and update their information sets.

Technically speaking, individuals in a rational expectations economy are assumed to know the probability distributions of the variables whose values they attempt to form expectations of. As we will see later in chapter 11, when these individuals 'guess', say, the current price level, their guess or expected value is in fact in the form of a guessed stochastic process governing p_t. When we study the solution technique used for the model in chapter 12, we will see how expectations are based on this distribution and are conditional on all available information. By solving for the parameters of the stochastic process in terms of the underlying structural parameters, the conditional expectations formed by agents will, on average, be correct. In terms of our simple example of imperfect information in the labour market, this translates into the following.

Let individuals have rational expectations now instead of adaptive expectations. Let the expansionary stabilization policies enacted in figure 5.1 be policies that are unanticipated. They are (for the sake of argument) unprecedented. The output–inflation trade-off has never been exploited before (or in the recent past, if you like) and individuals' information sets have no such experience stored in them.

The first time that the AS is manipulated to move right, it is very conceivable that individuals would be 'fooled' into supplying more labour, as they were adaptive exceptions. *But the story ends right here.* Any further attempts at stabilization in this rational expectations economy would be doomed to fail, as individuals counting on their recent experience would immediately attempt to renegotiate their contracts to maintain the purchasing power of their real wages.

However, this does not imply that rational expectations implies perfect foresight on the part of individuals; it does not. It only implies that individuals do not make continuous and repeated systematic errors; they can indeed make random errors. Furthermore, it is costly to obtain information and to 'renegotiate contracts every instant in the light of new information', according to Parkin.[6]

As Lucas demonstrates, people commit themselves to actions based on incomplete information, and they sometimes make mistakes.[7] It is this hedging behaviour on the part of unsure individuals that leads to the procyclical co-movements in prices and GNP. We will discuss rational expectations, and some common misconceptions associated with them, in chapter 6. Our next task is to use the framework that we have developed to explain stagflation.

Stagflation

I have argued that it was the incessant attempts at discretionary stabilization from the 1950s to the 1970s that eventually led the adaptive expectations AS curve to rotate counterclockwise till it reached its final vertical rational expectations position. Figure 5.3 is that of an economy at this final stage. The vertical rational expectations curve is called RE/AS.

Stagflation, which is 'increased inflation with stagnant output', took place because policy makers failed to interpret the gradual demise of their stabilization policies correctly. In figure 5.3(a), let y_A be some equilibrium recessionary output in the 1970s and let p_A be the equilibrium price level. Equilibrium initially exists at point A. The AD curve is shifted out to AD_1 by increased government expenditures. The AS curve, which is vertical (RE/AS), produces the new equilibrium point B, with output remaining unchanged at the recessionary value y_A and a new and *higher* price level p_B.

Policy makers, believing that the aggregate supply curve is still positively sloped (PM/AS), and therefore still capable of providing the output–inflation trade-off, attribute the output neutrality to insubstantial increases in expansionary policy. The goal of attaining point P in figure 5.3(a) was to be achieved by further demand-side stimulation.

They therefore redoubled their stabilization efforts by injecting larger doses of money and government spending into the economy which only resulted in the annoying phenomenon of even higher inflation with no accompanying change in output. In figure 5.3(a) we see that as frustrated policy makers yanked the AD curve further to the right from AD_0 to AD_2 by discretionary policies, the only result was an increase in the price level from p_B to p_C. Output stubbornly clung to its original value, y_A. Point P remained agonizingly elusive, with the successive equilibriums being A, B, and C.

Furthermore, these increases in government spending were now not matched by any increases in tax revenues, as incomes were unaffected due to the neutrality of output. Deficits, therefore, grew substantially larger during this period as we discussed in chapter 2. In the past, increases in government spending were offset to some degree by the accompanying increases in tax revenues stemming from higher national outputs and incomes. Not so any more.

Unfortunately, that was not all. The icing on the proverbial cake of policy impotence was provided by two events in the Middle East – the two oil crises of 1973 and 1979, the former due to the Arab oil embargo 'punishing' the US for its involvement in the Yom Kippur war, the latter due to the Iranian revolution that overthrew the Shah.

Oil crises shift AS curves, regardless of their shape, to the left, the intuition being that as the cost of inputs rises it causes producers to shift to less efficient means of production, or their 'second-best' options. Consequently, at each and every existing price level, the quantity of output supplied decreases, or the aggregate supply shifts to the left.

The final positions of the AD and AS curves are presented in figure 5.3(b), with RE/AS_{oil} being the new aggregate supply curve, post oil crises. The final equilibrium now is not C but point F, a point where the price level is now *even higher* than p_C and where the output is actually *lower* than p_A. The oil crises generated a higher price level, p_F, and a lower output, y_{oil}.

This was stagflation. Gone were the days of confident complacency for the macroeconomist policy maker. Gone were the days when all mothers wanted their daughters to marry slightly balding economists who manipulated entire economies with great dexterity. Macroeconomics was in a state of flux. The new and more technical rational expectations theories were viewed quite sceptically by most mainstream economists, and they still are. 'Fine-tuning' was gone; Camelot had played itself out.

Chapter six

Rational expectations: some common misconceptions

The theory of rational expectations has had an unusually hard time being accepted by the business community and, to some extent, by the economics profession itself. The rational expectations (RE) hypothesis was first introduced by John Muth in 1961, but its implications for macroeconomics in terms of well-articulated models of the business cycle were not seen till the seminal contributions of Robert E. Lucas in the 1970s.[1]

Today, almost two decades after the so-called 'rational expectations revolution', the concept still remains widely misunderstood. In my opinion there are two major misconceptions associated with the theory of RE that have seriously hampered the universal acceptance of this concept. Since the model implemented in chapters 11–13 is a rational expectations open-economy model, it is important that we clear these misconceptions.

Misconception 1: Rational expectations imposes unrealistic informational and computational burdens on individual agents. Therefore, it is inappropriate except in special idealized situations. After all, individuals do not have perfect foresight.
Answer: This is indeed a misconception. Rational expectations only means that agents use *all* the information available to them in an efficient manner. It is not, never, to be confused with perfect foresight.

Instead of imposing unrealistic information and computational burdens on individuals, the concept of RE actually treats the cost and difficulty of obtaining information quite explicitly. For instance, in the Lucas hypothesis of the business cycle, the 'driving' of the output–inflation trade-off is due to the inability of rational agents to infer if any changes in the price that they 'see' on their 'island' are caused by nominal or relative price shocks.[2] Lucas has markets on different 'islands' between which information flows sluggishly and incompletely. He shows that it is the *inability* of individuals to distinguish correctly relative price changes from aggregate price changes that gives rise to the output–inflation trade-off.

In an RE economy, agents know the *distribution* of the relevant economic variables, and they do not make systematic errors. This does not imply that they correctly guess the relevant variables with perfect foresight. In chapters 11–15 we will see how this knowledge of the distributions is a key element in the solution of the RE models.

Furthermore, rational expectations does not mean that all individuals possess the same knowledge or expertise in analysing the latest information signals from the Federal Reserve, Treasury, etc. If, however, some individuals are better equipped to analyse information, then this information will be disseminated quite rapidly as arbitrage would prevent any individuals (who might have greater computational skills) from exploiting any informational advantage. Thus there are no serious computational burdens placed on individuals.

In fact, without the concept of RE, it would be very difficult to explain the co-movements of prices and output, and at the same time be able to explain the brief, but sharp and independent, movements in prices and output evidenced during the 1970s.

The concept of RE is quite indispensable because, unlike the previous Keynesian and classical models, it does not treat expectations as being exogenously formed and remaining invariant with respect to changes in policy. In RE, expectations are endogenous, while in the previous framework there was no explanation of: (i) how expectations were formed, (ii) what caused them to change, and (iii) what their relationships to current and future economic activity were. If we accept the fact that expectations and changes in expectations of inflation have dominated economic history in the United States, then clearly the theory of RE discussed here would be best suited to the analysis of macroeconomic policy.

In conclusion, not only is the concept of RE a reasonable and well-defined one from the point of view of the informational burden, but also it is indispensable for understanding and formulating a well-articulated model of the business cycle.

Misconception 2: There is no role for discretionary fiscal and monetary policy in an economy where individuals have rational expectations, or, put differently, RE has no policy implications.
Answer: This misconception is, to some extent, understandable. In the previous chapter, while discussing the modified Phelps

model, we saw that there were indeed no policy implications for discretionary stabilization policy. Workers updated their information sets and contracted for nominal wage increases that would maintain their real wages, thus preventing the output–inflation trade-off.

In his 'Econometric policy evaluation: a critique', commonly known as the Lucas critique, Lucas shows how econometric models that do not embody agents' expectations, and provide a reasonable theory for these expectations, are flawed.[3] These models, according to Lucas, could be of some use for short-term unconditional forecasting only, and not for conditional forecasting (conditional on changing policy rules), because the parameters of these models remain invariant to future policy changes. More specifically, agents' actions are a function of the policy rules and (according to the Lucas critique) they change with actual or anticipated policy changes. The following example might assist in understanding this better.

First of all, it is important to note that 'macroeconomic policy' acquires a new meaning in an environment of rational expectations. The old-fashioned way of analysing policy was to determine the effect of, say, a 5 per cent increase in government spending, or maybe a 10 per cent cut in the money supply growth rate, on output, prices, and employment. Policy was treated as a *well-defined event*, and analyses concerning its effects covered only the period of duration of the policy. In our case the period would be that over which government spending actually increased by 5 per cent.

Keeping the Phelps exercise in mind, we know that it is simply not possible to analyse the effect of a single-event policy change without knowing if that change was anticipated or unanticipated.[4] We could analyse the effects on output, prices, and unemployment once we knew if agents did, or did not, anticipate the policy change. And since it is impossible to determine if a particular stabilization policy were anticipated or unanticipated by considering that event in isolation, or in a vacuum, it is necessary, therefore, to consider a whole string, or *process* of policies, stretching from the past, covering the present, and projecting into the future.

In an RE framework, 'policy' is no more a 'one-shot one-time-only' deal, but an entire process of policies, past, present, and future. It is only in doing so that we can study the evolution of our policy instruments and be able to divide them into their anticipated and unanticipated components.

The following is a simplified version of the Lucas critique.[5]

Let policy be defined by the sequence $\{x_t\}$, where $x_t = f(x_{t-1}, v_t)$. The policy in the current period, time t, is a function $f(.)$ of the last period's policy, x_{t-1}, and some random error, v_t. The rest of the model is given by $y_{t+1} = g(x_t, y_t, u_t)$, where (x_t, y_t) are state variables and u_t denotes the actions of agents, presumably derived from optimizing behaviour on their part. This says that the state of the economy in the next period, y_{t+1}, is a function $g(.)$ of the policy in the current period, x_t (which is a function of past policies x_{t-1}), and the actions of agents in the current period, u_t.

These actions are a function $h(.)$ of current policy and current and past states of the economy. We could represent this as $u_t = h(x_t, y_t)$, where both x_t and y_t are functions of past policies, x_{t-1}, and past states of the economy, y_{t-1}, respectively.[6]

According to the Lucas critique, the existing macroeconomic models were flawed because they *simply codified* past observations in the functions f(.), $g(.)$, and $h(.)$, which could be explicitly estimated and, once estimated, which *remained invariant* with respect to policy changes.

We know from our discussion of rational expectations, however, that agents' actions are not independent of policy changes. In fact, in an economy where individuals have rational expectations, their actions are functions of the policy rule, given by $h = T(f)$. Here $h(.)$ is the function of agents' actions and $T(f)$ is a function of the policy changes.

Therefore, until a good well-articulated model of the business cycle incorporating expectations is formulated, any activist discretionary fiscal and/or monetary policy would only serve to increase the level of uncertainty in the economy, as we saw in the stagflation experience. Consequently, Lucas advocates a well-announced and strictly adhered-to monetary policy, preferably instituted with a two-year lag to ensure its full and complete anticipation.[7]

This rather strong critique, coming on the heels of the disastrous policy results of the 1970s, naturally dealt a death blow to activist Keynesian stabilization policies. Now there was no role for fiscal and monetary intervention as the vertical RE supply curve prevented the shift to the right in the aggregate demand from producing any effects on output and employment.

Was there then no way to stimulate recessionary economies? Were output and employment doomed to prevail at their recessionary values? Should macroeconomic policy makers now be fired in droves and be replaced by a computer, as some noteworthy individuals had been advocating for years?

The solution, in theory, was actually quite simple. Since

demand-side policies had failed, why not shift the focus to the supply side! If policy makers could somehow *shift* the vertical aggregate supply curve to the right, then they would increase the output and hence the employment. Unlike the Keynesian demand-shifting policies, the emphasis would now be on the supply side.

Necessity is, after all, the mother of invention, and while the concept of an aggregate supply stimulation is not new to macroeconomics, the impetus provided by the failed policies of the 1970s in conjunction with a change in the political regime led to the birth of supply-side economics. According to some, this began a period of the longest sustained peacetime recovery in the United States. According to others, it was a period of great and grave fiscal irresponsibility. Let us find out for ourselves.

Chapter seven

Supply-side economics

It is important to distinguish between the two different types of 'supply-siders'. According to Martin Feldstein, the term originated as a way of describing an alternative to the demand-side emphasis of Keynesian economics.[1] In Feldstein's words, this alternative incorporated the view that 'capital accumulation, technical progress, improvements in the quality of the labor force, freedom from regulatory interference, and increases in personal incentives' would all tend to increase the aggregate supply. Viewed in this light, almost all economists are supply-siders.[2] In this sense, the proposition of 'supply-side economics' is not new at all; it existed in pre-Keynesian days extending all the way back to Adam Smith.

In the 1980s, however, 'supply-sider' has been used to refer to an economist who emphasizes a different aspect of the shift in aggregate supply. By this second usage, an economist is a supply-sider if he believes that an x per cent cut in tax rates will result in a higher incentive to work to avoid taxes and eventually in a decrease in tax revenues of less than x per cent.

'Reaganomics', as we will see later in this chapter, was a policy package that attempted to fuse the existing concepts of supply-side economics with the newer addition of the 1980s supply-siders. This resulted in what has been labelled by the media as some new or revolutionary concept of macroeconomic theory. Therefore, the term 'supply-sider' as used in this book will represent an economist incorporating the notions of capital accumulation, freedom from government regulation, and increases in personal incentives, with the notion of tax revenues falling by smaller percentages than cuts in tax rates.

Before we discuss how and why decreased government regulation might affect the output supply, let us understand if there is indeed a role for government regulation in the first place.

The role of government

Is there a role for government? And if there is, are governments productive?

Perhaps the most fundamental service provided by the government is the establishment of our property and human rights and the enforcement of contracts. If we could assign a monopoly in the 'legitimate use of coercion' to an economic agent, that agent would be the government.[3] This enables society to behave in a certain well-defined framework. Individuals entering into contracts with each other are now accountable to the government for any breach of their contract. The provision of national defence can be thought of as an extension of the government's role to maintain the order of society by seeking to guard the personal and physical property of its citizens against theft or damage by foreigners.

With this monopoly in coercion, individuals will find that it is more efficient to be protected by the collective provisions of a national defence scheme, since they can now switch resources from defending themselves and their property to pursue other more productive activities. The government's role here tends to increase national productivity by allowing individuals to spend more of their resources pursuing the activities that they are most proficient in, without being encumbered by having to provide for their own security.

Another important role for government is the provision of public health services. These include the provision of clean drinking water, sewage services, public inoculation, and the like. These services differ from private health services in that their benefits are felt by all individuals, regardless of individual contributions. It is highly probable, therefore, that in the absence of public health services, there would be no motivation for individual agents to come forward and bear the physical and financial responsibility of a public health service system. As a consequence, any outbreak of disease would reduce the effective productivity of that nation. In this sense, the government's role does maintain the overall productivity of its citizens by providing them with a public health system.

In addition to providing basic legal services and a public health service, the government provides other services. While some of these activities are productive, it is still controversial whether these services could be provided more efficiently by the private sector. Other activities of the government are clearly not productive at all. These involve the public violation of contract rights to take the place of private violations.

Some other examples of productive activities by the government are the provision of schools and universities, a road system, and various kinds of insurance. While some individuals have long argued for a minimal government role in the above activities (the Libertarians for example) it is not possible to determine conclusively if the private sector could undertake the provision and maintenance of schools and roads with greater efficiency than the government.

The range of public and private sector activities varies widely over countries. Countries like Switzerland seek to provide almost everything they can privately, whereas others like the Soviet Union seek to shrink the private sector to provide only a narrow range of consumer goods.[4]

While it is impossible to determine if the private sector can provide services other than the legal system and national security more efficiently than the government, it is conceivable that the more services the government provides, the more likely it is to encroach on areas where its productive expertise and efficiency are less than that of the private sector. This stands to reason as different organizations, or different individuals for that matter, generally tend to have their own different areas of expertise or specialization. This, after all, is the essence of the theory of comparative advantage. If these organizations or individuals attempt to diversify into areas other than the ones they excel in, then by definition they will not perform as efficiently as those that do.

Examples of activities indulged in by modern governments that are thought to have no productivity at all are those that involve income and wealth redistributions. Unfortunately, the negative effects stemming from these redistributions are not readily apparent in macroeconomics since we concentrate mainly on the overall (aggregate) figures of output, employment, income, and wealth, and hence tend to overlook the changes in the distribution *within* these aggregate figures.

It should be noted here that at present there do exist some rather well-designed schemes called 'negative income tax' schemes that propose to redistribute income and wealth in an efficient way by reducing the amount of bureaucratic involvement. While this might seem attractive, these tax schemes still remain highly controversial, and it is unlikely that the United States will change its current tax system within the near future.

In summary, there is clearly a role for government in certain well-defined areas such as the provision of law and order and national security, along with a public health system. The government, in providing these services, helps to maintain a certain level of national productivity. It is not clear whether the government can provide other services more efficiently than the private sector. However, as an agent that transfers wealth and income amongst individuals, the government is almost certainly inefficient.

Government activity, the production function, and labour demand

Let us now examine how productive government activity affects the short-run production function and the demand for labour. This is illustrated in figure 7.1. Figure 7.1(a) shows the production function for two economies. One economy has no government providing productive services, and its production function is denoted $f(n, g_0)$. Here n is employment and g is government spending (or government activity). The other economy is one in which the government provides a level of activity that supports a legal system, national defence, and public health services. The production function of this economy is denoted $f(n, g^*)$ and this is indicative of the maximum output possible when the government is providing g^* level of activity. Therefore, the provision of productive goods and services by the government shifts the production function upwards, and this will have special significance when we discuss specifically what the Reagan supply-side policy objectives were.

Just as productive government involvement shifts the production function, it shifts the demand for labour too. The demand for labour is nothing but the marginal product of labour. In figure 7.1(a), the marginal product of labour is very low in the economy without productive government involvement. The low labour demand curve is shown in 7.1(b) as $n^d(g_0)$. In contrast, the economy that has active and productive government involvement has a labour market where the marginal product of labour is much higher. This is presented in 7.1(b) as $n^d(g^*)$, and it is located above and to the right of $n^d(g_0)$. The marginal product of labour is also represented by the slope of the production function and hence the slope of function $f(n, g^*)$ is larger than $f(n, g_0)$. The difference in these slopes is reflected in the levels of the labour demand curves.

Labour supply and taxes

The understanding of the relationship between labour supply and taxes forms a crucial element in the supply-side theory. What is the

Figure 7.1 (a)

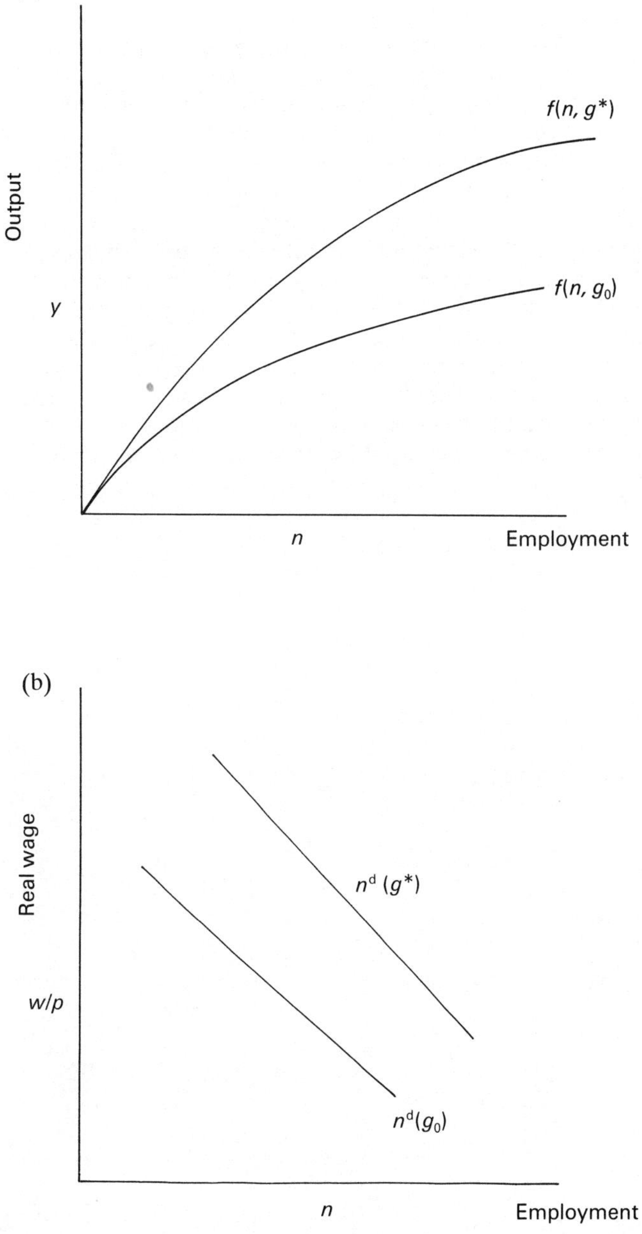

(a)
$f(n, g^*)$
Output
$f(n, g_0)$
y
n
Employment
(b)
Real wage
$n^d\ (g^*)$
w/p
$n^d(g_0)$
n
Employment

relationship between government involvement, taxes, and labour supply?

Government services are partly paid for by taxes. Let us assume, for the sake of simplicity, that all taxes are levied only on labour income. How does this affect the labour supply?

The enactment of taxes causes the labour supply to decrease, or the labour supply curve to shift to the left.[5] This is presented in figure 7.2. Let n^{s0} be the labour supply curve for the economy that has no productive government involvement. At the wage rate denoted $(w/p)_0$, the quantity of labour supplied is n_0. Now let the government impose a tax of t. In this situation what would the workers have to be offered in terms of real wage to supply n_0 labour? The answer is that the after-tax wage would have to be the same as what they earned before the tax was imposed. Thus, to induce a labour supply n_0, real wages would have to rise by t. This exercise holds true for any level of employment, so the entire labour supply curve would shift left from n^{s0} to n^{st}. And the larger

Figure 7.2

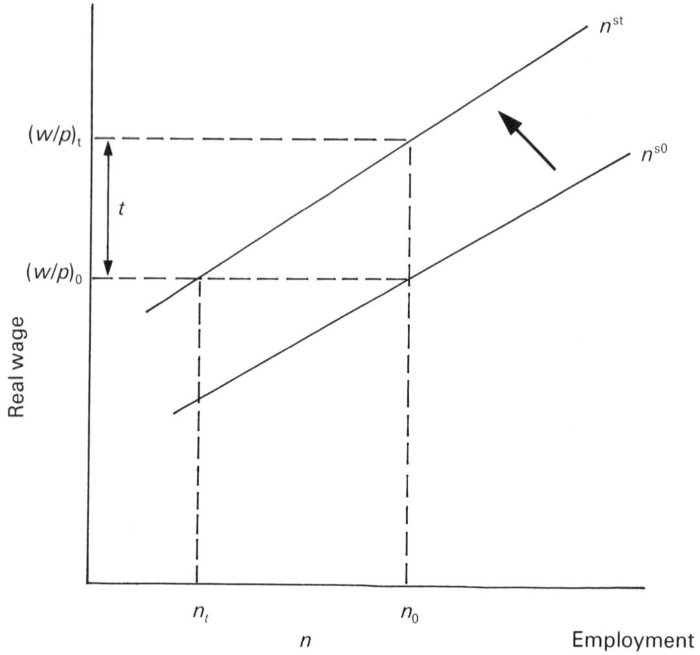

the tax increase, the larger the shift in the labour supply to the left. Another way of looking at this is that suppliers of labour are now willing to supply only n_t labour, at the initial real wage, after an increase in taxes.

Conversely, a *cut in taxes* would shift the labour supply curve *to the right.* In figure 7.3 we have an economy which has experienced a cut in taxes, t_c. We can see that to induce a labour supply of n_0 after the tax cut, the real wage would have to *decrease* to have this after-tax-cut real wage equal to that before the tax cut. Once again, this exercise performed for all levels of employment would result in the labour supply schedule shifting to the right.

Now downward adjustments in real wages are rare, almost non-existent in real life, so let us see what the labour supply would be if we were to hold the initial real wage constant. In other words, how much labour would workers be willing to supply if they were paid the same real wage *after* the tax cut? The answer is that they would supply n^* labour (figure 7.3), with n^* being *greater* than the

Figure 7.3

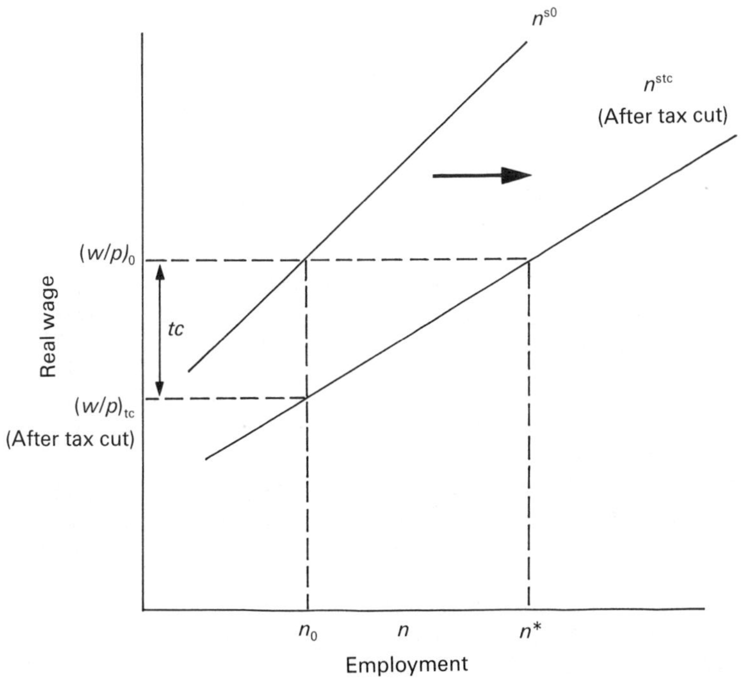

amount of labour previously supplied, n_0.

This then is one very crucial ingredient of Reaganomics: a cut in taxes results in *higher* amounts of labour supply at existing real wage rates.

Efficient government, output, and employment

We have seen how efficient government can shift the production function upwards and increase labour demand. We have also seen how the imposition of taxes tends to reduce labour supply or shift labour to the left. Let us now combine these two effects to obtain a rather interesting one – efficient government might actually raise output *and* employment. This is presented in figure 7.4.

In figure 7.4(b), the initial equilibrium in the labour market is at n_0 employment and $(w/p)_0$ real wage. Efficient productive activity on the part of government shifts the production function upwards in 7.4(a) and labour demand to the right to $n^d(g^*)$ in 7.4(b). The increase in government involvement is financed by levying taxes on labour income which in turn shifts the labour supply curve to the left, from n^{s0} to n^{st}. In this case, the expansionary effect of the shift to the right in labour demand *dominates* the left, or contractionary, shift in labour supply, resulting in a final equilibrium employment of n^*, the corresponding output y^*, and a rise in real wages from $(w/p)_0$ to $(w/p)^*$.

Thus, in this economy, government involvement has raised output, employment, and real wages. Of course, the government spending has to be paid for with taxes. Let the tax per worker be t^*. The total tax bill is then obtained by multiplying t^* by the equilibrium number of workers n^* to obtain the hatched area in figure 7.4(b).

This is the scenario for efficient government involvement – an economy consisting of productive citizens, free from any burden of protecting themselves or their property, and well cared for by an efficient public health and school system. These citizens can then devote all their resources to producing goods and services that they are most proficient in, and maximum possible output is thus attained.

Unfortunately, this is only one scenario – that of efficient, or should we say, optimal, government activity. Government involvement is, needless to say, not always optimal. As we saw earlier, government might actually *lower* overall productivity by encroaching into areas in which it is clearly not as specialized as the private sector. In the case of government, bigger need not necessarily be better.

Figure 7.4 (a)

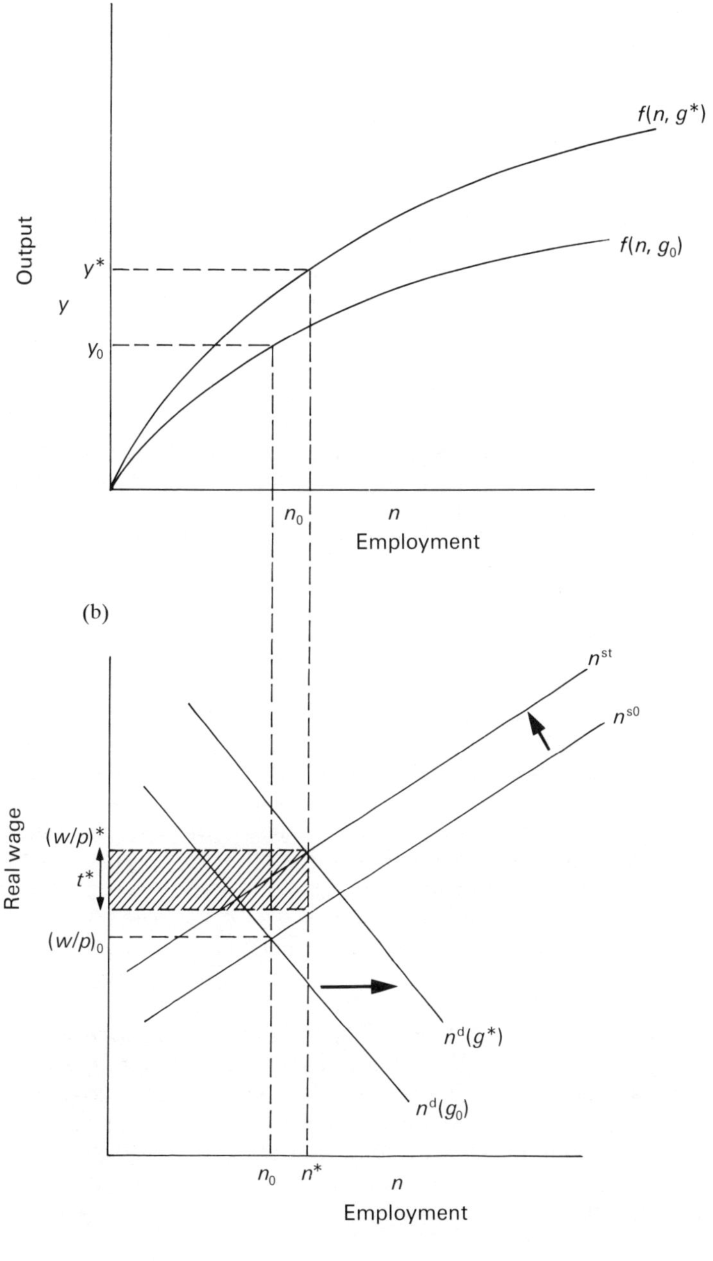
f(n, g*)
f(n, g0)
Output
y*
y
y0
n0
n
Employment
(b)
nst
ns0
Real wage
(w/p)*
t*
(w/p)0
nd(g*)
nd(g0)
n0
n*
n
Employment

We will now see how overgrown government might actually lower output and employment. Once we study this, we will be in a position to understand why the Reagan (and Carter) administration, convinced that government had indeed overgrown itself, took some bold and radical steps to trim it down to optimal size.

The adverse effects of large government

Figure 7.5 presents an economy where the government has grown too large, and in doing so a deterioration of national productivity has resulted. The output, y^*, employment, n^*, and real wage, $(w/p)^*$, are equilibrium values for an economy that has an efficient government. The equilibrium denoted y_0, n_0, and $(w/p)_0$ is that for an economy with no government involvement.

Let us now suppose that government grows bigger than the optimal efficient size. This government will have to raise taxes substantially to finance its now decreasingly productive activities. By definition, these taxes *will be larger* than what they would have been in the case of the smaller (and more efficient) government involvement that produced y^*, n^*, and $(w/p)^*$. It does not matter what the government does with these increased taxes. They could be used to redistribute wealth, to provide goods and services, or simply be squandered away. The point is that these tax revenues are not spent on any activity that can maximize the productivity of the economy, but are now spent on other options which are not the optimal ones.

This increase in taxes will shift the labour supply curve to the left, from $n^s(t^*)$ to $n^s(t_h)$ where t_h is 'higher taxes'. The new employment occurs at the point of equilibrium employment, n_1, and real wage $(w/p)_1$. The new output level is y_1, associated with n_1 employment. Clearly, levying taxes above the level necessary to maximize output has resulted in a distortion in the labour market that has reduced output and employment to levels below y^* and n^*.

The new equilibrium real wages, $(w/p)_1$, exceed those that occur when the economy has an efficient government $(w/p)^*$. Furthermore, after-tax wages are *lower* in the economy with an overgrown government, because of the disproportional tax increase as shown in figure 7.5(b). *This is the essence of the supply-side argument.* We can see from figure 7.5 that, by *reducing* taxes and *lowering* the amount of unproductive government activity provided with these taxes, we could once again *increase* equilibrium output, employment, and after-tax real wages to the levels y^*, n^*, and $(w/p)^*$ which were associated with the efficient government size.

Figure 7.5 (a)

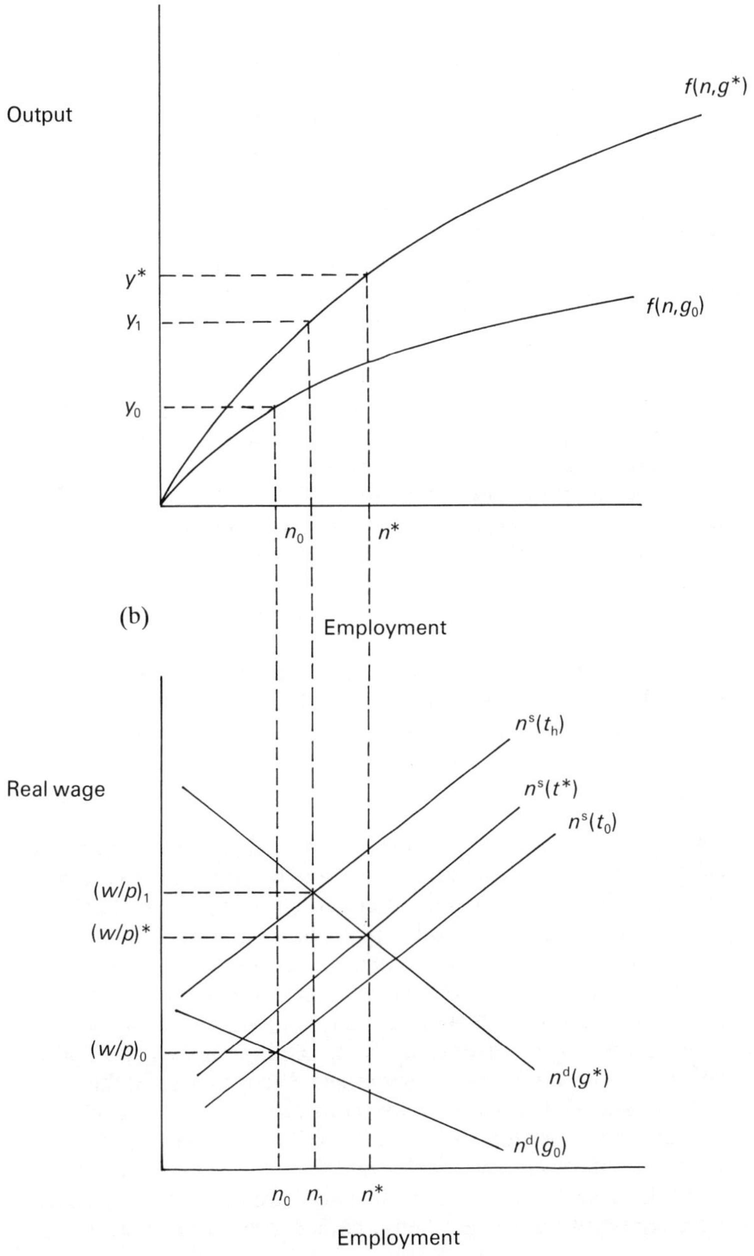

Output
f(n,g*)
y*
y1
f(n,g0)
y0
n0
n*
(b)
Employment
Real wage
n^s(t_h)
n^s(t*)
n^s(t0)
(w/p)1
(w/p)*
(w/p)0
n^d(g*)
n^d(g0)
n0 n1 n*
Employment

Therefore, trimming down overgrown government to its efficient size would cause ouput, employment, and real wages to rise. Intuitively, this last statement might seem obvious, but what is not immediately obvious is the underlying economics, namely the shifts in the production function, labour supply, the labour supply and demand curves, and the disproportionate tax revenues. Only a sound understanding of these concepts can allow responsible real-world policy decisions and evaluations to be made.

Speaking of the real world, while economists do not doubt the validity of the analysis accompanying figure 7.5, they do disagree on the empirical judgement concerning the productivity of government involvement. They feel that by reducing overgrown government and taxes, the production function might shift back down and the labour demand curve might shift back to the left from $n^d(g^*)$ to some new lower value. This would happen if government activity, although overgrown, were still slightly productive and the disincentive effects of taxes on labour supply were only slight. There is little agreement on whether reducing a too-large government shifts the production function downwards and the labour demand curve to the left (and hence lowers equilibrium output and employment) or whether the trimming causes output and employment to increase, as the supply-siders claim. Countless studies have been done, but there is little in the way of solid empirical evidence to settle this issue once and for all.

The above discussion, comparing an overgrown government with an efficient one, has led to a concept that some feel lies at the heart of the 'new' supply-side economics – the Laffer curve.

The Laffer curve

The Laffer curve is illustrated in figure 7.6. It is a curve that measures the tax rate on the vertical axis and tax revenues on the horizontal axis. The curve is named after Professor Arthur B. Laffer of the University of Southern California, who popularized it.

The Laffer curve is a strange and interesting economic phenomenon. It provokes either great derision or intense loyalty amongst macroeconomists – there are no individuals, to the best of my knowledge, who have ambivalent feelings about the Laffer curve. If this curve could be personified, I feel that it might come close to being a Napoleon. Some consider him to have been a totally reprehensible human being, while others fondly regard him as a great military and political strategist, capable of inspiring in men spontaneous bursts of heroism. There are no in-betweens, just as there are no in-betweens when it comes to the Laffer curve.

Figure 7.6

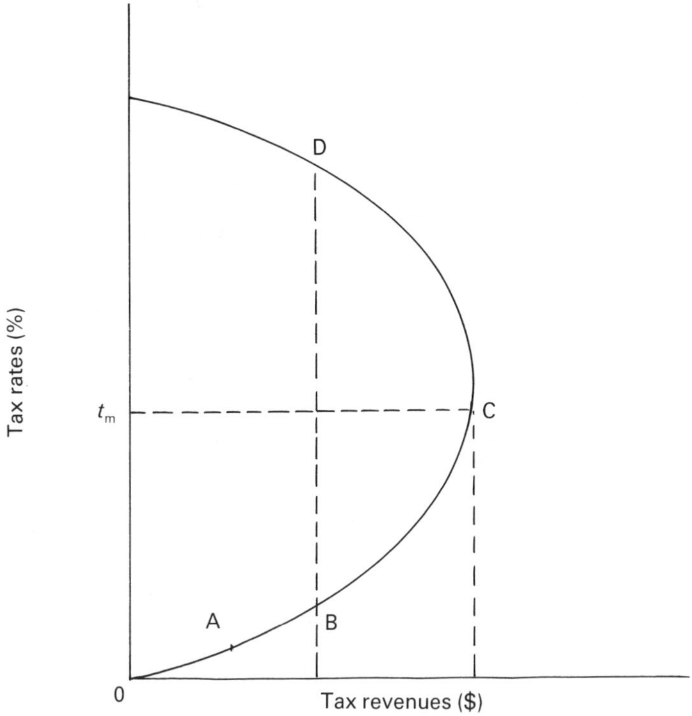

From figure 7.6 we can see that when the tax rate is zero, clearly no tax revenue will exist. When the tax rate is 100 per cent, presumably individuals would not want to do any work if all their income were to be taxed away, and tax revenues are again zero. For intermediate tax rates there is a range over which tax revenues will rise. This is the region 0ABC in figure 7.6. Tax revenues fall as tax rates exceed t_m, which is the tax rate that maximizes the tax revenues. It is shown to be 50 per cent only for illustrative purposes, and there is no presumption here that this is indeed the tax-revenue-maximizing rate. The tax rate t_m can be thought of as that imposed by the 'efficient' government of our earlier discussions resulting in maximum tax revenues (corresponding to point C in figure 7.6). The overgrown government would be at point D and too small a government would be at point B.

The 1980s supply-siders suggested that taxes were at a point corresponding to D, implying that the government had exceeded its efficient revenue-maximizing size. This government, they argued, could have obtained the *same amount* of tax revenues at a much lower tax rate, corresponding to point B, without imposing a cost on the rest of society over and above those that would be inflicted in a maximum revenue situation. In other words, equilibrium output and employment would be lower at point D when compared to point B. This is why paring government involvement and consequently reducing tax rates was strongly advocated by the supply-side economists in the early years of the Reagan administration.

Some economists contend that the idea behind the Laffer curve did not originate with Laffer. Laffer himself points out that the fundamental message of the Laffer curve – that tax rates above some level will actually reduce tax revenues – was stated in the fourteenth century by Moslem philosopher Ibn Khaldun, in the eighteenth century by Adam Smith, and in the nineteenth century by J.B. Say.[6] Fullerton and Blinder add Jules Dupuit, a French economist of the mid-nineteenth century to this list.[7]

The first attempt at directly implementing tax cuts based on the Laffer curve was made by Andrew Mellon's Treasury in the 1920s. Large increases in revenues followed Secretary Mellon's tax cuts from 73 per cent in 1921 to 56 per cent in 1922 and then to 46 per cent in 1924. In a 1924 speech, President Coolidge said that his economists had estimated the revenue-maximizing rate to be 25 per cent.[8] Other notables who concluded that tax cuts might raise the economy to a more optimal level of output, employment, and revenues were Milton Friedman in 1968 and of course the British economist J.A. Mirrlees, who concluded that the optimal tax rate was relatively flat and that the top tax rate should be about 20 per cent.[9]

Opposed to these advocates of trimming down government activity and cutting tax rates were (and still are) an equally formidable bunch of critics. First of all, we have those that totally deride the whole concept of tax cuts, resulting in a proportionately smaller decrease in tax revenues. Let us call them the 'derisionists'. Popular amongst these economists is the story that Laffer first drew the Laffer curve (or as they prefer, the 'Laughter' curve) on a napkin in a restaurant. The common sentiment among these individuals is that it should have remained there. But the response from the faithful was prompt. According to Martin Anderson, the restaurant in question was the exclusive Two Continents, where only expensive linen napkins are used. He claims that the story probably originated with one Jude Wanniski.[10]

The other more serious and more fundamental criticism is economic in nature and questions the validity of the Laffer curve itself.

According to these critics, a major criticism of the Laffer curve tax-cutting theory is that it is unlikely that the economy is at point D in the first place. The critics argue that the economy is more likely to be at point B, and a cut in taxes would only lead to *lower* tax revenues, taking the economy from B to A along the Laffer curve. They attribute the huge Reagan deficits to precisely this – cuts in taxes were implemented in an economy which they felt was at point B. These cuts were *not accompanied* by the reduction in government involvement which was the underlying motive behind them in the first place. The result, according to the critics, was a large and growing government involvement and shrinking tax revenues due to the tax cuts which caused the mega-deficits of today.

I relegate further discussion of Reaganomics, or the implementation of supply-side economics during the Reagan administration, to the next chapter. We will discuss these tax cuts in relation to specific government policies in more detail, and we will see how and why these seemingly outlandish claims by the supply-siders were accepted so widely and with such enthusiasm by policy makers in the UK, USA, and other countries.

Did the supply-siders tempt us to making important real-world experiments? Or did they cause us to implement misguided policies that have caused these tremendous budget deficits? Or are we in the middle of an ongoing, and therefore incomplete, supply-side revolution? Let us find out for ourselves by studying Reaganomics in the next chapter.

Chapter eight

'Reaganomics' and deficits: success, failure, or incomplete revolution?

In the last chapter, we examined the economics underlying some of the supply-side jargon used commonly, and in some cases mistakenly, by the media. We discussed why there should be a role for government, how the size of government is very crucial to national productivity, and what 'trimming the government' and 'revenue-maximizing tax cuts' actually mean. In this chapter we will see how these supply-side policies were implemented in the real world. My definition of 'Reaganomics' is that it was nothing but the active lobbying, marketing, selling, and implementing of the supply-side policies that we studied in the last chapter.

While the idea of supply-side stimulation is not new, the debate over marginal tax rates began to rage only after Laffer drew his curve and journalists, mainly Jude Wanniski and the *Wall Street Journal*'s editorial page editor, Robert Bartley, published it.[1] Different economists and politicians proposed supply-side policies, and tax cuts were in the air.[2] There was the Steiger amendment cutting the capital gains tax, proposition 13 in California, and Senator Lloyd Bentsen's joint economic committee proposed a tax-cut bill that did not make it in conference committee. The Kemp–Roth tax cut further advanced the cause but the secret ingredient was still missing. Supply-side economics still had to be sold to the general public as it had not yet become household knowledge.

Fortunately for the supply-siders, they enlisted into their ranks perhaps the most formidable salesman in the world, the Great Communicator himself – Ronald Reagan. After being partially persuaded by Kemp, the President put his weight firmly behind supply-side economics . . . and the word was out. The media labelled this as something new, a veritable revolution. After a decade of stagflation, the American people were ready for an economic miracle. And miracles, as we all know, are generally precipitated by some form of drastic action – there are no subtle miracles.

The Reagan policy measures were indeed drastic, and today the faithful claim that the longest peacetime expansion in the history of the United States is indeed miraculous. The critics point to the large deficits and claim victory too, while the doyens of academic research fear that it is still unfinished business.

Using the framework of chapter 7, let us see for ourselves.

Reaganomics in theory

Figure 8.1 illustrates the various salient features of Reaganomics. Let the initial equilibrium prior to the enactment of supply-side policies be n_0 employment, y_0 output, and (w/p_0) real wage. Let the production function be $f(n, g_r)$, where g_r is some level of 'high' or overregulated government. This does not necessarily mean that government was overgrown prior to the Reagan era, because the process of deregulation was actually begun during the Carter administration – in fact, most of the deregulation of the large industries was initiated by President Carter. This productive function only means that deregulation was *under way* and that the economy prior to the Reagan administration was relatively more regulative than that of the 1980s.

The original labour demand and supply curves are $n^d(t_0)$ and $n^s(t_a)$ respectively, with t_0 and t_a being some initial level of personal and corporate tax rates. AS_0 is the original aggregate supply curve and the initial aggregate demand is denoted AD_0. The aggregate supply curve is that for individuals with rational expectations. Its vertical nature implies that demand-side discretionary stabilization policies will not produce any real effects.

Let us first discuss the effects of the policies of the Reagan administration within the framework of figure 8.1. This will be followed by a discussion of the policy details.

In figure 8.1(b), the shift to the right of the labour supply and demand curves is due to the following reasons. First, we know from chapter 7 that overgrown government results in a decrease in labour supply stemming from the higher taxes imposed by the larger government. The decrease in regulation and the subsequent cut in taxes result in the labour supply shifting from $n^s(t_a)$ to $n^s(t_b)$ where t_b is a new level of lower corporate tax rates.

The labour demand curve shifts for two reasons. First, presumably, the labour demand curve had moved to the left, to $n^d(t_0)$, when the economy was highly regulated and the government was supposedly encroaching on the private sector's areas of expertise. Reducing the government to its efficient size would then cause the overall labour demand to increase as the aggregate productivity

Figure 8.1

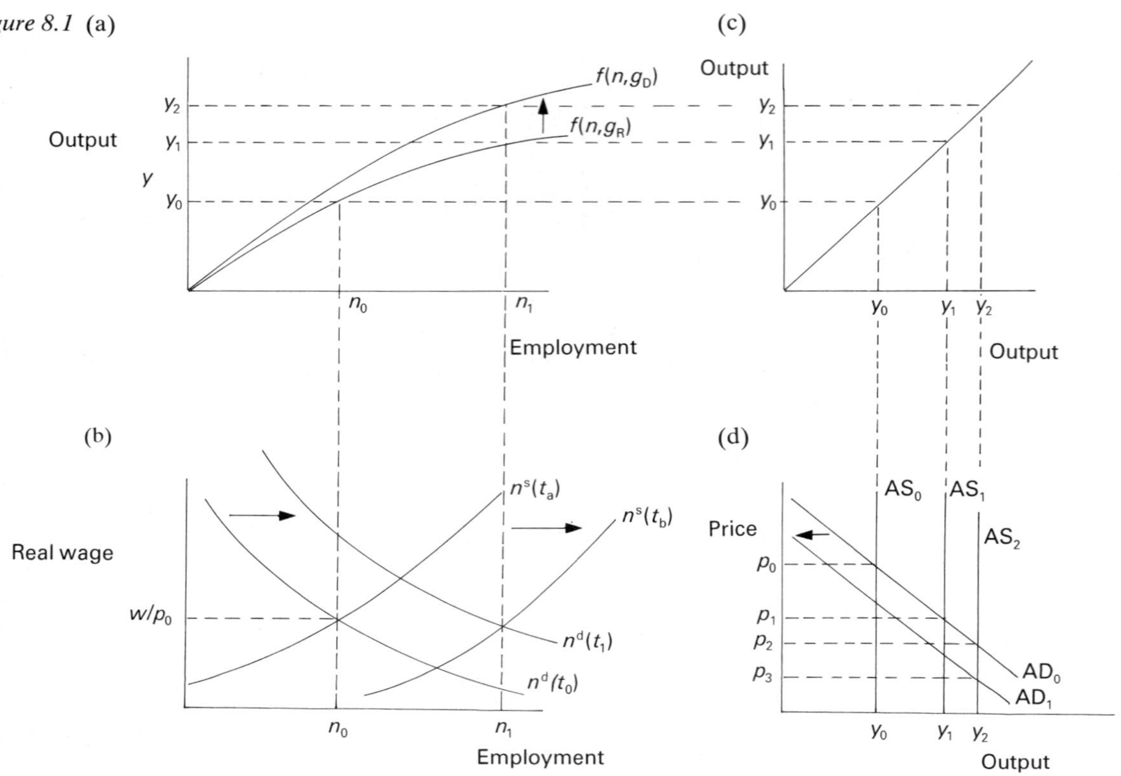
(a)
(b)
(c)
(d)
Output
y
y0
y1
y2
f(n,gD)
f(n,gR)
n0
n1
Employment
Real wage
w/p0
ns(ta)
ns(tb)
nd(t1)
nd(t0)
Price
p0
p1
p2
p3
AS0
AS1
AS2
AD0
AD1

would reach the maximum possible value. Second, the large Reagan corporate tax cuts might have resulted in a further increase in the demand for labour. Both the effects would cause the labour demand curve to shift from $n^d(t_0)$ to $n^d(t_1)$, with t_1 being the lower corporate tax rate.

In terms of intertemporal substitution, the shifts in both these curves could be interpreted in the following manner. Individuals (workers and producers) view the personal and corporate tax cuts as temporary policy changes. When taxes get lowered, workers supply more work in the current period (as their take-home pay increases) and consume more leisure in the next period when they expect the tax cuts to be removed. This is true because labour and leisure are both normal goods and substitutable intertemporally.

The new equilibrium output is now y_1 with higher employment n_1 and price level p_1. Some economists agree that an overgrown government might actually cause the production to be lower, so if the function $f(n,g_R)$ corresponds to the lower production function for a regulated economy, then with deregulation it might shift to $f(n, g_D)$, with g_D being a deregulated economy or a government of efficient size of the kind discussed earlier. If this were true, we would obtain an even higher equilibrium GNP of y_2 and a lower price level, p_2.

In either case, the point to be noted here is that the increase in output and employment has been a result of policies designed to shift the aggregate *supply* curve. Any changes in government spending or the money supply would only shift the aggregate demand curve over a vertical AS curve without any change in output or employment. The only result of an increase in AD in this AD/AS framework, without the shifts to the right in AS, would be an increase in the price level.

This brings us to the one demand-side discretionary policy that *was* enacted during the Reagan administration. It was, however, not designed to have any real effects on output and employment, but only nominal effects on the inflation rate.

The United States entered the 1980s with double-digit inflation – 10.4 per cent – and the Federal Reserve under Paul Volcker was determined to kill inflation once and for all. A change in the operating procedure, coupled with a decrease in the rate of growth of the money supply in the early 1980s, resulted in the aggregate demand shifting to the left from AD_0 to AD_1. This reduction in money growth, accompanied by the dampening effect on the price level already exerted by the shift to the right in aggregate supply, resulted in a two-pronged suppression of inflation, from over 10 per cent in 1979 to 5.5 per cent in 1986. As we saw in an earlier chapter, the 1980s have been characterized by disinflation. The new lower price level, in figure 8.1(d), is now p_3.

The research model in chapter 11 explores the possibility of sustaining the Reagan deficits in an economy characterized by the contractionary monetary policy of the early 1980s.

Some specific policies

Now that we understand the theoretical framework underlying the concept of Reaganomics, an examination of some of the specific policy measures is in order as it is very likely that the present Bush administration will continue most of these policies. There were essentially four key features of the Reagan supply-side program. They were: (i) the provision of more national defence; (ii) reductions in supposedly inefficient domestic programmes; (iii) tax cuts; and (iv) deregulation.

First, the increase in defence spending may be thought of as an increase in productive (efficient) government involvement. The argument for increased defence spending is that more national defence provides for a greater measure of security than would otherwise be available. This would result in domestic and foreign individuals having a higher measure of confidence in the future of US political stability, which would then encourage them to a greater volume of savings and investment.

The reduction in inefficient government programmes is viewed as the elimination of unproductive government activity. This reduction, in conjunction with the increase in government spending, can be interpreted as a re-allocation of revenues from unproductive to productive use, which in turn would shift the aggregate production function upwards.

The tax cuts were designed not only to shift the labour supply and demand curves to the right, but also to stimulate capital formation. The following is a brief description of the various tax policies which formed the backbone of the 'Reagan revolution'.

Accelerated depreciation

A company investing in a new machine or factory is not permitted to take the entire cost of that asset as a tax write-off in the year it is purchased. Instead, the cost is spread out over the lifetime of the asset in a series of depreciation allowances. Many latter-day supply-siders argue that by speeding up or 'accelerating' these depreciation allowances, firms and individuals will have greater incentive for investment. With this objective in mind, President

Reagan and Congress took a course of action in 1981 to allow investors to reduce the 'lifetime' of a machine for tax purposes from, say, 10 years to 7 years, and hence reap the benefits of tax savings from faster depreciation.

Reducing the corporate income tax

Another type of tax cut instituted by the Reagan administration was one that reduced the statutory rate of taxation on corporate income. Companies were allowed, in this tax scheme, to retain more of their pre-tax income. In doing so, it was argued, government would create an atmosphere of greater investment, and create more investable funds by letting companies keep more of their earnings.

It should be noted here that the above two kinds of tax cuts were aimed primarily at spurring investment. This can also be interpreted as tax cuts designed to increase the demand for loanable funds (investment). But this increase in demand, without any accompanying increase in the *supply* of loanable funds, would result in an increase in the cost (or price) of loanable funds which is, of course, the nominal interest rate.

This is shown in figure 8.2. Here interest rates rise from i_0 to i_1, due to a shift to the right in the demand for loanable funds from d_0 to d_1 (caused by the *three* tax cuts described above), with no accompanying shift in the supply of loanable funds, s_0.

This rise in interest rates would eventually retard economic growth by making the cost of borrowing prohibitive. To prevent this from happening, the following tax policies were adopted to increase the supply of loanable funds, or to *increase savings.*

Reducing taxes on income from savings

The first and most extreme form of this proposal planned to exempt all income from interest and dividends from taxation. The income tax changes of 1981 did contain several steps in this direction. In 1981 and 1982 individuals benefited from tax-sheltered retirement accounts and a new form of tax-free savings certificate. Beginning in 1985, substantial amounts of interest income were exempted from taxation. Since capital is not the only factor of production, efforts were also made to expand the supply of labour, as we discussed earlier.

Figure 8.2

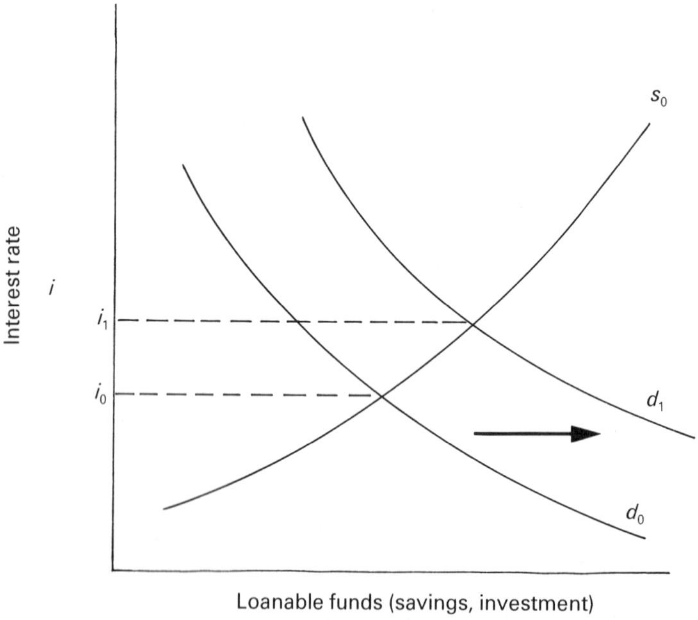

Lowering personal income tax rates

Sharp cuts in personal taxes were the corner-stone of Reaganomics. At the urging of President Reagan, Congress passed a massive three-stage reduction in personal income taxes. Tax rates were reduced by 5 per cent in 1981 and an additional 10 per cent in 1983. The top tax rate in the United States fell from 70 per cent in 1980 to 50 per cent in 1985 and finally to 33 per cent in 1988.

Table 8.1 lists these figures for various industrialized countries. These large cuts in taxes were supposed to bolster incentives to work, to save, and to invest. The increase in the supply of loanable funds, or savings, was to have a dampening effect on interest rates, as shown in figure 8.3.

In this stylized diagram, the supply of loanable funds is supposed to shift from s_0 to s_1 due to the two tax policies designed to enhance savings. This would leave the original interest rate i_0 unaffected and thus allow the economic recovery to continue unabated.

Table 8.1 The top marginal tax rate on individual income in various Western industrialized countries

Country	*Top tax rate in 1985*	*Top rate in 1986 or later*
Australia	60	49 (from 1987)
Canada	43[2]	29 (effective 1 July 1988)
Denmark[1]	73	68 (from 1987)
France	65	50 (from 1988)
Ireland	65	58 (from 1986)
Italy	65	56 (from 1988)
Japan	70	60 (from 1988)
New Zealand	66	33 (effective 1 October 1988)
United Kingdom	60[3]	40[4]
United States	50[5]	33 (from 1988)
West Germany	56	53 (from 1990)

Sources: Tanzi, V. (1987) 'The response of other industrialized countries to the U.S. Tax Reform Act', *National Tax Journal* XL: 3: 344; Japanese and New Zealand Consulates; Fraser Institute; *Wall Street Journal*; Henderson (1988).

Notes: [1]Includes tax to primary and county authorities and church tax.

[2]In 1979 and early 1980s.

[3]Top rate was 98 per cent on investment income and 83 per cent on 'earned' income in 1979.

[4]Introduced in British budget, 14 March 1988.

[5]Top rate was 70 per cent in 1980.

Figure 8.3

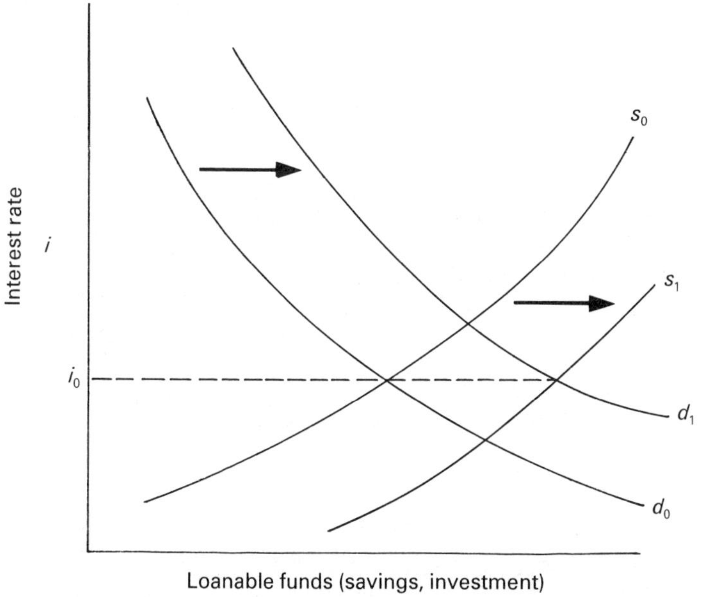

Tax credits for research and development

Since aggregate supply depends on the state of technology, the supply-siders used taxes as policy instruments to encourage technological programmes. Under a 1981 law, companies that spent money on research and development were entitled to reductions in their tax bills.

The last key feature of the Reagan supply-side programme is one that we have already discussed briefly within the theoretical framework of Reaganomics – deregulation. We can think of deregulation as being equivalent to the reduction of taxes and unproductive government expenditure. Regulation is tantamount to the imposition of a tax that diverts revenues from voluntary to involuntary uses – mainly from voluntary consumption and savings activity to the involuntary payment of taxes.

Furthermore, regulation requires government to employ a huge clerical staff to monitor the activities of those being regulated and enforced. This results in additional government expenditure and additional diversion of private resources from voluntary uses. In these terms, the reduction of regulation would involve a reduction of government spending and taxes, and as we have seen earlier the effect would be the same as trimming unproductive government and the high taxes associated with it.

Has Reaganomics worked? It must be admitted that the theoretical framework is intuitively quite appealing. The labour supply and demand curves shift appropriately, and the vertical rational expectations aggregate supply curve shifts obligingly to the right. Output and employment increase, and there is a *dampening* effect on inflation.

During the days of the Keynesian stabilization policies, an increase in output was bought at a cost of higher inflation – our familiar output–inflation trade-off. There was no ‘free lunch’ in the era of discretionary Keynesian stabilization policies, but now, in the theoretical Reaganomics framework, in a sense there *is* a free lunch – higher output *and lower inflation.*

Unfortunately, free lunches have a nasty habit of making their costs felt, usually at some time in the distant future. Our next task is to begin with some of the achievements of Reaganomics and then proceed to a list of criticisms of the supply-side policies of the 1980s.

Accomplishments of Reaganomics

Let us examine the economic success of the 1980s that advocates of supply-side economics directly attribute to the policies of the Reagan administration. These are presented in figure 8.4.

> 1. The United States has experienced the longest period of peacetime economic recovery since 1796 and the highest continuous peacetime real rate of economic growth during any six-year period in this nation's history. (The detractors violently beg to disagree, as we will soon see.) Economic growth lies in the range of 4.1–4.5 per cent for the period 1983–6.
> 2. Total employment increased by approximately 12 million jobs between 1980 and 1987. In fact, unemployment fell to a fourteen-year low of 5.3 per cent in June 1988, prompting some economists to want to change the definition of 'full-employment' from 6 per cent to 5.5 per cent unemployment.
> 3. Inflation has ceased to be an economic problem; the consumer price index (CPI) fell from 12.4 per cent in 1980 to 1.1 per cent in 1986. The doublt-digit inflation of the 1970s is only a distant memory. Arthur Okun's Misery Index (figure 8.5), comprising the sum of the unemployment and inflation rates, demonstrates a healthy downward trend since 1980.[3]
> 4. The supply-siders also chalk up a productivity success. In 1974–80, output per hour of work grew at the abysmal rate of 0.9 per cent a year. The administration promised a startling increase of 2.5–3 per cent as the supply-side policies gradually took effect.[4] In fact, productivity growth in 1980–7 averaged between 1.3 and 1.5 per cent. While this fell below the supply-side goal, it nevertheless exceeded that of the preceding six years.
> 5. Perhaps the most significant success that the Reagan supply-siders could claim for themselves, in my opinion, is not in terms of macroeconomic rates of growth and performance figures, but rather in terms of a philosophical, or if you will, a psychological, victory of sorts.

The supply-siders led us through one of those rare periods in history characterized by distinct, deliberate, and dramatic policy changes. The Keynesian economists had been arguing that the United States was trapped in a permanent state of stagflation and that little could be done to spur economic growth and reduce inflation. They insisted that government might indeed have to grow and become more active in order to ensure a better distribution of income.

The major opposition to this view came from the supply-siders,

Figure 8.4

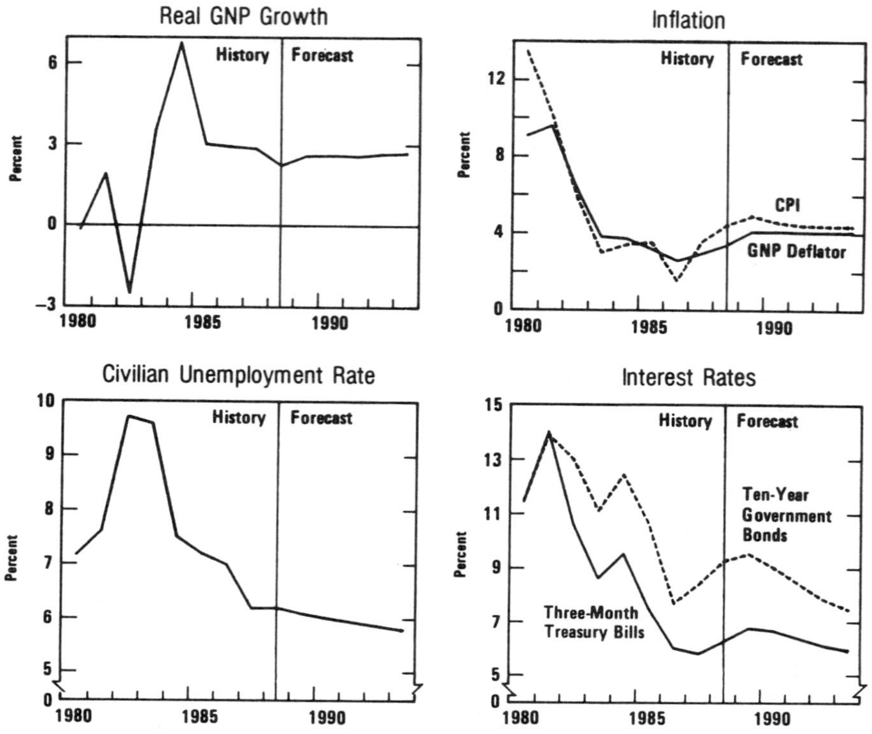

Sources: Congressional Budget Office; Department of Commerce, Bureau of Economic Analysis; Department of Labor, Bureau of Labor Statistics; Federal Reserve Board

Figure 8.5

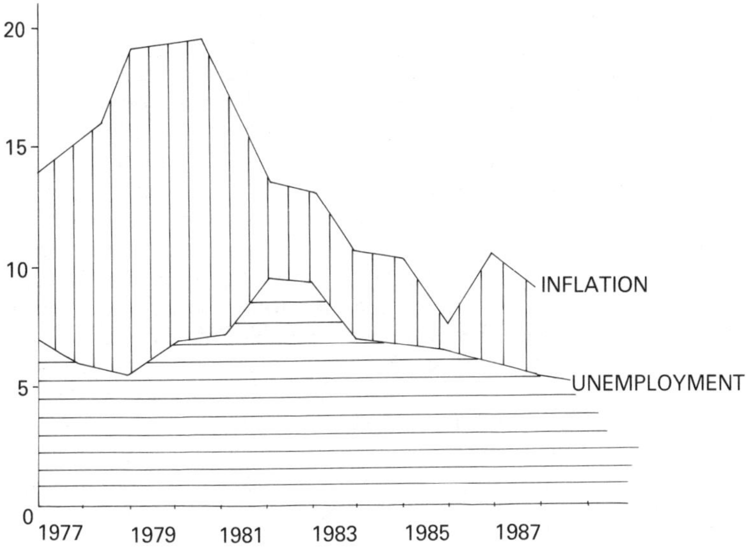

Source: Congressional Budget Office, *Outlook* 1988

not just in the United States but in a host of Western industrialized countries (see table 8.1). If these policies were wrong, argued the supply-siders, then why were they *so widely imitated*? And if the polices were indeed wrong, then why have the apocalyptic predictions of the Keynesians not come true? In this sense, the supply-siders could claim a philosophical and psychological victory.

Criticisms of Reaganomics

The critics of the last administration's supply-side policies can be divided into three groups. The first group acknowledges a macroeconomic success, but attributes it *not* to Reaganomics but simply to the final effects of the policies implemented by the Carter administration and the Federal Reserve Board under Paul Volcker, a Carter appointee, and the business cycle. According to this group, the deregulation policies which the supply-siders claim as theirs were actually initiated by President Carter, and to a large extent they were. The increase in national defence preparedness, they argue, could be traced to Carter again – primarily the upgrading of the US Navy. And finally, the demise of inflation, which the Reaganists claim to be a direct result of their policies, has in fact very little to do with the Reagan administration's policies. This group of critics points out that it was the sharp and continuously maintained contraction in the growth rate of the money supply from 1980 to 1982 that caused inflation to be curbed. This was a policy instituted by the Federal Reserve under Paul Volcker, which technically is independent of, and not influenced by, the political regime.

This group, therefore, agrees with the supply-siders that there is indeed a period of commendable aggregate macroeconomic performance – but the applause should not be directed towards the White House, but instead towards a small town in Georgia called Plains.

The second, and perhaps most vociferous, group is composed of a whole bunch of macroeconomic heavyweights. These economists either vehemently deny that there have been any macroeconomic successes during the 1980s, or in some cases grudgingly concede that minor gains have indeed been made. They claim that while the supply-siders point to the common 'media' variables such as unemployment, output, and inflation as signs of success, they ignore all the negative and insidious effects of the Reagan policies. They argue that these perverse effects, being subtle, will manifest themselves only at some point in the future, a point when it will be too late to reverse the damage done by the huge tax cuts and spending increases of the Reagan administration.

Perhaps their most important criticism is that the deficits during the Reagan administration are quite different in nature and magnitude from the previous ones. It is on the issue of the sustainability of the Reagan deficit legacy that we will converge towards the end of this chapter. Now, let us briefly discuss the specific criticisms of this second group of detractors.

Reaganomics came under savage criticism right from the early 1980s. The detractors were ruthless in their condemnation of supply-side policies. Comments about 'voodoo economics' by the then Vice President, George Bush, and caustic remarks by a sulking David Stockman, served only to fan the flames of ridicule. The 1980–2 recession brought about by the contraction in the money supply and the accompanying rise in interest rates had severely damaged the supply-side credibility. Here are some early quotes:

> Supply-side economics may yet prove to be the irritant, which like the grain of sand in the oyster shell, produces a pearl of new economic wisdom. But up to this point, the pearl has not appeared.

This was an early attack (19 March 1980) by Herbert Stein in 'Some supply-side propositions' in the *Wall Street Journal.*

> What I am ready to predict and to promise is that the effect of the President's program will not be . . . to cut the inflation rate more than in half. Whatever effects it would have on the inflation rate surely would work in the opposite direction . . .

This by Gardner Ackley, former chairman of the Council of Economics Advisers, in congressional testimony on 4 March 1981. He goes on to say that the administration's projection (of) inflation from 11.1 per cent in 1981 to 4.2 per cent in 1982, would 'truly be a miracle'.

Our final quote is by MIT's Lester Thurow, and his prediction of economic doom might be considered dire enough to drive even the most laid-back individual to a crash course in survivalism. He wrote:

> The engines of economic growth have shut here and across the globe, and they are likely to stay that way for years to come.[5]

The facts prove him wrong. One month after Thurow's pronouncement of permanent global recession, the expansion began. And Professor Ackley was quite wrong about inflation.

Other critics raise some valid points. Alan S. Blinder points out that the growth rate of real GNP of 2.4 per cent fell short of Reagan's promise of 3.0 per cent during the period 1980 through 1986.[6] Since the actual growth rate of 2.4 per cent is *actually below* the growth rate of real GNP during the previous six years from 1974 to 1980, he concludes that there is really *no* huge peacetime recovery in terms of GNP growth. Therefore, according to him, score one for the critics.

What about the 12 million new jobs claimed by the supply-siders? Blinder concludes that while 10.5 million jobs were created between 1980 and 1986, the *same* (and possibly greater) number of jobs were created in the previous six years! However, I feel that the inclusion of the labour statistics incorporating the latest 1988 figures would refute this claim.

Unfortunately for the supply-siders, the increase in productivity and the decline in unemployment have not translated into real wage gains. Real compensation per hour has risen only 0.5 per cent a year since 1980 compared to 1.1 per cent a year from 1974 through 1980. Score another point for the critics.

The last group of detractors believe that the *theoretical* supply-side framework that we studied in the previous chapter is simply fancy economic armchair theorizing. This group believes that the performance of the economy in the 1980s can be explained very easily by the conventional Keynesian stabilization framework without resorting to all the supply-side shifts, etc. In the next chapter we will briefly examine this alternative framework which, incidentally, provides its own interpretation of the economic recovery.

Next, let us evaluate the most important criticism, common not only to all three groups of detractors but to some supply-siders as well – the problem of the sustainability of the Reagan budget deficits.

A legacy of non-sustainable deficits?

The national debt incurred to finance the mounting deficits has increased by $1.2 trillion during the Reagan years; it is larger than the deficits accumulated under all previous administrations combined. According to Alan Blinder, the original Reagan economic plan promised a budget surplus by fiscal 1986, despite massive tax cuts.[7] It was believed (according to the critics) that the tax cuts *accompanied by the trimming of excess unproductive government* would result in higher tax revenues, lower government spending, and therefore lower deficits.

The increases in tax revenues were to be realized by moving down the appropriate side of the Laffer curve, as we discussed in chapter 7. These increased tax revenues never materialized and the critics contend that the economy was in fact at point B to begin with and *not point D*, in figure 7.6. Thus, a cut in the tax rates simply took the economy from B to A instead of from D to C, as the supply-siders had hoped. The result was *even lower* tax revenues – exactly the opposite of what was desired!

The deficit situation was aggravated still further by the failure of the final component of the policy package to fall into place, namely the cut in government spending or the paring of the 'over-grown' and highly regulative government.

Government spending was to be eventually reduced to 19 per cent of GNP. This was, needless to say, quite unrealistic. Federal outlays in 1986 actually increased to 23.8 per cent of GNP, and the deficit was $221 billion. While the trend since 1986 has been towards a gradual reduction in government spending and deficits as a percentage of GNP (figure 8.6), the fact remains that the deficits measured in any way (actual, inflation-adjusted, or full-employment) have trended upward during the 1980–6 period.

The supply-siders responded to this barrage of criticism in the following manner. According to them, and contrary to a widely accepted myth, neither President Reagan, nor any of his economists, assumed or stated that the Reagan tax cuts would be self-financing! They claimed that the simplistic Laffer-curve diagrams with the large tax cuts resulting in convenient increases in tax revenues were never seriously incorporated in their policy planning. As Anderson shows, according to Reagan's economists the originally proposed '30 per cent' tax cut and accelerated depreciation schemes would lead to a static revenue loss of $192 billion.[8] This would be offset by a modest supply-side revenue gain of only $39 billion. Clearly, overall tax revenues would decrease. In fact, according to Lindsey, the final figures were not far off the mark.[9]

The Reaganists claim that, contrary to public opinion, they never believed that deficits would miraculously disappear in the near future. Implicit in this economic agenda was the fact that *in the short term* budget deficits would actually *rise*.

The logic was that President Reagan, who had preached the private sector gospel for years, had realized full well the impossibility of trimming down what he perceived as overgrown government. So he cut taxes *first*, and in doing so he put the onus of reducing government size on the spenders. In essence, he attempted to *force* fiscal responsibility on a spendthrift government by slashing taxes, causing the deficits to reach astronomical proportions and hopefully giving the spenders no alternative but to reduce the size of the public sector in the long term. He said 'we can lecture it [spendthrift government] about extravagance until we're blue in the face, or we can discipline it by cutting its allowance'.[10]

Remarkably, as shown in figure 8.6, under pressure from the mounting deficits, spending as a percentage of GNP peaked in

Figure 8.6

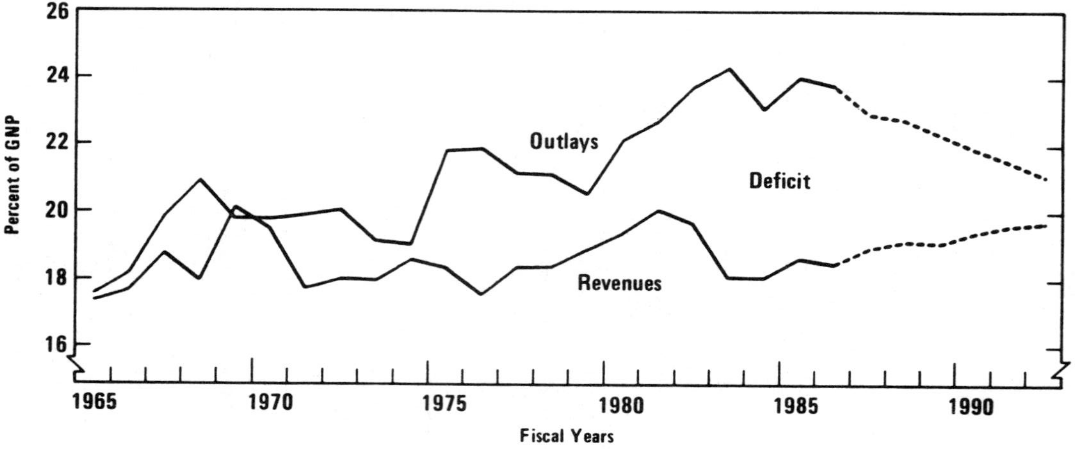

Sources: Congressional Budget Office; Office of Management and Budget; Department of Commerce, Bureau of Economic Analysis

1983 and has been on a gradually declining trend since then.

In this sense, Reaganomics can be thought of as an incomplete revolution – incomplete because the last item on the policy agenda, a reduction in government spending, has yet to manifest itself in significant proportions. We will discuss the implications of this incomplete revolution in greater detail in chapters 9 and 10.

Let us now summarize the response of the supply-siders to the critics who derisively point to the phenomenal Reagan deficits as proof of the failure of the supply-side policies.

According to the supply-siders:

1. They never claimed that the tax cuts would be self-financing. What they did claim was that an *x* per cent cut in the tax rate would result in less than an *x* per cent decrease in revenues. They point out that it was Laffer, and not they, who made the preposterous claim that the tax cuts would 'in overall revenues, be self-financing in less than two years'.[11] They feel that the critics, particularly the news media, have confused Laffer's comments with those made by the Reagan economists.
2. The supply-siders also agree that while there has in fact been a tax revolution, it did not originate in the United States, but in the United Kingdom. In 1979, newly elected Prime Minister Margaret Thatcher slashed the top rate on earned income from 83 per cent to 60 per cent. In 1988, she cut it further to 40 per cent. In the United States, the top rate fell from 70 per cent in 1980 to 50 per cent in 1982, and to 33 per cent in 1988.

   As table 8.1 shows, this revolution in tax policy has been mimicked by a host of industrialized countries. New Zealand's top personal tax rate fell from 66 per cent in 1985 to 48 per cent in 1986, and to 33 per cent from 1 October 1988. Canada has followed suit with a cut in federal taxes. Its top rate fell from 43 per cent in the early 1980s to 29 per cent in 1988. Tax rate cuts have also been experienced in Australia, Denmark, France, West Germany, Ireland, Italy, and Japan.

   Therefore, the supply-side revolution, as it pertains to tax policy, is not endemic to the Reagan administration. It is not a policy formulation devised by a small select bunch of Reagan supply-siders, but, on the contrary, it is an internationally accepted policy agenda. The proponents of supply-side economics further argue that if the concept of an *x* per cent cut in tax rates leading to less than an *x* per cent cut in tax revenues is theoretically and practically flawed, then why have the tax-cutting policies of the UK and the USA been so widely imitated?

3. The supply-siders agree that deficits would undoubtedly increase in the short term, but as the final component of Reaganomics (decreased government spending) eventually falls into place, there should be a gradual reduction in the budget deficit. Total outlays as a percentage of GNP, they point out, have already begun to edge downwards.

As we all know, in economics, 'short term' and 'long term' are very mysterious time frames. While it is indeed true that total outlays have decreased marginally, the fact remains that the budget deficits still assume their large proportions, and will continue to do so over at least the next two administrations. These deficits have to be financed by borrowing, and the interest payments, according to some studies, have been financed by 100 per cent borrowing.[12]

Reaganomics might have succeeded or failed depending on which economic framework is followed, but the deficits – the bond-financed deficits – whether intentionally created in the 'short term' to pressure government to curtail spending, or incurred as a result of a macroeconomic agenda gone awry, are very real. And they are here to stay.

Our purpose in this book is to see if they are sustainable. We have understood how and why the deficits have been created, and we have discussed the views of both sides. Our next task is to understand and study the method by which deficits are financed. We will include the foreign sector and see how capital inflows finance large portions of these Reagan deficits. Most importantly, we will see if these inflows of capital and private lending to the government might make the deficits sustainable.

If they are sustainable, then the Reagan gamble will have paid off. He will have had his tax cuts and let future administrations, beginning with that of George Bush, worry about cutting government spending.

If they are not sustainable, then there will be a very interesting period of macroeconomic manoeuvring, and the supply-siders would then be held culpable for perhaps the most irresponsible fiscal policy experiment of all time – creating a deficit monster that inexorably grows larger with each interest payment.

The mechanics of deficit financing is presented in chapter 10. In the next short chapter I present an alternative framework for analysing the economic 'recovery' and interpreting the Reagan deficits. I use the word 'alternative' because this is the framework used frequently by the detractors of Reaganomics, and it does not incorporate the rational expectations aggregate supply curve.

Chapter nine

Another view of the 1980s deficits

In the last three chapters we studied the economic framework of Reaganomics and some of the positive and negative features of the so-called 'revolution'. We also discussed the criticisms of two groups of detractors. The first group agreed with the supply-siders that an 'economic miracle' was under way – not because of President Reagan's policies *per se*, but mainly because of the continuing of President Carter's policies by the Reagan administration.

The second group conceded that only very marginal gains were made by the supply-siders, and the economy was in fact on the verge of a major collapse. According to this group, this would be caused by the huge build-up of debt that the Reagan administration had accumulated by its irresponsible cutting of tax rates and by its inability to stem the growth of government spending.

The third and last group of critics oppose Reaganomics on theoretical grounds. According to this group, the behaviour of the key macroeconomic variables in the 1980s can be explained perfectly well by the standard Keynesian model. They attribute the economic expansion and the rise in budget deficits to traditional fiscal demand-side stabilization policies. They feel that there was no supply-side revolution but a plain and simple demand-side expansion resulting from increased government spending and the cutting of tax rates. They oppose supply-side economics on theoretical grounds which we will discuss in this chapter.

We studied the economic framework of the supply-siders in chapter 7; now let us study the framework within which the critics base their arguments. Then, armed with these two frameworks, we will be in a good position to decide which framework is best suited to explain the events of the 1980s and to predict those of the near future.

Theoretical objections to the supply-side tax cuts

The ambiguity of supply-side effects

The first objection is that it is by no means clear that the aggregate supply curve will shift to the right as the supply-siders claim. It is easy to enact policies cutting taxes which would simply increase take-home pay. The critics argue that while cutting tax rates is very easy in a political sense, this does not in itself guarantee that people will actually supply more labour.

Instead, suppliers of labour may find that they can now afford the goods and services they want by supplying fewer hours of labour, and they might then work *less*. Similarly, if tax cuts increase the return on savings, then individuals' savings goals will be reached more easily with the tax cuts. Again, workers would react to this by saving less.

These critics point to the statistical evidence that suggests that it is unrealistic to expect tax reductions to lead to huge increases in either labour supply or household savings. They therefore expect very modest increases in labour supply and saving – definitely far below the level claimed by the supply-siders. Charles Schultze, Chief Economic Adviser to President Carter, said 'there's nothing wrong with supply-side economics that division by ten couldn't cure'.[1]

Demand-side effects

We have touched upon this point earlier. The contention of the critics is that what was experienced during the 1980s was a plain and simple demand-side expansion caused by spending increases and tax cuts. The argument is as follows.

Individuals will certainly *spend* more with a cut in taxes. As we saw earlier, this is tantamount to the aggregate *demand* curve shifting to the right due to an increase in spending from cuts in personal and corporate taxes. This 'certain' increase in spending is to be contrasted with a 'possible' increase in labour supply as a result of tax cuts. In other words, with a cut in personal taxes, individuals *might possibly* work more and shift the aggregate supply curve to the right, but they will *definitely spend* more and thus shift the aggregate *demand* to the right.

The initial plan of the supply-siders was to negate this inflationary effect of a shift in aggregate demand caused by the increase in spending, by sharp reductions in government spending. This, hopefully, would cancel out the demand-side effects..

Since total aggregate demand is given by

$$Y = C + I + G + NX \text{ (net exports)}$$

the increase in consumption C, and investment I, would then (in theory) be offset by reductions in government spending G. This would result in a shift in the aggregate supply without any spending-stimulated shift in the aggregate demand, as shown in figure 9.1.

Unfortunately, the problem with this reasoning was that large tax cuts had been implemented. Therefore, to prevent any overall increases in aggregate demand, relatively large cuts in government spending would have to accompany them.

As it turned out, by accident or by intent, the expenditure cuts proposed by the Reagan administration wound up being much smaller than the tax cuts. This is why the critics claim that it was, after all, a demand-side effect, as shown in figure 9.2.

The cut in taxes, accompanied by the high levels of government spending, causes the AD curve to shift and rotate from AD_0 to

Figure 9.1

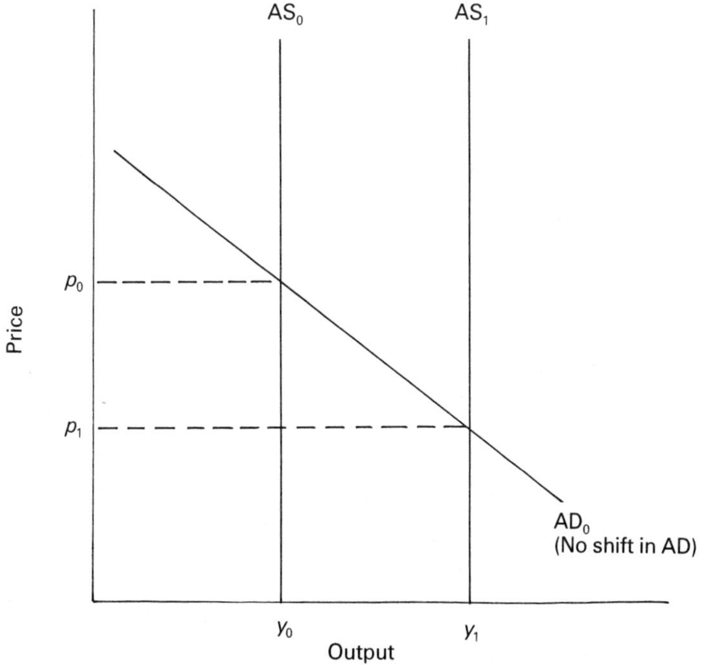

Figure 9.2 (a)

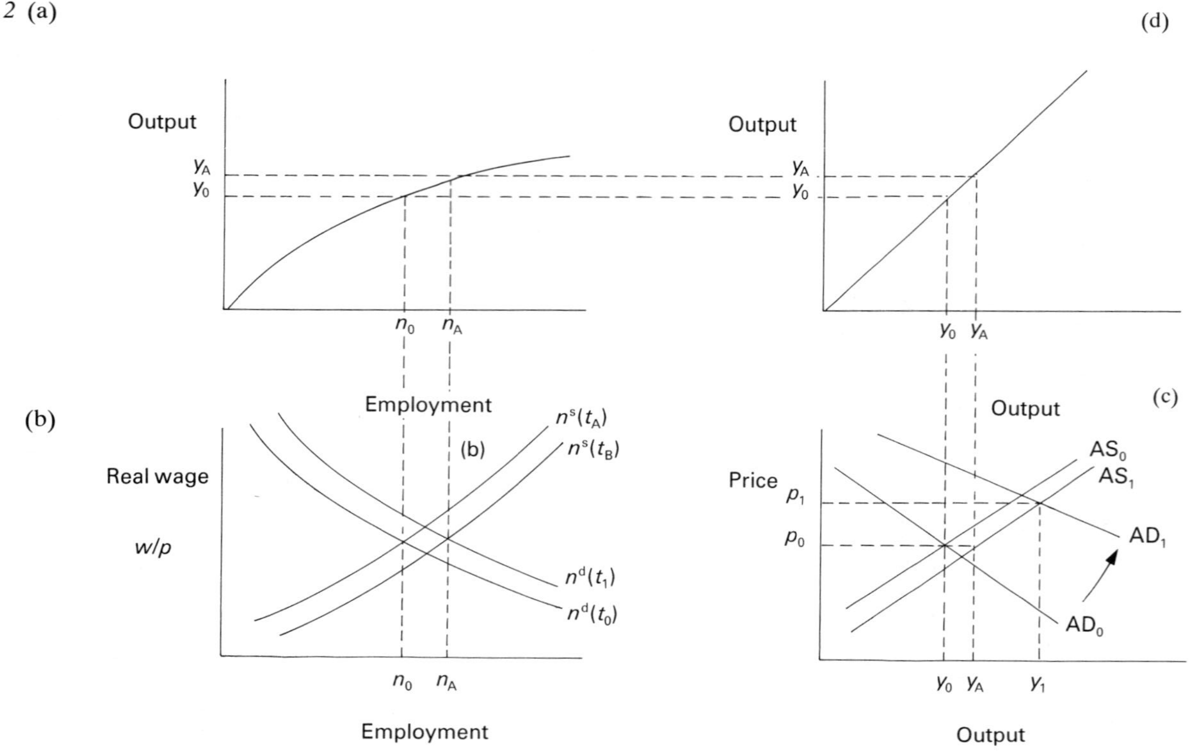
(d)
Output
y_A
y_0
n_0 n_A
Output
y_A
y_0
y_0 y_A
(b)
Employment
Real wage
w/p
(b)
$n^s(t_A)$
$n^s(t_B)$
$n^d(t_1)$
$n^d(t_0)$
n_0 n_A
Employment
(c)
Output
Price
p_1
p_0
AS_0
AS_1
AD_1
AD_0
y_0 y_A y_1
Output

AD_1 in figure 9.2(c). The labour market in this framework is presented in figure 9.2(b). The shifts to the right in the labour supply and labour demand curves are *not nearly* as pronounced as they were in the framework of the supply-siders in chapter 7. The new equilibrium employment in the labour market increases very marginally from n_0 to n_A, with output increasing from y_0 to y_1.

The overall effect for the whole economy is shown in figure 9.2(c). The shift in the aggregate demand clearly dominates the weak aggregate supply shift, i.e. AD_0 shifts out further than AS_0. The result is an increase in GNP from y_0 to y_1 and employment from n_0 to n_a, and very moderate inflation from p_0 to p_1.

Investment lags

By the policies of accelerated depreciation, the supply-side tax cuts hoped to encourage greater business investment. But investment does not mean an instantaneous increase in plant capacity. New investment projects take time because the financing has to be arranged, and there are delivery lags on machinery and implementation lags for the new systems. The point here is that expenditures on investment goods *precede* capacity expansion. Thus, 'even if supply-side policies are successful, aggregate *demand* expands first and aggregate *supply* follows later', according to Blinder.[2]

This again ties in with the framework discussed in figure 9.2 – the recovery was primarily due to a large shift to the right in the AD due to increases in consumption and investment expenditures.

Effect on inflation

The supply-siders perhaps bit off too much when they claimed that their agenda was a permanent cure for inflation. Inflation, unfortunately for them, is always a monetary phenomenon. The dampening effect on prices due to a shift in the aggregate supply curve would produce a one-time-only decrease in the price level. If this shift in the aggregate supply were stretched out over a period of time, then a case could be made for the supply-side policies having a dampening effect on the inflation rate over a finite period of time (till the AS stopped shifting).

Blinder points out that supply-side policies, by themselves, would lower inflation marginally – about 1 percentage point. Inflation depends on the difference in the rates of growth of aggregate demand and supply. While the rate of growth of aggregate demand can be easily manipulated by changes in fiscal or monetary policy, the long-term rate of growth of the aggregate supply *cannot.* The latter, by definition, is the product of the amount of labour available multiplied by the amount of output, or the productivity of labour. The long-term growth rate of labour cannot be manipulated; it is basically a function of population growth. The supply-side policies might increase labour supply in the short term, but never in the long term.

The historical growth in productivity of the United States lies between 2 and 3 per cent. A huge increase in productivity (50 per cent, according to some supply-siders) would, according to these critics, border on the ridiculous. Furthermore, if it did take place, it would give rise to unprecedented inflation, especially if the increase in supply was accompanied by an increase in demand caused by cutting taxes.

It its noteworthy here that the dramatic decrease in inflation experienced during the 1980s was a product of the 'tight money' policies of the Federal Reserve during that period. Care should be taken to distinguish between 'inflation' and 'changes in the price level'; the former is always determined by the rate of growth of the money supply, while the latter is due either to brief changes in real variables like labour supply and demand, or to exogenous nominal or real shocks.

In the real world, however, it is very difficult to distinguish one from the other as even 'brief' policy changes in real variables take months and sometimes years, resulting in a continuous series of changes in price levels. On the other hand, the distinction between the two might be blurred because the shock to the economy that produces a once-and-for-all rise in the price level may have effects that are drawn out. This is why in the past few chapters we have used 'inflation' and 'changes in the price level' interchangeably.

The income distribution problem

The critics claim that supply-side policies further exacerbate income inequality. This is because the bulk of the tax cuts and capital gains cuts are aimed at the rich who earn most of the capital gains, interest, and dividends.

Economists of varying persuasions are surprisingly united when it comes to the issue of income distribution. In the United States, the extremes of the income scale have increased in number while the middle class has lost ground. In 1987, for instance, the top fifth of American families – those earning more than $50,000 – got approximately 45 per cent of all family income, a post-war high. The bottom fifth, earning less than $13,200, got 4.7 per cent, the lowest in twenty-five years. Families earning $15,000–$35,000 a year, adjusted for inflation, fell to 35 per cent of the total, down from 46 per cent in 1970.

While economists are universal in the recognition of this inequality, they disagree as to its cause. Some of the explanations are related to the decrease in manufacturing jobs, the increase of women in the work-force, the baby-boomers with their dual-income families, and, of course, the Reagan tax policies that they claim strongly favoured the rich.

Increases in deficits

The critics predicted that the Reagan tax cuts would not be offset by increasing tax revenues, but, on the contrary, tax revenues would fall drastically, leading to monstrous budget deficits. Since we have discussed both the views regarding the Reagan deficits in some detail in chapter 8, I have just listed this theoretical argument here for the sake of completeness.

Now comes the time of reckoning. We have studied all the views and the pros and cons of the Reagan policies. I have quoted eminent economists and politicians and whipped out neat intuitive frameworks to study entire policy prescriptions. But the question, inevitably, is asked by a student either in the front row or from somewhere in the murky back of the auditorium, for reasons that I have not yet begun to fathom. The question is clear, maybe with a hint of challenge. Like every good macroeconomist I have finally to make my stand, to present *my* opinion.

Here is the question.

But what do *you* think, Professor Langdana?

My answer is divided into two parts. First, I feel that it is still too soon to tell if the Reagan supply-side policies did succeed. Second, I subscribe to the view that Reaganomics is still unfinished business, 'unfinished' in the sense that the large deficits experienced in the 1980s have made cuts in government spending not just desirable, but absolutely necessary. Let us discuss these points in some detail.

I say that it is too soon to tell if Reaganomics has indeed succeeded because it is vital to distinguish the immediate effects of supply-side policies from the secondary, or final, effects. There is strong empirical evidence to indicate that, in the short term, the responsiveness of labour supply and the accumulation of savings are quite small. The main reason for this is that there are very real costs incurred when individuals change their pattern of labour supply. Furthermore, if individuals perceive the tax cuts to be *temporary*, then naturally they would be reluctant to supply more labour during the period of reduced taxes, only to cut back when taxes are increased again, because of the adjustment costs involved.

Since 1986 there has been a growing feeling amongst economists and policy makers that an increase in taxes in the future is 'inevitable'. Nervousness about the large bond-financed deficits compounded by doomsday predictions in the media have convinced workers that the tax cuts are temporary. This has stunted the outward shift of labour supply and labour demand. It remains to be seen if the present administration does keep taxes at the low levels of 1987 and 1988, or conveniently ignores election year promises and raises them.

If tax cuts do remain low, then this will provide greater impetus to the shifts in labour supply and demand by lending an air of permanence to tax policy. This is why I say that it is too soon to tell if President Reagan's policies have succeeded when it comes to the labour market.

In this world of individuals with rational expectations, the results of the policies of any one administration are strongly contingent on the *expectations* of individuals regarding the continuation of these policies by *succeeding administrations.* Once again, we must remember that policy is not a one-shot deal, but a 'rule' or a sequence extending into the future and the past.

The second part of my answer concerns the incompleteness of the Reagan agenda. 'Incomplete revolution' might perhaps be too much; let us just refer to it as an unfinished policy programme.

Budget deficits are financed by issuing government bonds to domestic and foreign residents (borrowing) or by issuing bonds to the Federal Reserve (monetizing the debt). The processes of government spending, taxes, and money creation are linked quite explicitly by the arithmetic of the intertemporal budget constraint.[3]

As we saw earlier, by cutting taxes and convincing (or persuading) the Federal Reserve to curtail the rate of money creation, the Reagan administration has made the cutting of government spending absolutely imperative. The arithmetic of deficit financing shows that if government spending were not cut, and the deficit consequently not reduced, then there would come a point when domestic and foreign individuals would *stop lending* funds to the US government. It would be impossible to sell any more government bonds. My research, presented in chapters 11–13, indicates that without any help from government spending cuts the present bond-financed deficits are *not* sustainable.[4]

Thus, in my opinion, it is this underlying intuition that prompted the Reaganists to pursue their unilateral tax cuts and thereby exacerbate the deficits. In this sense it is unfinished business because the next phase – that of actually cutting government spending – is hopefully about to begin.

Our next task is to study the government budget constraint. We will understand how deficits are financed and examine the issue of the debt explosion. We will also explicitly define 'sustainability' and review some previous research on the subject.

Chapter ten

Financing budget deficits

In the previous chapter we saw how the Reagan administration incurred large deficits (intentionally or unintentionally) and thereby exerted pressure on Congress to reduce current and future levels of government spending. The arithmetic of the government budget constraint is crucial to the notion that Congress will indeed have to relent by cutting its spending *if* the tax policy and money creation stay unchanged.

Let us begin with the extremely interesting analogy of Neil Wallace where he compares policy forming between the administration, Congress, and the Federal Reserve to a 'game of chicken'.[1]

Sargent's version of Wallace's game of chicken

I subscribe to Neil Wallace's interpretation of the financing of the Reagan deficits as a 'game of chicken'. Budget deficits are financed by issuing government bonds to domestic and foreign residents (borrowing), or by issuing bonds to the Federal Reserve (monetizing the debt). We will discuss both these mechanisms later in this chapter, but for now let us just say that deficits are financed by either borrowing from individuals and businesses, or by money creation by the Federal Reserve.

Wallace has different branches of the US government as different players in the game. These different branches have different preferences about what the size of government ought to be. Reducing the size of government is the objective of one of the players. Another player is strongly opposed to this objective. The game is played by three players, each of whom 'controls' one of the three policy instruments of government expenditure, tax collection, and money creation. The Reagan administration, in the spirit of the deliberately incomplete agenda, is the player whose main objective is to reduce the present value of government expenditure. The other players are described below.

There is a government expenditure authority, the Congress, that determines the sequence of government expenditures. There is a central bank, the Federal Reserve Board, that determines the process of money creation. Finally, there is the tax authority, whose role is assigned to the Reagan administration and whose responsibility it is to select a process for tax collection.

On a day-to-day basis, the three players are not forced to co-ordinate their strategies regarding tax policy, money creation, and government expenditure. As we shall see in the next chapter, they are, however, forced to co-ordinate their policies in the long term by virtue of the intertemporal government budget constraint.

According to this game of chicken played during the Reagan administration, the tax and monetary authorities both have the reduction of government expenditure, along with a stable price level, as their objective. While both these players have *no direct control* over this objective, Congress, the player that *does* control it, is assumed to have an insatiable thirst for more government spending. More specifically, Congress is assumed to desire a larger expected present value of government expenditures than the tax authority (the Reagan administration).

To achieve its purpose, the tax authority plays the following game. The present value of tax collections is reduced by a once-and-for-all reduction in taxes. The tax authority (the Reagan administration) then encourages the Federal Reserve to adhere to a Friedman-like x per cent growth rate. According to Sargent, Wallace refers to these as 'plays' made by the President and the Federal Reserve. Since these two plays are 'fixed', the only optional policy is that of a reduction in government spending by Congress. Let us examine this statement in the context of the government budget constraint.

The government budget constraint

The government's budget constraint is presented below in equation (10.1):

$$P(G-T) = \Delta B_f + \Delta B_p = \Delta H + \Delta B_p \tag{10.1}$$

This states that the nominal budget deficit, $P(G-T)$, is financed by borrowing either from the central bank, ΔB_f, or from the private sector, ΔB_p. The change in the central bank's holdings of government bonds (usually discounted treasury bills and bonds) is financed by additional money creation, so we can say that the budget deficit is financed by either issuing bonds or increasing the money supply.

When the Treasury finances its deficit by borrowing from the private sector, it engages in debt financing. In this case, the Treasury sells Treasury bonds or bills (T-bills) to the private sector. Individuals, firms, and banks pay for these securities with cheques which are usually deposited in Treasury accounts at private banks or at the central bank. The funds can then be spent at the discretion of the Treasury, just as if they were tax revenues.

Treasury bills are perhaps the most common form of government bond issuance.[2] Before the Second World War, the amount of Treasury bills outstanding rarely exceeded $2.5 billion. By 1945, however, the total had risen to $17 billion, at the beginning of this decade the outstanding volume was $216.1 billion, and they reached the record-high of $403.4 billion in 1986. Figure 10.1 shows net borrowing from the public and net borrowing by major source category.

T-bills are sold in minimum accounts of $10,000 and multiples of $5,000 above the minimum, although smaller denominations have been offered sometimes. These bills sell at a discount through competitive bidding with the return to the investor being the difference between the purchase price of the bill and its face, or par, value. The scheduled offerings of 91- and 182-day bills are regularly made on a weekly basis, and that of 52-week bills is made on a monthly basis.

When the Treasury borrows from the central bank to finance its deficit, it indulges in money financing. In this case, the central bank purchases debt directly from the Treasury. There is a major difference between borrowing from the public and borrowing from the central bank. When the central bank buys government bonds (Treasury debt), it pays for the debt by giving the Treasury a cheque on the central bank – in other words, by creating money. The money supply is increased when the Treasury spends the deposit it has received at the central bank in exchange for selling the government bonds, thus leaving the private sector with larger money holdings. This is commonly referred to as monetizing the debt.

Now let us return to Wallace's game of chicken. From constraint (10.1) we can see that if taxes were cut (T were reduced) and the Federal Reserve were persuaded to monetize smaller amounts of debt (ΔH were reduced), then *increases in deficits due to the tax cuts would have to be financed by selling more bonds.* Furthermore, any increases in government spending (G), with taxes and money creation held fixed, would mean that

Figure 10.1 **FEDERAL DEBT**

Total net borrowing from the public amounted to $1,906.3 billion in FY 1987, an increase of $157.2 billion from FY 1986. This chart has been presented to graphically show the increase in net borrowing from the public and the interest expense.

NET BORROWING FROM THE PUBLIC WITH INTEREST EXPENSE, FY 1977-87

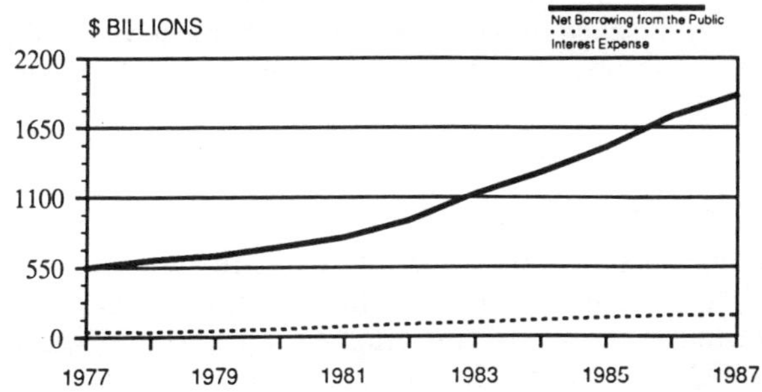

The Federal Debt schedule which follows reflects information on the borrowing of the Federal Government needed to finance the Government's operations. This table supports the balance sheet caption, "Debt issued under borrowing authority," which is shown net of intragovernmental holdings and unamortized premium or discount. Intragovernmental holdings represent that portion of the total Federal debt held by Federal entities, including the major trust funds. The distribution of 1987 net borrowing from the public by major source category is graphically depicted.

NET BORROWING BY MAJOR SOURCE CATEGORY

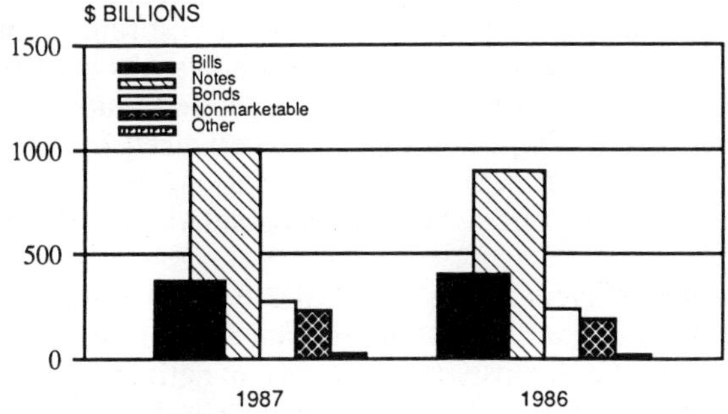

Source: Congressional Budget Office, *Outlook*, *Treasury Bulletin*

these increases would have to be financed by an equivalent amount of borrowing by issuing yet more bonds.

How long can this go on? My theoretical research indicates that increases in government spending cannot be perpetually financed by increases in bond sales, in the above situation.[3] Someone, or some 'player', will have to give in. In this case, since tax and money policies are fixed, the player that will be forced to relent due to the arithmetic of the government budget constraint is Congress – spending will *have* to be cut.

This is the essence of Wallace's game of chicken, and this is the view that I subscribe to when I refer to Reaganomics as unfinished business.

The backfire scenario

What if this massive gamble were to backfire? Or, to put it differently, what if Congress, despite the pressure to cut spending, is unable to make any significant progress in trimming expenditures? This is a nightmarish situation for the macroeconomist.

In this case, one (or both) of the other players would have to relent. Either taxes would have to increase (the administration relents), or the Federal Reserve would have to start monetizing larger amounts of bonds outstanding (the Fed. relents). The latter is perhaps more likely as monetary policy is more flexible than fiscal policy; changes in tax policies take years. Additionally, the Federal Reserve is sometimes forced to chicken out due to outside pressures. This happened in August 1982 and at the beginning of 1985.[4]

In 1982 the Fed. was responding to the Mexican crisis and the threat it posed to US financial stability. Monetary policy was eased and real interest rates were temporarily pushed down (figure 10.2). Beginning in 1985, the Fed. partially capitulated again from its tight money policy by trying to lower real interest rates in attempts to drive down the value of the dollar. This move was in response to the surge of protectionism that swept the United States as a result of the sharply escalating trade deficits experienced by Americans. As we will see later, these huge trade deficits are one consequence 'of the string of government deficits associated with the game of chicken'.[5]

Of the three players in the game, the Federal Reserve finds it the most difficult to adhere to its original fixed strategy of maintaining tight money because of pressures emanating from the international sector. For this reason I have analysed two economic scenarios in my research.

Figure 10.2

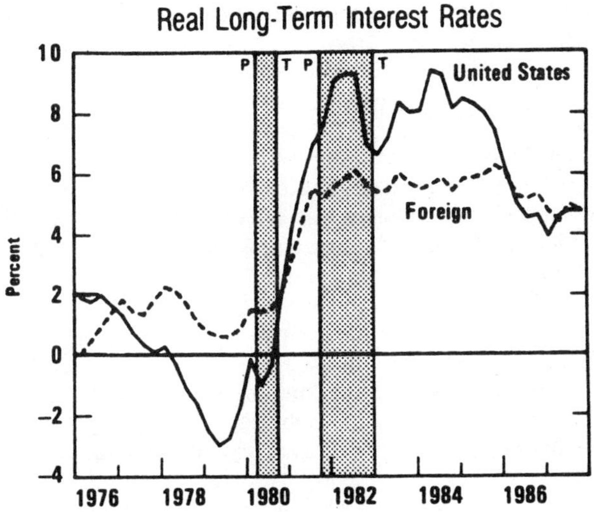

Sources: Congressional Budget Office; Federal Reserve Board; International Monetary Fund

The first scenario, case I, is that of an economy resembling the early 1980s when the Federal Reserve and the Administration clung doggedly to their fixed strategies. The second scenario, case II, is one that reflects the policies of the Federal Reserve after 1985. In this case, the monetary authority has been forced to relent from its tight money position, or to chicken out, and hence monetize significantly more debt.

While the authorities have been playing this game, we have observed significantly higher real interest rates on government debt during the 1980s. The result of these higher real interest rates on government debt and the existence of higher primary deficits is a growing real value of the stock of interest-bearing government debt.

The continuing rise in the stock of government debt is a clear signal that the game is very much in progress and that monetization, however large, is still insignificant. In relation to GNP, the real stock of interest-bearing federal debt *continues to grow* to unprecedented levels, with the $2 trillion barrier long broken.

Let us now study the causes and ramifications of this dramatic increase in government debt.

The debt explosion of the 1980s

Public debt as a percentage of GNP is presented in figure 10.3. We can see that this has been declining since the end of the Second World War. In 1945, public debt was 1.2 times the GNP. By 1948, the ratio of debt to GNP had fallen to 34 per cent. Between 1981 and 1987 the national debt rose from 27 per cent to about 43 per cent of GNP.

If these figures were to include the private debt of families (consumer installment credit plus mortgages), then debt would have risen from 58 per cent of personal income in 1975 to 75 per cent in 1986. The amount of personal debt accumulated by American families, on average, equals three-quarters of one year's income after taxes.

Over 20 per cent of federal government expenditures are devoted to interest payments, and the burden of private debt appears to be of the same magnitude as that of public debt. During the decade 1977 to 1987, per capita consumer debt almost tripled. Latin American countries are generally considered to be steeped in debt, but the combined debt of Mexico, Brazil, and Argentina is less than that of 2½ million US farmers.

This rapid escalation of government debt that resulted from policies adopted by the administration, the Federal Reserve, and Congress (note: all three players are responsible) has led to some bogus arguments about the burden of debt. Let us discuss these before dealing with the real problems that arise when the government spends more than it takes in through taxation.

Argument 1: It will bankrupt the nation. Like any family or business, a nation has some maximum amount of borrowing that it can indulge in. If this maximum amount of debt were exceeded, then the nation would be unable to meet its principal and interest payments and default on the debt.

Answer: This is a false analogy. The US government need never fear defaulting on its debt because, unlike private debtors, it has the enormous ability to raise revenues by taxation. Furthermore, the debt is paid back in US dollars, and in a crisis the central bank would certainly intervene by monetizing large amounts of debt.

Figure 10.3 Federal debt held by the public

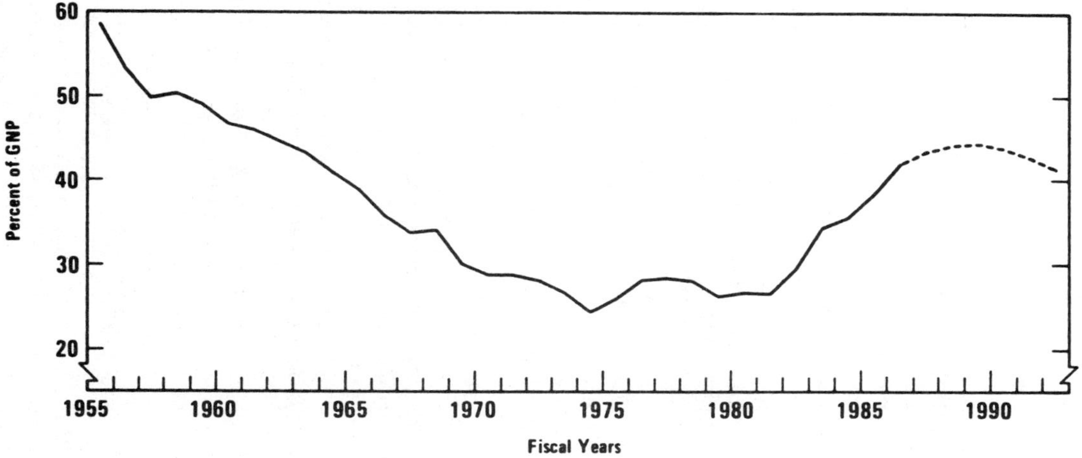

Sources: Congressional Budget Department; Office of Management and Budget; Department of the Treasury; Department of Commerce, Bureau of Economic Analysis

Another extremely important reason why the above argument might not hold is that as long as GNP continues to grow at the same or greater rate than the public debt, the burden of the debt will remain the same or decline. Therefore, economic growth is the best protection against an increasing debt burden. We will discuss what 'sustainability' exactly means in the context of this statement right after we finish refuting the following bogus arguments about deficits.

Argument 2: Future generations, namely our children and grandchildren, will be burdened by heavy interest payments. Taxes will eventually have to rise to meet these payments.
Answer: This is an understandable sentiment given that the massive deficits have caused the administration to borrow more than half a billion dollars a day for debt service. If monetary policy and government spending were to stay unchanged, then the administration would have to give in by virtue of the arithmetic of the budget constraint, and taxes would eventually have to be raised.

But let us not forget that the same generations that pay these higher taxes will also be reaping the fruits of higher interest payments. Thus one group of Americans will be making payments to another. Blinder writes that 'while some people will gain and others will lose, the future generation as a whole will come out even'.[6]

The only problem with the above argument, according to some economists, is that substantially large amounts of government bonds are bought by foreigners. The inclusion of the foreign sector raises a host of issues such as: (i) How does the inflow of capital from abroad affect the sustainability of US budget deficits? (ii) Is there a link between the budget deficit and the trade deficit? If so, what is it? (iii) How does the government borrowing affect exchange rates? To provide answers to these questions, a review of macroeconomic policies incorporating the foreign sector (the open economy) is in order.

Budget deficits, trade deficits, and exchange rates

The US economy today is characterized by large trade deficits and equally large capital inflows. Both of these are a continuous source of concern to a large number of people. The former is taken to be a sign of some national malaise, while the latter has proved worrisome in that 'foreigners are buying up America'.

Foreigners are indeed buying substantially large amounts of government debt. For instance, since just 1987 the Japanese have increased their purchase of US government bonds by as much as 65 per cent. By some estimates, anything from 30 to 35 per cent of US government debt is bought by foreigners (figures 10.4 and 10.5).

In this case, interest payments on debt will not simply be a transfer among two different groups of Americans, but will constitute a net outflow of funds from the country. The potential decrease in national wealth has worried some economists and forced other, more strident ones to make statements such as 'foreigners are holding the US economy hostage.' Let us examine these concerns in the framework presented in figure 10.6.

Figure 10.4 Net purchases of long-term domestic securities by selected countries. Calendar years 1984 through 1988, second quarter

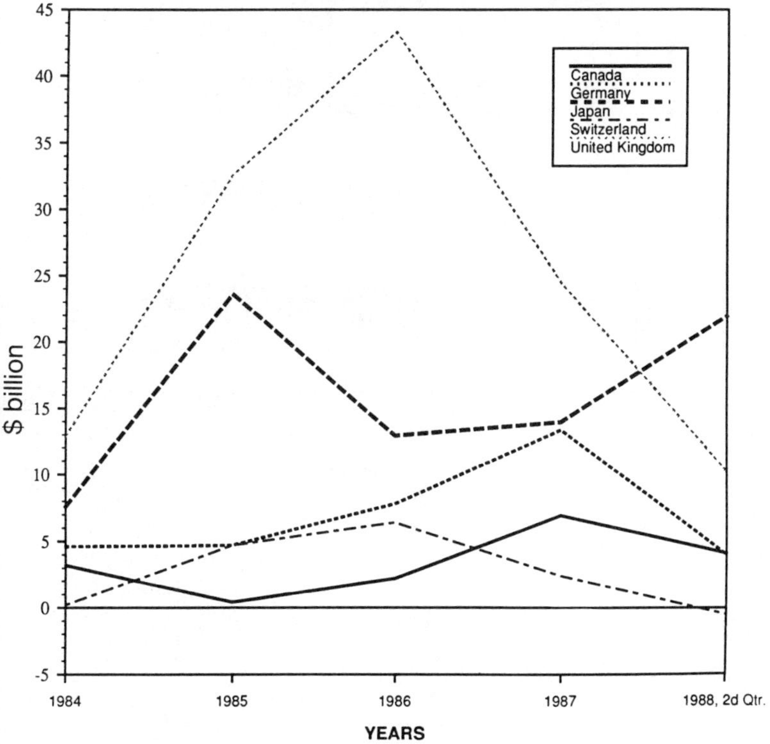

Source: Congressional Budget Office, *Outlook, Treasury Bulletin*

Figure 10.5 Liabilities to foreigners. Calendar years 1983–8 (reported by international banking facilities and by banks in the United States)

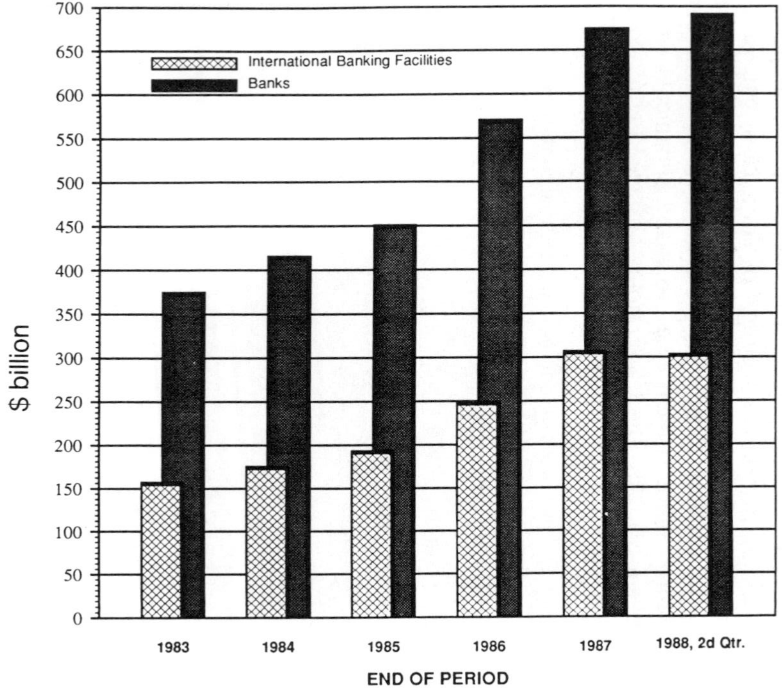

Source: Congressional Budget Office, *Outlook*, *Treasury Bulletin*

Figure 10.6 (a)

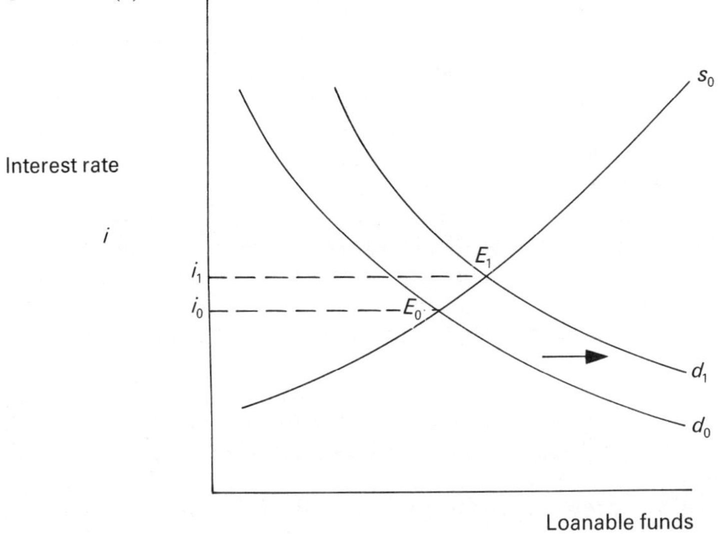

(b)

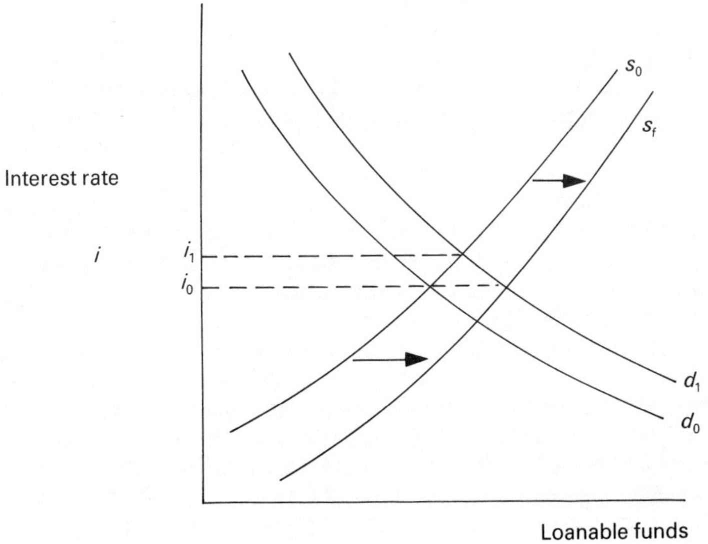

Figure 10.6(a) is a diagram of the market of loanable funds: s_0 and d_0 are the initial supply and demand curves, and equilibrium is at E_0 with the prevailing interest rate being i_0. We assume here that the government incurs a budget deficit and finances it by borrowing from the domestic public. Domestic money creation is held fixed. This will cause the demand for loanable funds, d_0, to increase and shift out to d_1. The new equilibrium is now at a *higher* interest rate i_1.

Increased government borrowing, in this case, has caused the finite supply of loanable funds to be more 'expensive', or the interest rate to escalate. This, as we have studied earlier, is detrimental to private investment as private investors are crowded out of the market of loanable funds as costs of borrowing are now prohibitive.

The time has finally come to extend our analysis to the foreign sector. How would foreign investors react to this? What are the implications of these high US interest rates for international capital flows?

As domestic and foreign investors realize that the American rates exceed those of the rest of the world, they rush to take advantage of these high yields. Individuals switch from holding foreign securities to US securities. This, in turn, increases the demand for US currency as these bonds have to be purchased in US dollars. As foreigners flock to exchange their own currency for US currency (which is now in great demand thanks to the high rates), the US currency gets more expensive in terms of units of foreign currency.

For example, before the increase in American interest rates, 170 yen might have been exchanged for 1 US dollar, but now, with the higher interest rates, 240 yen might be exchanged for 1 US dollar. The dollar, in this case, has gotten 'stronger', or the domestic currency has 'appreciated'.

In the mid 1980s, as US nominal and real rates rose to new heights in the wake of the severe monetary contraction of 1980–2, the US dollar reached unprecedented strength by achieving its record-high in 1985, as shown in figures 10.7 (a) and (b).

This extraordinary appreciation of the US dollar resulted in American goods becoming more 'expensive' to foreigners, as they now had to exchange more of their currency for one unit of US currency. Similarly, foreign goods became increasingly more affordable to US residents, with the net result that Americans were buying more of these 'cheaper' goods and services from abroad than they were exporting. Thus, it can be argued that the pressure on the demand for loanable funds arising from the need to finance the large deficits led to the eventual strengthening of the dollar and

Figure 10.7 (a) Real long-term interest rates; (b) Real exchange rate and relative interest rates

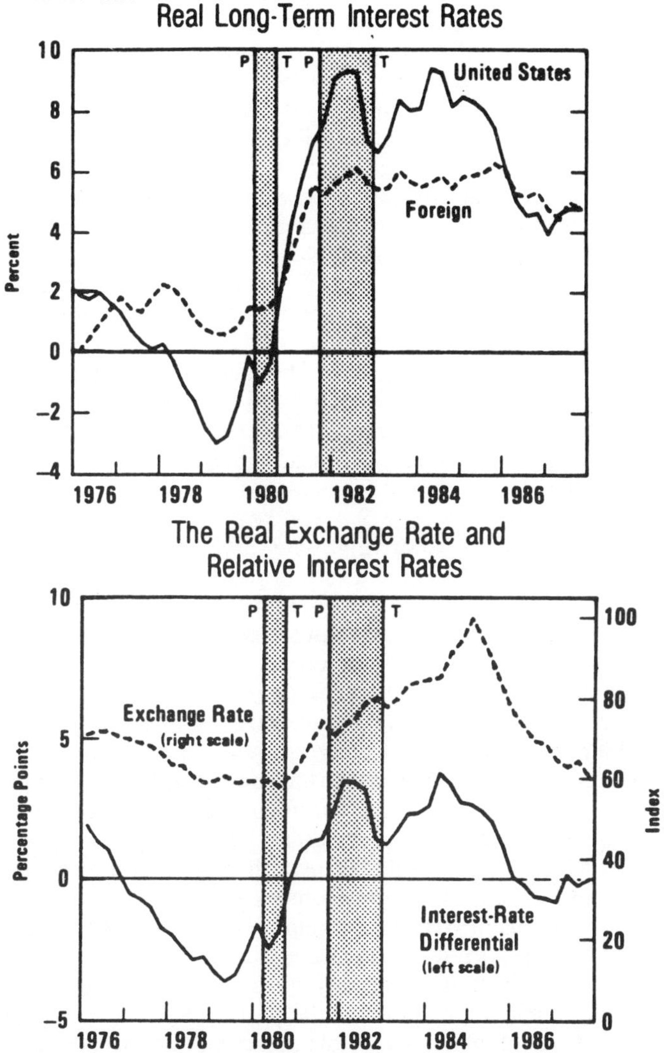

Source: Congressional Budget Office; Federal Reserve Board, International Monetary Fund

Note: The real exchange rate is a trade-weighted average of dollar exchange rates adjusted for consumer price inflation. Expected inflation is proxied by a two-year centred moving average of actual and projected CPI inflation. The foreign real interest rate is a GDP-weighted average of the rates of other major industrial countries. The interest rate differential is the US rate less the foreign rate.

the consequent deterioration of the US's trade balance during the 1980s.

The current account deficit, which is the deficit in goods and services traded internationally, increased quite dramatically till it matched the budget deficit in 1986–7 at about $200 billion. The current account, shown in figure 10.8, is usually referred to as the trade deficit by the media. Its full definition is that it is the account of the balance of payments in which the value of the flows of goods and services that are internationally traded, and the current receipts and payments between domestic and foreign residents, are recorded.

The deterioration of the US export sector, particularly the manufacturing sector, has led to a tremendous amount of pressure on the Fed. to weaken the dollar and stimulate exports by making them 'cheaper' to foreigners. The Fed. has complied to some extent, and the dollar has fallen quite substantially with respect to some currencies – by as much as 30 per cent with respect to the Japanese yen. However, US trade deficits have declined *only marginally*. This is due to four reasons:

1. US residents, perceiving some foreign goods to be of superior quality, have developed a certain product loyalty and hence are willing to pay marginally higher prices.
2. The percentage increase in the price of imported goods has been *far lower* than the percentage decline in the strength of the dollar. This is primarily due to the fact that foreign exporters, mainly the Japanese, have allowed the effect of the weaker dollar to 'pass through'. They simply cut their profit margins in attempts to avoid the sharp and traumatic price increases of their exports that might have resulted from the deliberate weakening of the dollar. In this sense, they let the effects of the weaker dollar 'pass through' their export sector without having any serious consequences.
3. Some South-east Asian countries like Taiwan and South Korea, that currently experience budget surpluses with the US, have their currencies 'pegged' to the US dollar. Therefore, any deliberate manipulations on the part of the Fed. to weaken the dollar would only result in the currencies of these countries weakening proportionately, leaving the trade balance unchanged.
4. Central bank intervention in foreign currency markets either to strengthen or to weaken the national currency would only have temporary effects at best. *As long* as there are sizeable deficits, the private and the public sector will be forced to

Figure 10.8 The real trade balance

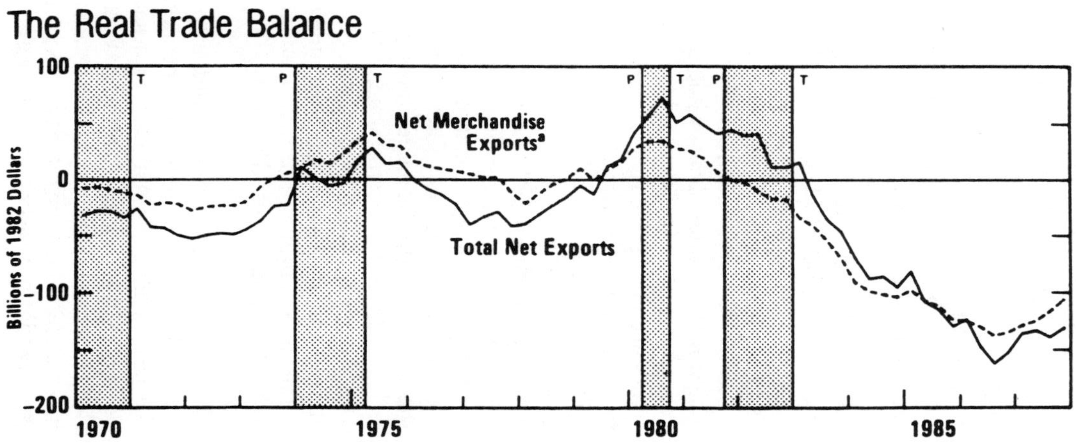

Sources: Congressional Budget Office, Department of Commerce, Bureau of Economic Analysis
Note: Net merchandise exports are non-petroleum non-agricultural merchandise.

compete for a finite supply of loanable funds. As we have seen, this will inevitably result in higher domestic interest rates and, eventually, a stronger national currency.

Furthermore, intervention would only temporarily affect the nominal exchange rate, which is the domestic currency price of foreign currency. To affect the trade deficit, the real exchange rate, which is the relative price of foreign goods in the domestic currency with respect to the price of domestic goods in the domestic currency, would have to change. The real exchange rate is *not* a policy instrument and it is extremely difficult to manipulate as it is a function of the nominal exchange rate, as well as the domestic and foreign inflation rates. We will study both these exchange rates in detail in Chapter 11.

As the US trade deficits worsen, domestic residents acquire imported goods and services, while foreign residents accumulate US dollar deposits which they *re-invest* in the United States to take advantage of the high interest rates. Thus, while the United States suffers a current account deficit, it also benefits from a net capital inflow, or a capital account surplus, which helps partially to finance the deficit. The capital account is defined as the account of the balance of payments that records the receipts from non-residents and payments made to non-residents arising from the issuance of new debt, or the repayment of existing debt.

Going back to figure 10.6(b), we see that this inflow of capital results in the increase in the supply of loanable funds from s_0 to s_f, where s_f denotes domestic savings *plus* foreign inflows. This shift to the right in the supply of the loanable funds curve exerts an ameliorating effect on domestic interest rates. The equilibrium interest rate now falls from i_1, which is the initial equilibrium rate without capital inflows and with increased government borrowing, to i_0, which is the new equilibrium rate resulting from the increased supply of loanable funds due to the foreign capital inflows.

Thus, while it is true that interest paid on bonds to foreigners is 'lost' from the national wealth, it must also be noted that this interest paid is the cost incurred in maintaining domestic interest rates to levels *below* i_1 (not necessarily all the way back to i_0, but below i_1). These lower interest rates prevent the excessive crowding out of private investment which might have taken place at the higher rate i_1, when we did not incorporate the foreign sector and the capital inflows associated with it.

Foreign capital inflows

The financial flows that have accompanied the large US current account deficit have transformed the United States from a net international creditor of $141 billion in 1981, the record-high, to a net debtor of $264 billion in 1986. Gross US liabilities to foreigners have risen accordingly, from $689 to $1,401 billion. As the budget deficits and the higher interest rates (in the United States) are expected to persist over the near future, current account deficits and capital inflows are expected to grow accordingly.[7]

Another factor that has contributed significantly to the increase in the capital inflows experienced by the United States is the ongoing deregulation of financial markets, combined with the extensive liberalization of international capital flows, particularly in Japan. For instance, the maximum allowable proportion of foreign securities in the portfolios of banks in Japan has been raised from 6 per cent in 1983 to about 16 per cent in 1988.

While these capital inflows finance the budget deficits to some extent, they have, however, raised several concerns about their effects. One major concern is that there will come a time when foreign investors will simply refuse to absorb any more debt. This might happen if there exists an upper limit, or a 'satiation' point, in the amount of US government bonds that foreigners might want to include in their portfolios. If this should happen, the Federal Reserve would have no other recourse but to create money to meet the principal and the interest payments on existing debt. This unanticipated money creation would result in a rapid escalation of the price level accompanied by a currency collapse reminiscent of the German hyperinflation of the 1920s.

This is indeed a legitimate concern, and I have specifically recreated and researched this scenario in case II in chapter 13. In fact, some economists believe that foreign investors have already begun to shift away from holding US liabilities. They feel that it is only the manipulation of the dollar by the central bank that has sustained the aggregate level of capital inflows without any major increase in US interest rates.

I think that this concern is premature. While it is true that foreign-held private holdings of US Treasury securities did slow down between 1985 and 1986, and declined in 1987 (see figure 10.4), foreign private purchases of *corporate securities* increased sharply after 1986. Direct investment in automobile plants, electronics, and joint ventures also continues to grow. Therefore, it seems that what we perceive as a dangerous slowing-down in the purchase of US debt by foreign investors is actually an attempt by them to diversify their portfolios.

Another concern is that the huge inflow of capital is mirrored by an equally large deterioration in the current account deficit (or, loosely speaking, the trade deficit). We have seen how current account deterioration is the mechanism that allows foreign savings to supplement domestic savings in financing domestic government deficits (figure 10.6). US residents consume larger amounts of the cheaper (and, in some cases, perceived to be better) imported goods as the dollar appreciates (gets stronger), while foreigners accumulate dollar deposits which they eventually 'turn around' and re-invest in America.

This is particularly troublesome to certain specific lobby groups that contend that the United States is 'losing jobs to foreign competition' and that the nation will eventually be a service-oriented economy, weak in heavy manufacturing – a nation of 'hamburger flippers'. This is an entirely bogus argument and a false concern. There is no evidence of any positive correlation between US trade deficits and civilian unemployment. In fact, as trade deficits have soared, unemployment has *decreased* as we saw earlier. This economy has been hovering at or below the full-employment rate of 6 per cent since 1987, as shown in figure 10.9.

While it is undoubtedly true that certain sectors have suffered unemployment due to foreign competition, at the aggregate level more jobs have been created as foreign companies set up in the United States to manufacture goods independently (Nissan and Toyota in Tennessee, Honda in Ohio), or by means of joint ventures with their US competitors. Additionally, the consumer has benefited by being able to choose from a wide variety of domestic and foreign goods. US producers have been *forced* to snap out of the lethargy that mysteriously gripped them in the 1970s and to compete in terms of quality and price with foreign manufacturers.

Furthermore, the trade deficit by itself is not really an accurate summary of how well (or how poorly) US businesses do abroad. The trade deficit includes *only* those goods that clear customs; in the case of Japan, for instance, it includes only the goods shipped back and forth across the Pacific. It excludes altogether the billions in sales racked up by some 250 US companies with production and sales operations *within* Japan.[8] These businesses range from over 470 McDonald's restaurants to Coca-Cola (Japan's best-selling soft drink) to IBM. All of these companies manufacture and sell within Japan and thus their sales cannot be included as US 'exports' to help balance the trade 'deficit'. And yet these sales

Figure 10.9 Civilian unemployment rates

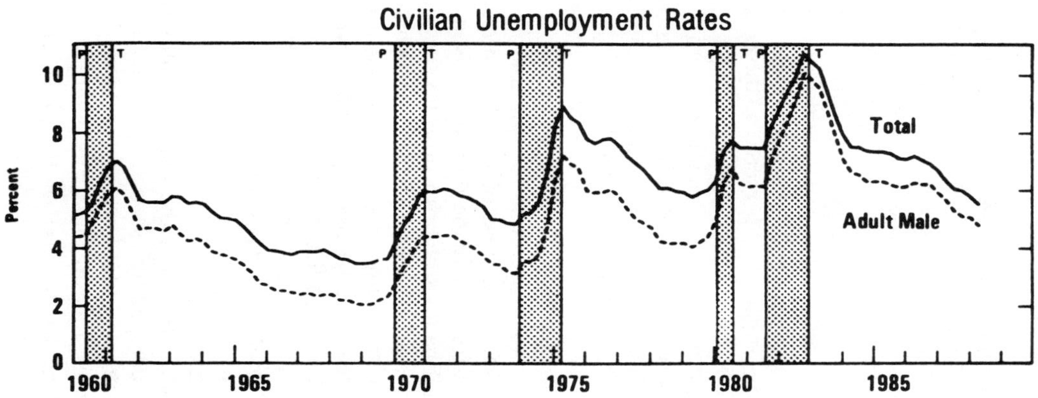

Sources: Congressional Budget Office, Department of Labor, Bureau of Labor Statistics; Department of Commerce, Bureau of Economic Analysis eventually benefit Americans in both increased jobs and higher returns to shareholders.

I do not imply that trade deficits do not exist, but only that we should recognize that the numbers by themselves tend to distort the picture and make an already nervous public even more vulnerable to protectionist sentiments.

Unfortunately, the strong and strident protectionist lobby in the United States refuses to acknowledge that trade deficits do not imply higher unemployment rates and that the average consumer is indeed better off in an economy free of protectionist tariffs and barriers. This group also raises the concern 'what if all the foreign investors were to pull out their money simultaneously?' They feel that this situation is tantamount to the United States being held hostage to the whims of foreign investors. This, again, is another false concern, and my response to these xenophobes is as follows. The argument that foreigners will pump the dollars back into the United States only as long as they perceive it (the country) to be a safe haven, is full of holes.

The first experience in recent memory, with large capital inflows, was at a time when the United States was far from being a safe haven. This occurred during the crippling stagflation of the 1970s when the OPEC countries pumped back large quantities of petro-dollars, which they had suddenly (and happily) accumulated as a result of their embargoes.

Another reason for the increase in foreign holdings of US debt during this period was not because of high US interest rates and the strong dollar, but for exactly the opposite reason. In the early 1970s foreign central banks sought to prop up the rapidly falling dollar by buying dollar-denominated assets, particularly Treasury bonds. Also, foreign banks used the US dollar as a reserve asset and thus increased their holdings of dollars. These were held in the form of T-Bills and bonds, in lieu of gold, sterling, or other assets. In short, the sharp increase in foreign ownership of US debt took place for reasons *that are independent of US budget deficit concerns*, which is what really bothers those who worry about foreigners financing the deficits.

Concerning the comment that the United States is gravitating towards being a completely service-oriented economy, my response is that if this is indeed where the United States has a comparative advantage, then by all means it should specialize and exploit this advantage to the best of its ability. In all fairness, though, I must add that it is still not clear why the United States is moving towards a service-oriented society. Is it due to 'crowding out' due to high interest rates caused by excessive government borrowing that eventually results in foreign goods becoming 'cheaper'? Or are the interest rates higher due to government borrowing alone, or to government borrowing *in conjunction* with the strong demand for loanable funds from a healthy and growing private sector?

The empirical evidence is strongly divided, but if high interest rates are a result of increased government borrowing, then continually growing budget deficits would result in a decline in long-term capital accumulation. The effects of changes in the real interest rate due to government borrowing are included in the extension of case I of my research model in Chapter 11.

The last myth that we are about to explode is that sooner or later the United States will have to pay off its debt, and that when the fateful day of reckoning arrives the economy will simply collapse. Dante would have a field day.

This takes us to the next subject, namely the economics of making the principal and interest payments on existing government debt.

'Rolling over' the government debt

Argument: The huge government borrowing will ruin the nation when this enormous debt is repaid.
Answer: Once again, the confusion lies in comparing the nation with a private entity. Unlike the latter, the nation need never pay off all its debt. Instead, each time the principal and interest payments are due, the US Treasury can simply roll over its debt by floating more debt. And this is precisely what the Treasury does.

According to research done by W. Michael Cox of the Federal Reserve Bank of Dallas, 100 per cent of all the interest payments since January 1971 have been totally debt financed. Over the 1950–81 period, he finds an average of 60 cents of every $1 of interest payment to be financed by simply borrowing more.[9] The question then is: 'How long can the United States keep financing its deficits by "rolling over" the debt to domestic and foreign residents?' This, after all, lies at the core of the issue of the sustainability of deficits.

Sargent and Wallace explore this issue of sustainability in 'Some unpleasant monetarist arithmetic' by examining a closed economy. By definition, this approach ignores the foreign sector and the capital inflows and deficits associated with it.[10] To understand the intuition underlying Sargent and Wallace's notion of sustainability, let us take the following simple example.

Let the government have an initial stock of bonds outstanding, say $100, on which the rate of interest is, say, 10 per cent per annum.[11] In year 2 the government would have to sell $10 worth of bonds to pay for the interest on the initial $100. It has simply 'rolled over' the interest payment. (We assume that the Fed. does not monetize any debt here.) In year 3 the government would have to issue $11 worth of bonds to pay the $10 interest on the original $100 plus the $1 interest on the $10 bond issued in year 2. This process would continue indefinitely with the stock of bonds growing at 10 per cent per annum.

Since the rate of interest on bonds is composed of two components, the real rate and the inflation premium, the real stock of government bonds outstanding would not be growing at the same rate of interest. The growth of the *real* stock would, in fact, equal the *real* rate of interest which is determined by the rate of growth of the economy, namely the growth in population, stock of capital equipment, and overall wealth.

Thus, provided the economy is growing, the government can exploit the device of rolling over the debt (borrowing to pay interest and principal), only to the extent that it permits its stock of bonds outstanding to grow at, or below, the rate of growth of the economy as a whole.

But what would happen if the stock of government bonds grows faster than the growth of total wealth in the economy? This is an extremely important and pertinent question, because this did in fact happen in the United States in the early 1980s, and since 1986 the two rates have remained dangerously close.

Sargent and Wallace begin their analysis by assuming that the real rate of growth of government bonds is greater than that of the economy. As we will see later, they conclude that such a method of bond financing is not sustainable. One of the three 'players', the Federal Reserve in this case, would have to step in and monetize large portions of the outstanding debt, causing a resurgence of inflation and thus making the arithmetic 'unpleasant'. I extend their analysis to take into account the large capital inflows that mirror the current account deficits and determine if 'rolling over' might succeed if the foreign sector is incorporated. This is done in chapters 11–13.

Coming back to our simple framework here, in an economy where the rate of growth of government bonds exceeds that of the growth of the economy, the fraction of government bonds held in the portfolios of households and firms will steadily rise. Eventually, all private sector assets will consist of nothing but government bonds. Individuals will not hold physical capital or corporate debt, as government bonds will be the only debt in existence. Since government debt *does not* generate any real return while real capital does, the interest payments on government debt would simply amount to a transfer of wealth from taxpayers to bondholders. This is why an economy with runaway debt issuances will be characterized by a deteriorating capital stock and macroeconomic decline.

Our next task is to study the open-economy rational expectations models of sustainability. We will begin with a review of Dornbusch's model of sustainability and move on to determine if the US's bond-financed deficits are any more or less sustainable after taking into account the large capital inflows experienced in the 1980s.

Chapter eleven

The sustainability of deficits: model description

This chapter presents a framework for exploring the sustainability of bond-financed deficits in the presence of capital inflows. A 'sustainable' deficit-financing policy is defined as one in which the combination of debt financing and seigniorage prevents the deterioration of the domestic current account balance and an exodus of domestic real wealth. A policy in which the combination cannot prevent a growing current account deficit and a depletion of real wealth is a 'non-sustainable' policy, with non-sustainability further divided into 'strong' and 'weak' non-sustainability. This will become clearer when we discuss the results of our policy experiments.

We have seen in earlier chapters that the present state of the US economy can be characterized by large domestic and current account deficits, increasing amounts of capital inflows, and a dollar that has only recently come off its 1985 record-high. This scenario, coupled with the renewed and vigorous attention devoted to the twin deficits following the stock-market crash of 19 October 1987, has raised a host of issues, some of which are:

1. Can the government continue on a path of large fiscal deficits without accommodation from the monetary authority, or how long can the government 'roll over' its debt by issuing more bonds and without any increased monetization from the monetary authority?
2. How does the inflow of capital affect the sustainability of domestic budget deficits, or how is the 'rolling over' policy affected in a milieu of large capital inflows?
3. How should fiscal and monetary policy be conducted in the above situation, and what are the effects of these policies on key macroeconomic variables such as the price level, nominal and real interest and exchange rates, and individuals' wealth holdings?

4. Most importantly, is there an upper limit on the amount of debt the government can roll over by issuing new debt? Will monetary accommodation be inevitable, and if so, when? In other words, how sustainable is the US budget deficit in the presence of capital inflows and under the present policies of rolling over a substantial portion of the existing debt by issuing new government bonds?

Before we proceed with an overview of the current literature, a review of the standard approach to determining sustainability is in order. This approach is applicable only in the case when increases in government spending are financed solely by issuing more bonds; there is no increased monetization on the part of the Federal Reserve, and this case corresponds to case I, discussed later in this chapter. While this approach is quite different from that taken in the research model, it nevertheless provides us with a good intuitive feel for the subject of sustainability.

The Dornbusch model of sustainability

The following simple example of a closed economy, with no domestic money creation, illustrates the meaning of a 'sustainable' debt-financing policy as used in the context of this book.

Let P be the price level, y the real output or GNP, D the real primary deficit (the non-interest part of the actual deficit), i the after-tax gross nominal interest paid by the government on its debt, and B the nominal debt outstanding. The change in the real value of the debt, B/P, over time can be shown to be

$$\frac{d(B/P)}{dt} = D + r\,B/P \tag{11.1}$$

Here r is the real interest rate and the right-hand side is the primary deficit D plus the real interest on public debt, or the inflation-corrected deficit, while the left-hand side is the increase in real debt.

Defining the ratio $d = D/y$ as the primary deficit as a fraction of GNP and the ratio $b = B/Py$ as the debt to income ratio, equation (11.1) can be written as

$$\text{inflation-corrected deficit as a fraction of GNP} = d + rb$$

The important question is that, given d and r, what is the behaviour of b? The examination of the deficit–GNP ratio over time has been one of the central issues in determining the sustainability of domestic deficits.

Using the definition of b, and $g = \dot{y}/y$, the growth rate of output, we have the following expression:[1]

$$\dot{b} = d + (r - g)b \tag{11.2}$$

Models incorporating various forms of this equation have been fairly common in the deficit dynamics literature. In equation (11.2) the debt–income ratio rises if the primary deficit, d, exceeds the debt–income ratio multiplied by the excess of the real interest rate over the growth rate of output. Equation (11.2) has been used to analyse the existence, and the behaviour, of steady states in which b reaches a constant level.

From equation (11.2) it can be seen that if the primary deficit, d, is positive, and if the real interest rate, r, exceeds the economy's growth rate, g, then the debt–income ratio *keeps on increasing.* Given a positive primary deficit, there can be no steady-state debt–income ratio *unless* the growth rate exceeds the real interest rate. The intuition behind this is that with a primary deficit the government is always issuing new debt, and the only way the debt–income ratio can be kept from increasing is if income is growing fast. But if the interest rate on existing debt exceeds the growth rate of GNP, the rate at which interest payments on the debt mount up outweighs the effects of the growth of GNP in permitting debt issues that do not increase the debt–income ratio. With debt rising relative to income, one or more of the following three things must eventually happen: (i) The government raises taxes to increase revenue with which to serve the debt and slow down the growth of the debt to below the rate of income growth. (ii) The government creates a big unanticipated inflation to wipe out the debt in real terms. (iii) The public debt is repudiated or written down. In this book, a 'weakly non-sustainable' deficit-financing policy is defined as one in which the primary debt, d, is positive, the real interest rate, r, exceeds g, the economy's growth rate, and the fiscal/monetary authorities are *forced* to resort to one of the three extreme measures listed above. It is assumed here that the second option, the large-scale monetization of the deficit resulting in a large unanticipated inflation, is the one most likely to occur and therefore a weakly non-sustainable debt-financing policy is taken to be one in which monetary accommodation is expected in the future.

We define a 'strongly non-sustainable' debt-financing policy as one in which the monetary athority has had to purchase a large amount of government debt due to the reluctance of the public to accept any more government bonds in their portfolios. This economy is characterized by an exploding price level and a collapse of the domestic currency. Both the weak and the strong forms of non-sustainability will be made clearer with the discussion of the results of cases I and II, respectively.

In the period following the Second World War till 1982, the growth rate of the output, *g*, has been in the 3–4 per cent range, while the real after-tax rate on US Treasury securities has been of the order of 2–3 per cent. Consequently, debt dynamics have never been explosive. After 1982, however, the real rate has either exceeded the growth rate, or come dangerously close to it. This economic backdrop makes the issues that this book tackles timely and pertinent.

Sargent and Wallace (1981, 1985) show that in a closed economy where the monetary base is closely connected to the price level and the monetary authority can raise seigniorage, the monetary authority's control over inflation is very limited. By assuming that the real rate of return exceeds the growth rate of the economy, they establish inherently unstable debt dynamics. They give particular attention to the inflation option, especially when fiscal policy 'dominates' monetary policy. In this case they have the fiscal authority independently setting its budgets and announcing all current and future deficits and surpluses, thereby determining the amounts of revenue that must be raised through the sale of government bonds and seigniorage. Sargent and Wallace demonstrate that if the demand for government bonds implies an interest rate on bonds greater than the economy's growth rate, then, in the presence of deficits, the monetary authority is unable to contain the growth rate of the money supply for ever, i.e. monetary accommodation is inevitable.

The objective of the research in the next three chapters, in a specific sense, is to extend the Sargent and Wallace analysis by incorporating the foreign sector and to determine if bond-financed deficits are indeed non-sustainable *even when* domestic savings are supplemented by foreign savings in the form of capital inflows. These inflows are a direct consequence of the large current account deficits experienced by the United States since 1980, and their present persistently large rate of growth makes this an important topic.

Furthermore, the model constructed in these chapters is amenable to an analysis of price and exchange rate volatility in a regime of forward-looking individuals with rational expectations. Exchange rate volatility, in particular, must emerge as fluctuations either in the prices of tradable goods or in the profits of the firms producing them. This is especially important in a situation such as the present where studies indicate that Japanese firms are choosing to sacrifice profits by absorbing any systematic downward movement in the dollar resulting from the international exchange rate accords, thereby leaving the trade, in real terms, unchanged. We will study these accords and their relative successes and failures in chapter 13.

In addition to determining the sustainability of bond-financed deficits and the volatility of domestic prices and exchange rates, we will also discuss the case incorporating the real interest rate effects on sustainability. Before proceeding with the model description, a brief overview of the recent related macroeconomic research is in order. This undertaking follows next.

Related research

Currently there are two broad classes of macroeconomic models of the open economy. The first class is one in which the models represent a short-term partial equilibrium portfolio balance perspective. In this class (Mundell-Fleming 1962, Driskill and McCafferty 1980), the recent strengthening of the US dollar from 1982 to 1985, for example, could be explained in terms of the effect the increased government spending has on the domestic and foreign interest rate differential. High and rising US real interest rates associated with domestic budget deficits, in this view, have created an interest rate diferential that has attracted foreign capital inflow. The inflow has, in turn, caused a temporary appreciation of the dollar exchange rate above long-term equilibrium value associated with purchasing power parity. In this class of models, for the example under consideration, the real value of the dollar would gradually fall back to its former level either because interest rates would eventually fall, or because investors might become reluctant to invest an increasingly large share of their portfolios in dollar-denominated securities.

The second class of models not only considers the short-term portfolio adjustments, but also incorporates the long-term effects on goods markets and interest rates in a world of perfect capital mobility. This broader asset market approach (Dornbusch 1976, Branson 1977, 1985, McTaggart 1985) assumes two-way causation. The exchange rate, in this view, is determined proximately by financial market equilibrium conditions. It, in turn, influences the current account balance. The latter, in its turn, is the foreign rate of accumulation of domestic national debt, and this feeds back into the financial market equilibrium. Thus, the general equilibrium asset market approach contains a dynamic feedback mechanism in assets and exchange rates.

This second class of models has various sub-classes. One of these is the equilibrium models based on first principles of explicit utility maximization subject to budget constraints – primarily overlapping generations and two-period models. The models of Frenkel and Razin (1984a, b) are good examples of these. These general equilibrium models have been used quite frequently in the recent literature to assess the effects of permanent versus transitory fiscal policies as well as changes in countries' net debtor positions on world rates of interest, domestic and foreign wealth, and spending. However, even modest complications render these models quite intractable. For instance, most of these models are simplified 'real' models, and hence they ignore the effects stemming from the interaction of fiscal and monetary policy. These effects, on the contrary, are deemed to be of central importance in this thesis, as (i) the sustainability of domestic and current account deficits is viewed in the context of expected future monetization, and (ii) the behaviour of prices and particularly exchange rates is explained in terms of present and anticipated monetary and fiscal (primary tax) policies. For the reasons mentioned above, the model implemented in this dissertation is not of the general equilibrium class of models.

McTaggart (1985, 1988) constructs a model that lies within another sub-class of the second class of models. The two-sector open-economy log–linear rational expectations model is rich enough to capture the important feedback effects from asset markets to the product markets, and vice versa. It is specified so that solution techniques developed in conjunction with linear rational expectation models can be applied and the evolution of the economy be simulated under different policy experiments. McTaggart explicitly models a medium to large economy producing a single tradable good in an economy where the markets are those of domestic output, domestic money, domestic bonds, and foreign exchange. The agents are domestic households, the Treasury, the Federal Reserve, foreign residents, and later, when the model is extended to two sectors, agricultural and manufacturing households. Omission of any simplifying assumptions and the explicit inclusion of all the various different goods and agents render this model suitable for stochastic simulation methods.

Another important paper in the above sub-class is that by Turnovsky (1976) where he provides a good brief survey of the important contributions up to and including 1976. He found that much of the closed-economy research was essentially static and that the models did not address the intrinsic dynamics of the economy. Some examples are Helliwell (1969) and Takayama (1969). Others such as Oates (1966) and McKinnon (1969) have recognized the role of the government budget constraint in an open economy, but emphasis here has been only on the equilibrium steady state of the system with the dynamics being ignored by the analysis. Yet others such as Tower (1972) and Floyd (1969) explicitly considered the dynamics of the capital flows but ignored the manner in which the deficit was financed.

Turnovsky extends the work of Blinder and Solow (1973) to analyse the dynamics of fiscal policy in a small open economy with a fixed exchange rate.[2] The research done by Blinder and Solow shows how the government's deficit-financing mechanism affects the stability of fiscal policy and the long-term real effects of government expenditure.[3] They find that if the deficit were financed entirely by money creation, then the system will be stable, but if it were purely bond financed, then fiscal policy would not be stable. Furthermore, they demonstrate that if it were stable, then the long-term efforts of increased government expenditure would be more expansionary than in the pure money case.

Turnovsky emphasizes three aspects which are lacking in the studies prior to 1976.[4] He introduces two policy parameters: (i) the mix of money and debt financing, and (ii) the extent to which the monetary authority indulges in the sterilization of changes in foreign reserves through open-market operations. By introducing these parameters which have impacts on the supply of domestic financial assets, he, in effect, endogenizes the government's fiscal and monetary policies. The model constructed in this book incorporates certain features of the Turnovsky flexible rate model. The similarities and differences will become apparent in case II.

Model description

The log–linear rational expectations model constructed in this book incorporates the feedback effects betwen the goods and the asset markets. This two-way causation (Dornbusch 1976, Turnovsky 1976, 1983, 1986, Branson and Frenkel 1985, McTaggart 1985, 1988) has the exchange rate determined proximately by financial market equilibrium conditions. It, in turn, influences the current account balance. The latter, in its turn, is the rate of accumulation of national claims on foreigners, and this *feeds back* into the financial market equilibrium. In this manner, the asset market approach incorporated in the following model contains a dynamic feedback mechanism in foreign assets and exchange rates.

The model lies within the Turnovsky (1976) and McTaggart (1985) class of open-economy macromodels and provides a sufficiently rich theoretical framework within which the issues of sustainability can be studied. The analysis here is purely theoretical and subscribes to a trade-off between greater computational ease and a loss of richness of structure, relative to McTaggart/Turnovsky.

The outline of this section is as follows. First, the conceptual framework is presented within which the model is constructed. The next two sections then describe the model under two monetary regimes, and the final section presents the model summaries for cases I and II, respectively.

Conceptual framework

The mechanism by which budget deficits influence the current account, and the channels through which this influence is transmitted under a floating exchange rate regime, are described here. The basic reason the budget and current account deficits are related is because budget deficits represent a 'use' of saving, and current account deficits a 'source' of saving. This may be seen from the national savings identity:[5]

$(G - T)$	$=$	$(S - I)$	$+$	$(M + R - X)$
budget deficit or surplus		private domestic saving surplus or deficit		current account deficit or surplus

The government budget deficit (expenditures less taxes, $G - T$) must equal, or be financed by, the excess of private domestic saving, S, over private investment, I, plus the current account deficit.

In flow of funds technology, the budget deficit and private investment constitute competing 'uses' of savings. The 'sources' of this saving are private domestic saving, S, and the funds from the foreign sector represented by the current account deficit. Not only does a current account deficit require a net inflow of foreign funds to finance it, but a nation can sustain a net financial inflow from abroad *only* by incurring an equal current account deficit, in a regime of floating exchange rates.

One possible mechanism linking the budget deficit to the current account deficit could be the following: in an open economy, large and growing domestic budget deficits, in the absence of accommodative monetary policy, might cause domestic real interest rates to exceed those of the rest of the world. This will cause investors to attempt to shift out of foreign assets and into domestic assets in order to take advantage of higher domestic real yields. The rise in demand for domestic assets, in turn, will put upward pressure on the domestic currency in the foreign exchange market. As investors move to sell foreign currency for domestic currency and use the receipts to puchase higher-yielding domestic bonds, they will bid up the exchange rate.

Real domestic currency appreciation associated with higher real interest rates also represents a rise in the price of domestically produced goods relative to those produced abroad. This weakens export demand and spurs imports, causing the current account balance to deteriorate gradually. Current account deterioration, in turn, is the mechanism that allows foreign savings to begin to supplement domestic savings in financing domestic government budget deficits and private domestic investments, as in the post-1980 period in the United States.

In an economy characterized at present by ballooning levels of government spending, it is important to identify the various mechanisms by which the government can obtain a larger share of the current output.[6]

First, it is reasonable to suppose that the increased deficit has resulted from the government attempting to increase its consumption share of current output while not directly reducing the share going to private consumption (via increased taxation). As the demand for current output rises, short of an increase in output stemming from a Keynesian response, some prices have to rise to ration national current domestic output and induce voluntary transfers from private consumption to government consumption. There are several ways in which this price rationing can occur. The aggregate price level might be pushed up by the excess demand, resulting in inflation even in the absence of monetary influences. Individuals will then be induced to save more to restore their eroding real cash balances, and in this way the inflation tax releases resources from private consumption to current government consumption.

The second, third, and fourth mechanisms by which the government can achieve a larger share of current output are related to the manner of deficit financing. Influences through the asset markets will be of importance when deficits are financed by borrowing from the private sector. The increased supply of government debt drives down bond prices. Yields on these bonds increase, with arbitrage pushing up interest rates generally. If prices are stable, this rise in both the nominal and real interest rates will reduce current private consumption and increase current savings (or expected future consumption). This is because the real interest rate is the opportunity cost of current consumption in terms of future consumption, and the higher nominal rates cause some crowding out by increasing the cost of real investment. The reduction in both private consumption and investment release current output directly to government consumption. The higher domestic interest rates attract a capital inflow from overseas which in turn enables the government (Treasury/Congress) to increase its current consumption, and this has been described earlier.

Finally, an 'inflation tax' can be imposed upon the public by simply having the Federal Reserve purchase government debt directly – or monetize the debt. The prices are generally presumed to increase in proportion to the increase in the money supply, and this releases real resources to government consumption.

This conceptual framework forms the underlying superstructure on which the model is constructed. Case I incorporates the first three mechanisms, while case II incorporates all of them.

Model description: case I

Consider a small country that produces a good that is imperfectly substitutable with goods in the rest of the world.[7] This small country exports part of its output to the rest of the world and the quantity exported depends on the real exchange rate (relative price of foreign output in terms of domestic output) and the level of foreign income. Similarly, the country imports output from the rest of the world and the level of imports is a function of domestic income and real exchange rates. The system is a 3 × 3 matrix system with the endogenous variables being the domestic price level, p_t, the nominal exchange rate s_t, and the domestic real wealth balances, w_t. Domestic private consumption is a function of real disposable income and wealth holdings, and government consumption is a function of domestic income.

These considerations imply the real private domestic demand of domestic output in levels (a ^ signifies a level):

$$\hat{Y} = \hat{C}(\hat{Y}^{\mathrm{d}}, \hat{W}) + \hat{X}\left(\hat{Y}^{*}, \frac{\hat{S}\hat{P}^{*}}{\hat{P}}\right) - \frac{\hat{S}\hat{P}^{*}}{\hat{P}}\,\hat{M}\left(\hat{Y}^{\mathrm{d}}, \frac{\hat{S}\hat{P}^{*}}{\hat{P}}\right) + \hat{G}(\hat{Y}) \tag{11.3}$$

where $\hat{C}$ is the consumption demand or domestic absorption, $\hat{X}$ and $\hat{M}$ are the levels of exports and imports, respectively, $\hat{S}$ is the nominal exchange rate which is in units of domestic currency per unit of foreign currency, $\hat{P}$ is the domestic currency price of domestic output, and $\hat{G}$ is government demand or the level of government spending. Because of the small-country assumption, the domestic residents view $\hat{P}^*$ and $\hat{Y}^*$ as some exogenous stochastic processes. The real disposable income, $\hat{Y}_{\mathrm{d}}$, is given by

$$\hat{Y}_{\mathrm{d}} = \hat{Y}(1 - \tau)$$

where $\hat{Y}$ is the level of gross real income and τ is the marginal tax rate.

Assuming that the level of trade is initially balanced, the following equation is derived as a log–linear approximation of equation (11.3). All coefficients are non-negative and all lower-case variables, other than interest rates, are in natural logarithms:[8]

$$y_t = K^{\mathrm{d}} - \gamma_0\tau_t + \gamma_1 w_t + \gamma_2 g_t + \gamma_3\rho_t + \gamma_4 y_t^* + \varepsilon_t^{\mathrm{d}} \qquad (11.4)$$

where the variables, not yet defined, are: K^{d}, the exogenously determined trend component of domestic output; g_t, the real government consumption of domestic output; ρ_t, the real exchange rate, which is the relative price of foreign goods in the domestic currency with respect to the price of domestic goods in the domestic currency. In levels $\hat{\rho}_t = \hat{p}_t{}^* s_t / \hat{p}_t$, where the variables are as defined earlier.

The parameter γ_3 captures the substitution of both domestic and foreign residents towards domestic goods as their relative price falls. It is thus a measure of the responsiveness of the trade account to relative price changes. The ε_t is a series of iid (independent, identically distributed) shocks, with zero mean and a constant variance. It is assumed that the government (Treasury/Fiscal authority) can fix the fraction of output that it wants to consume and to obtain as tax revenues (T_t). In levels, this is

$$\hat{G}_t = K_1 \hat{Y}_t \qquad 0 < K_1 < 1$$
$$\hat{T}_t = \tau \hat{Y}_t \qquad 0 < \tau < 1$$

and the domestic deficit is equal to $\hat{G}_t - \hat{Y}_t = (\kappa_1 - \tau)\ \hat{Y}_t$.

These functional forms are chosen for analytical convenience and conceptually they could be thought of as being derived from some time-variant government utility maximization problem.

Domestic and foreign bonds are assumed to be perfectly substitutable in this economy. Capital is therefore 'perfectly mobile' internationally with 'perfect capital mobility' being defined as uncovered nominal interest parity. The operative criterion of this interest rate parity is

$$i_t = i_t^* + (E_t s_{t+1} - s_t) \tag{11.5}$$

where $(E_t s_{t+1} - s_t)$ is the expected percentage depreciation of the dollar over the coming period. In other words, investors respond to any differentials in expected returns so as to arbitrage them away. It is assumed here that investors are risk neutral, or exchange risk is completely diversifiable.

While capital is thus defined to be perfectly mobile in the sense of uncovered nominal interest parity, stemming from the perfect substitutability of domestic and foreign bonds, it should be noted that real interest parity, $r_t = r_t^*$, need not exist in this economy. This is because real interest parity exists *only* when *both* the following conditions are met: (i) nominal interest arbitrage exists; (ii) purchasing power parity holds, or there is perfect substitutability between domestic and foreign goods. Since the goods are *not* perfectly substitutable here, condition (ii) is not met, and real interest parity therefore need not exist, i.e. $r_t \neq r_t^*$.

This inequality of the real interest rates is a crucial mechanism for ensuring a flow of capital across national boundaries. hence the presence of the real exchange rate, ρ_t, implying the absence of perfect substitutability in the goods market, cannot be overemphasized.

But would not the real interest differences be arbitraged away just as the nominal interest rates are? The answer lies in the fact that international portfolio investors have reason to arbitrage away gaps in countries' nominal rates of return when expressed in a common numeraire, but they have *no reason* to arbitrage away a gap between the domestic rate of return expressed in terms of domestic goods and the foreign rate of return expressed in terms of foreign goods, when these goods are not perfect substitutes.

The output supply for the small domestic country is given by[9]

$$y_t = \bar{y} + \gamma(p_t - E_t p_{t+1}) + \varepsilon_t^s \tag{11.6}$$

where y_t is the logarithm of domestic output, p_t is the logarithm of the domestic price level, ε_t^s is an iid supply-side shock, $\bar{y}$ is a systematic supply term that is intended to capture systematic changes in technology, population, etc., γ is the absolute value of the relative price elasticity of current output supply, and E_t is the mathematical expectation operator conditional on information possessed at date t. More formally, the relevant price expectation could be written as $E_t p_{t+1} / \Omega_t$, where Ω_t is the information set which includes knowledge of all variables through time t as well as knowledge of the structure of the model.

This equation embodies the 'natural rate' hypothesis and any deviations of output from this 'natural rate' respond positively to the term $p_t - E_t p_{t+1}$. As in Barro (1976) this can be viewed as an effect of speculation over time associated with the intertemporal substitutability of leisure.

The money supply is given by

$$m_t^{\mathrm{s}} = \psi_{\mathrm{d}}\, d_{t-1} + \bar{f} + \varepsilon_t^{\mathrm{m}} \tag{11.7}$$

where m_t^{s} is the nominal supply of domestic money, d_t is the domestic component of the domestic money supply, ψ_{d} is a feedback policy parameter of the money growth process, $\varepsilon_t^{\mathrm{m}}$ is an iid shock, and $\bar{f}$ is the volume of foreign reserves which is a constant amount in this economy of floating exchange rates. The d_t is supplied exogenously by the Federal Reserve, in this model, by means of open-market operations, and is of the form

$$d_t = \psi_{\mathrm{d}} d_{t-1} + \varepsilon_t^{\mathrm{m}}$$

In this economy, the fiscal authority independently chooses K_1 and announces it, while the monetary authority (the Fed.) maintains a money supply given above.

The domestic demand for real money balances depends on the nominal interest rate and the level of real output. This is given by

$$m_t^{\mathrm{d}} = \gamma_5 y_t + p_t - \gamma_6 i_t \tag{11.8}$$

the variables being as defined earlier. The domestic trade sector is assumed to be small and hence the price level in question is not a weighted average of domestically consumed and imported goods.

The exports for the small domestic country, which were described in levels earlier in equation (11.3), are

$$X_t = K_{\mathrm{x}} + \gamma_7 y_t + \gamma_8 \rho_t + \varepsilon_t^{\mathrm{x}}$$

where the variables are as defined earlier.

The imports are

$$I_t = K_n + \gamma_9 y_t - \gamma_{10}\rho_t + \varepsilon_t^n$$

The net exports, therefore, can be written as

$$X_t - I_t = K_N + \gamma_7 y_t^* + (\gamma_8 + \gamma_{10})\,\rho_t - \gamma_9 y_t - \varepsilon_t^N$$

where $K_N = K_x - K_n$. Therefore, the balance of payments equation, which is the sum of the current and capital amounts, is (for a flexible exchange rate regime)

$$0 = [K_n + \gamma_7 y_t + (\gamma_8 + \gamma_{10})\,\rho_t - \gamma_9 y_t] + \gamma_{11}\,(r_t - r_t^*) \qquad (11.9)$$

The first term in the brackets on the right-hand side is the net exports expression (or the current account). The second term is the short-term capital flow (capital account) which is assumed to be a function of $r_t - r_t^*$, the domestic and foreign real interest differential, given by $\gamma_{11}\,(r_t - r_t^*)$. This specification is similar to that of Turnovsky (1976) and Krugman (1985).

Using the expression for uncovered nominal interest parity (11.5) and the Fisher equations

$$r_t = i_t - (E_t p_{t+1} - p_t) \quad \text{and} \quad r_t^* = i_t^* - (E_t p_{t+1}^* - p_t^*)$$

where the real rate is the difference between the nominal interest rate and expected inflation for the domestic and foreign economy, respectively, and the definition of ρ_t, $\rho_t = p_t^* + s_t - p_t$, the following expression for the real interest rate differential is obtained:

$$r_t - r_t^* = E_t\,\rho_{t+1} - \rho_t = (E_t p_{t+1}^* - p_t^*) + (E_t s_{t+1} - s_t) - (E_t p_{t+1} - p_t) \qquad (11.10)$$

The real interest differential is thus equal to the expected depreciation of the real exchange rate.

The domestic budget deficit, in any particular time period, is financed by domestic bond holdings and foreign capital inflow, and this is achieved by the Treasury's sale of one-period discounted government bonds to domestic and foreign residents. The domestic money creation, seigniorage, is obtained by the Federal Reserve's indulging in open-market operations. There are only two assets held in the portfolios of the domestic private sector: domestic money and bonds. Private citizens at home and abroad do not hold foreign currencies as assets and the Treasury does not hold cash balances. The bonds are viewed by domestic and foreign residents as perfect substitutes and therefore equation (11.5) holds, as discussed. For the sake of simplicity, the foreign country is assumed to possess a balanced budget.

The consolidated budget constraint is given by (in levels)

$$(\hat{B}_t^d/1 + i_t) + \gamma_{11}\hat{p}_t(r_t - r_t^*) + \hat{D}_t = \hat{p}_t(\hat{G}_t - \hat{T}_t) + \hat{B}_{t-1}^p$$

$\hat{B}_t^d$ is the domestic demand in period t for one-period discounted government bonds with \$1 face value and $\hat{B}_t d/(1 = i_t)$ represents the current nominal value of bond sales to the domestic residents, $\gamma_{11}\hat{p}_t(r_t - r_t^*)$ is the bond sales to foreign residents, and D_t is the nominal money creation (seigniorage) or bond sales to the Federal Reserve. The first term on the right-hand side is the budget deficit and $\hat{B}_{t-1}^p$ is the amount required to retire the last period's debt, *both* domestic and foreign. It is assumed that the domestic budget was balanced at, and prior to, time $t - 2$, and this initial condition is necessary to pin down a unique solution in the following section.

The amount needed to pay the principal on the last period's debt, B_{t-1}^p, is simply the total demand of domestic and foreign residents in period $t - 1$ for the one-period discounted government bonds. The balanced budget assumption for, and prior to, period $t - 2$ precludes the presence of principal repayments in time $t - 1$.

The consolidated government budget constraint in logarithmic form is given by

$$\gamma_{12}b_t^d - \gamma_{13}i_t + \gamma_{11}(r_t - re_t^*) + \gamma_{14}d_t$$
$$= (p_t + y_t)(\gamma_{15} - \gamma_{16}) + \gamma_{15}K_1 - \gamma_{16}\tau + \gamma_{16}b_{t-1}^p \quad (11.11)$$

The definition for domestic real wealth is[10]

$$w_t = \gamma_{20}b_{t-1} + \gamma_{21}d_{t-1} - p_t \quad (11.12)$$

where w_t is the real wealth with which individuals enter period t, or, in levels, $\hat{B}_{t-1} + \hat{D}_{t-1}$ represents the current dollar value of household wealth carried over from the last period. Individuals in this economy view deficits as permanent because government bonds are not backed by taxes, and they incorporate these bonds into their wealth holdings. Consequently, Ricardian equivalence does not hold in case I.

Model description: case II

The model with an accommodative monetary policy regime is

described in this section. Domestic money creation is endogenized here as opposed to the fixed money rule in case I. The system is a 4 × 4 matrix system with the endogenous variables being the domestic price level, p_t, the nominal exchange rate, s_t, domestic demand for one-period discounted government bonds, b_t, and domestic real wealth balances, w_t.

The equations for the real private demand for domestic output, and the supply of domestic output, are identical to equations (11.4) and (11.6) in case I. However, domestic real wealth holdings are not defined as in case I, where they (the real wealth holdings) comprised domestic bonds and money. In case I, when the possibility of debt monetization was non-existent and the tax rule was clearly defined, bonds were incorporated into the definition of wealth. But now, with the endogenized domestic money supply, there is always some accommodation, the extent of which depends on the 'mix' of money and bond financing and the exact amount of which is fixed by the fiscal and monetary authority, as explained later in this section. Hence, real wealth, w_t, is an endogenous variable, without any imposed *a priori* definition of its components, and the extent to which w_t is affected by money and bonds is determined endogenously within the model.

The real government spending, g_t, and tax revenues, t_t, are given by the following announced, and adhered to, rules (ψ_g and ψ_t are the rates of growth of government spending and taxes, respectively):

$$g_t = \psi_g g_{t-1} \tag{11a}$$

$$t_t = \psi_t t_{t-1} \tag{11b}$$

These rules imply that once again, the fiscal policy dominates the monetary policy because by fixing these rules the Treasury has announced the string of deficits that it is going to incur into the future.

The domestic money supply is given by

$$m_t^s = d_t + \bar{f} + \varepsilon_t^m \tag{11.13}$$

Here d_t, the component of domestic money creation, is an endogenous variable and $\bar{f}$ and ε_t^m are as defined earlier.

The domestic demand for real money balances depends on the nominal interest rate and the level of real output. This is identical to that of case I and is given by

$$m_t^d = \gamma_5 y_t + p_t - \gamma_6 i_t \tag{11.8}$$

The balance of payments is again identical to equation (11.9) in case I and is given by

$$0 = [K_N + \gamma_7^* y_t + (\gamma_8 + \gamma_{10})\,\rho_t - \gamma_9 y_t] + \gamma_{11}(r_t - r_t^*) \qquad (11.9)$$

where the domestic and foreign real interest rate differential is once again

$$r_t - r_t^* = E_t\rho_{t+1} - \rho_t = (E_t p_{t+1}^* - p_t^*) + (E_t s_{t+1} - s_t) - (E_t p_{t+1} - p_t) \qquad (11.10)$$

The real interest rate differential is thus equal to the expected depreciation of the real exchange rate.

The financing of the domestic budget deficit is radically different from the financing mechanism in case I. In this economy a sequence of deficits is announced and it extends into future periods, by virtue of the rules 11(a) and 11(b). These deficits, in any particular time period, can be financed by sales of government one-period discounted bonds to domestic and foreign residents, with the discrepancy between total amounts needed to finance the deficit and total bond sales made up by domestic money creation. The amount of debt that is 'rolled over', or the proportion of the principal plus interest on debt issued in the last period that is retired by selling yet more bonds, is 'fixed' in this economy. This value, θ_1, is fixed by some assumed co-ordination between the Treasury and the Federal Reserve, and a higher value of θ_1 implies a larger proportion of debt being 'rolled over'.

Similarly, as an example, let the amount of the primary deficit that is financed by issuing one-period government bonds be fixed by the parameter α_1. If α_1 and θ_1, which are percentages of the primary deficit and the principal plus interest payments, have values of $\alpha_1 = 1$ and $\theta_1 = 1$, then this would imply an entirely bond-financed economy with no reason for domestic money creation.

It should be noted that even though α_1 and θ_1 arc fixed by the Treasury and the Fed., the quantities of government bonds issued and the amount of domestic money creation are *still endogenously* determined by the model because the nominal interest rates that prevailed between time $t - 1$ and t, and the domestic price level, are both endogenous. It is *only* the extent of the rolling over of domestic debt that is exogenously determined in this economy.

The bonds sold to domestic and foreign residents can thus be expressed by, in levels:

government bonds sold in period t to domestic and foreign residents

$$= \alpha_1 \hat{p}_t(\hat{g}_t - \hat{t}_t) + \theta_1(\hat{B}^{p}_{t-1}) \tag{11c}$$

where the first term on the right-hand side is the fraction of the current period nominal deficit and the second term is the fraction of the principal plus interest payments ($\hat{B}^{p}_{t-1}$) that are bond financed. here $\hat{B}^{p}_{t-1}$ is the total demand by domestic and foreign residents in period $t-1$ for government bonds. The domestic budget is once again assumed to be balanced for, and prior to, period $t-1$, and this precludes principal repayments in time $t-1$.

In this model, for the sake of computational simplicity, it is assumed that the *entire* primary deficit and a portion θ_1 of the principal and interest payments are bond financed, i.e. $\theta_1 < 1$ and $\alpha_1 = 1$. This means that domestic money is created to finance the remainder of the principal plus interest payments – *it does not* finance the primary deficit in the current period at all.

Here we have log [government bonds sold to domestic and foreign residents] = [log (nominal time t deficit)] + θ_1 [log (principal plus interest payments to retire last period's debt)].

Denoting bonds sold to domestic residents as b_t and those to foreign residents by the expression for net capital inflow, $\gamma_{11}(r_t - r^*_t)$, we have the following expression for bond financing:

$$\begin{aligned}\gamma_{12}b^{d}_t - \gamma_{13}i_t + \gamma_{11}(r_t - r^*_t) &= (\gamma_{15} - \gamma_{16})p_t \\ &+ \gamma_{15}g_t - \gamma_{16}t_t + \theta_1(\gamma_{15} - \gamma_{16})\,p_{t-1} \\ &+ \theta_1\gamma_{15}g_{t-1} - \theta_1\gamma_{16}(\mathrm{t}_t/\psi_t) - \theta_1[s_{t-1} - (i^*_t/\psi_t) - \phi]\end{aligned}$$

Substituting for i_t from the expression for uncovered nominal interest arbitrage, and for $(r_t - r^*_t)$ from expression (11.10) we obtain:

$$\begin{aligned}\gamma_{12}b_t + (\gamma_{13} - \gamma_{11})s_t + [\gamma_{11} + (\gamma_{15} - \gamma_{16})]p_t &= \gamma_{11}E_tp_{t+1} + (\gamma_{13} - \gamma_{11})E_ts_{t+1} - \theta_1 s_{t-1} \\ &+ \theta_1(\gamma_{15} - \gamma_{16})p_{t-1} + \gamma_{15}g_{t-1}(\theta_1 + \psi_g) \\ &- \gamma_{16}t_{t-1}(\theta_1 + \psi_t) - \gamma_{11}(1 - \psi^*)p^*_t \\ &+ i^*_t[\gamma_{13} + (\theta_1/\psi^*_i)] + \theta_1\phi\end{aligned} \tag{11.14}$$

where the variables are as defined earlier and ϕ is $E_t(\mathrm{E}_{t-1}s_t)$. The domestic money creation is given by, in levels: d_t = [total amount required for principal plus interest payments on last period's debt net of amount of debt rolled over by issuing new debt]. The logarithmic expression for domestic money creation is then:

$$\begin{aligned} d_t = {} & \theta_2 p_{t-1}(\gamma_{15} - \gamma_{16}) + \theta_2 \gamma_{15} g_{t-1} \\ & - \theta_2 \gamma_{10} t_{t-1} + \theta_2 i^*_{t-1} + \theta_2 \phi - \theta_2 s_{t-1} \end{aligned} \quad (11.15)$$

where $\theta_2 = - K_1\theta_1$, i.e. a greater amount of debt rolled over necessitates less domestic money creation.

It should be noted here that the rule (choice of θ_1 and θ_2) for determining the amount of debt financing need not necessarily be a conscious deficit-financing strategy hammered out by the Treasury and the Fed. It could be the *result* of the independent behaviour of the above two decision-making bodies. W. Michael Cox (1985) has determined that a 'rule' similar to the one used in this thesis does, in fact, exist. Over the period 1950–81, according to Cox, each $1 of interest paid on the Federal Government's debt was, on average, financed with only 41 cents in taxes. The 59 cent remainder was deficit financed. Furthermore, a statistical analysis of federal deficits has revealed a shift in this 'rule' in the early 1970s – interest payments since January 1971 have been *totally* deficit financed. In the economy of this thesis, tax rates are held exogenously fixed and any change in the expected time paths of these revenues is fungible between principal and primary deficit financing.

Model summary: case I

A summary of both cases of the model is presented in the following subsection.

1. $y^d_t = k_d - \gamma_0 \tau + \gamma_1 w_t + \gamma_2 g_t + \gamma_3 \rho_t + \gamma_4 y^*_t + \varepsilon^d_t$

Note that $\rho_t = p^*_t + s_t - p_t$.

2. $y^s_t - \bar{y} + \gamma(p_t - E_t p_{t+1}) + \varepsilon^s_t$

3. $m_t = \psi_d d_{t-1} + \bar{f} + \varepsilon^m_t$

4. $m^d_t = \gamma_5 y_t + p_t - \gamma_6 i_t$

5. $0 = [K_n + \gamma_7 y^*_t + (\gamma_8 + \gamma_{10})\rho_t - \gamma_9 y_t + \varepsilon^n_t] + \gamma_{11}(r_t - r^*_t)$

6. $r_t - r_t^* = E_t\rho_{t+1} - \rho_t = (E_tp_{t+1}^* - p_t^*) + (E_ts_{t+1} - s_t)$
$- (E_tp_{t+1} - p_t)$

7. $\gamma_{12}b_t^d - \gamma_{13}i_t + \gamma_{11}(r_t - r_t^*) + \gamma_{14}d_t$
$= (\gamma_{15} - \gamma_{16})(p_t + y_t) + (\gamma_{15}K_1 - \gamma_{16}\tau) + \gamma_{17}b_{t-1}^p$

8. $w_t = \gamma_{20}b_{t-1} + \gamma_{21}d_{t-1} - p_t$
   (a) $g_t = K_1 + y_t$
   (b) $t_t = \tau + y_t$
   (c) $i_t = i_t^* + [E_ts_{t+1} - s_t]$
   (d) $r_t = i_t - [E_tp_{t+1} - p_t]$
   (e) $r_t^* = i_t^* - [E_tp_{t+1}^* - p_t^*]$

where y_t^d is the demand for domestic output, y_t^s the real domestic output supply, p_t the price of domestic output in units of domestic currency (dollars), s_t the nominal exchange rate (the number of units of domestic currency per unit of foreign currency), i_t the domestic nominal interest rate, w_t the real domestic wealth, τ the tax collection (marginal rate), K_1 the government's consumption share of current output, g_t the real government consumption of domestic output, ρ_t the real exchange rate (the relative price of foreign goods in the domestic currency with respect to the price of domestic goods in the domestic currency), p_t^* the price of foreign output in units of foreign currency, y_t^* the foreign real output, $\bar{y}$ the trend rate of growth of the domestic output, m_t the total money supply, d_t the domestic component of the money supply, f_t the level of reserves, b_t^d the domestic nominal demand for one-period discounted government bonds, b_t^p the principal repayment for government bonds purchased in period t by domestic and foreign residents, and ε_t the iid shock with zero mean and finite variance.

Equations (11.4), (11.6)–(11.8) are the goods and money market supplies and demands. Equation (11.9) is the balance of payments equations, (11.10) is the expression for the difference in domestic and foreign real interest rates, (11.11) is the consolidated budget constraint, (11.12) is the definition for real wealth, and (11.1), (11.2), and (11.5) are definitions of fiscal policy, uncovered nominal interest parity, and the Fisher equations.

Model summary: case II

The equations for supply and demand in the goods and money market, as well as the expressions for the balance of payments and the real interest rate difference, are identical to those of case I, i.e. equations (11.4), (11.6), (11.10), (11.11). The equations specific to case II are:

$$\begin{aligned}\gamma_{12}b_t^d + (\gamma_{13} - \gamma_{11})s_t + [\gamma_{11} + (\gamma_{15} - \gamma_{16})]p_t \\ = \gamma_{11}E_t p_{t+1} + (\gamma_{13} - \gamma_{11})E_t s_{t+1} \\ - \theta_1 s_{t-1} + \theta_1 (\gamma_{15} - \gamma_{16})p_{t-1} \\ + \gamma_{15}g_{t-1}(\theta_1 + \psi_g) - \gamma_{16}t_{t-1}(\theta_1 + \psi_t) \\ - \gamma_{11}(1 - \psi_p^*)p_t^* + i_t^* [\gamma_{13} + (\theta_1/\psi_i^*)] + \theta_1\phi\end{aligned}$$

$$\begin{aligned}d_t = \theta_2 p_{t-1}(\gamma_{15} - \gamma_{16}) + \theta_2 \gamma_{15} g_{t-1} \\ - \theta_2 \gamma_{15} t_{t-1} + \theta_2 i_{t-1}^* + \theta_s \phi - \theta_s s_{t-1}\end{aligned}$$

These are the expressions for the 'rules' of bond and money financing incorporated into the government budget constraint. Here, θ_1 is the fixed portion of principal payment that is rolled over, and $\theta_2 = -K_1\theta_1$, where θ_2 is the portion of principal payment that is paid off by domestic money creation.

Chapter twelve

The solution technique for rational expectations models

The solution technique and the solutions for cases I and II are presented here. This technique is an adaptation of the method of undetermined coefficients to a matrix system and is similar to that of Aoki and Canzoneri (1979). In earlier chapters we studied the general economic concept of rational expectations and we will now see how this concept is indispensable for solving large and complex rational expectations models.

Solutions for case I

The system of equations for case I is reduced to a system of three equations in quasi-reduced form, with p_t, s_t, and w_t as the endogenous variables. This 3 × 3 matrix system is presented in appendix A.

We define the following vectors:

$$\mathbf{P}_t = [p_t \ \ s_t \ \ w_t] \qquad \mathbf{p}_t^* = [p_t^* \ \ y_t^* \ \ i_t^*]$$

$$\mathbf{d}_{t-1} = [d_{t-1} \ \ \tau \ \ K_1] \qquad \bar{y} = [\bar{y} \ \ \bar{f} \ \ \phi] \qquad \varepsilon_t = [\varepsilon_t^s \ \ \varepsilon_t^d \ \ \varepsilon_t^m]$$

Using this vector notation, it is possible to reduce the model to the quasi-reduced form

$$A\mathbf{p}_t = BE_t\mathbf{p}_{t+1} + \lambda\mathbf{p}_{t-1} + C\bar{y} + D\mathbf{d}_{t-1} + E\mathbf{p}_{t-1}^* + F\varepsilon_t \tag{12.1}$$

where $\mathbf{p}_t$ is the vector of endogenous variables, $\mathbf{p}_t^*$ is the vector of exogenous disturbances emanating from the rest of the world, $\mathbf{d}_{t-1}$ is the vector of domestic policy instruments, and $\boldsymbol{\varepsilon}_t$ is the vector of domestic and foreign unobservable taste shift disturbances. $\boldsymbol{\varepsilon}_t$ represents the underlying uncertainty in the model and it is assumed to be iid with zero mean and finite variance. A, B, λ, C,

D, E, and F are all 3 × 3 matrices with model parameters as the elements.

Suppose that

$$p_t^* = \psi^* p_{t-1}^* \tag{12.2}$$

That is, domestic residents perceive the foreign price level, interest rate, and output to follow an exogenously determined process given by equation (12.2) above – the United States is considered 'small' relative to the rest of the world, and hence it takes foreign prices, output, and interest rates as exogenously given. Again, ψ is a 3 × 3 matrix. The above process is assumed to be not really restrictive, as any general autoregressive process or a relatively large class of general ARMA (Autoregressive Moving Average) processes could have been chosen.

In equation (12.1) the current and expected future values of the vector of foreign prices, output, and interest rates have been expressed in terms of the values of the above three variables lagged by one period. This has been accomplished by applying the Weiner–Kolmogorov procedure to equation (12.2). This procedure is described in appendix B.

Using the method of undetermined coefficients for a matrix system, we 'guess' the following solution and then verify that it is in fact correct. A reasonable guess is

$$\boldsymbol{p}_t = \pi_0 \boldsymbol{p}_t^* + \pi_1 \boldsymbol{d}_t + \pi_2 \bar{y} + \pi_3 \varepsilon_t \tag{12.3}$$

The next step is to solve for the unknown coefficients π_0–π_3, where each coefficient is a 3 × 3 matrix of unknowns. To substitute (12.3) into (12.1), the following manipulations have been made.

Leading equation (12.3) by one period, taking expectations at time t, and applying the Weiner–Kolmogorov procedure:

$$E_t \boldsymbol{p}_{t+1} = \pi_0\, \psi^{*2}\, \boldsymbol{p}_{t-1}^* + \pi_1\, \psi_d^2\, \boldsymbol{d}_{t-1} + \pi_1\, \psi_d\, E_t \varepsilon_t + \pi_2 \bar{y} + \pi_3\, E_t\, \varepsilon_{t+1} \tag{12.4}$$

The vector $E_t \varepsilon_{t+1}$ is zero by definition, but $E_t \varepsilon_t$ is not. This is because the conditional expectation of the vector ε_t, $E_t[\varepsilon_t/\Omega_t]$, where Ω_t is the set of all available information, namely the current observed price level, the nominal exchange rate, domestic wealth, and the exogenously given policy and trend variables, is non-zero. From equation (12.3) it can be seen that if agents observe the vector of endogenous variables, $\boldsymbol{p}_t$ (which they do) and if $\boldsymbol{p}_t^*$, $\boldsymbol{d}_t$, and $\bar{y}$ are exogenously given and known to all, then the expectation of ε_t, conditional on the observed pieces of information, can be explicitly determined by agents so that $E_t[\varepsilon_t/\Omega_t]$ is simply ε_t. It should be noted that since $E_t\varepsilon_t$ can be explicitly determined in this economy, agents are never in doubt regarding the source of the fluctuations (i.e. stemming from real or nominal shocks) in the observed endogenous variables, p_t, s_t, and w_t, and consequently they are not forced to indulge in the signal extractions characterized by a Lucasian economy. Three combinations of the three shocks, ε_t^s, ε_t^d, and ε_t^m are observed here, and this reduces the signal extraction process to a simple conditional forecast.

Lagging the guess (12.3) by one period we obtain

$$\boldsymbol{p}_{t-1} = \pi_0 \boldsymbol{p}^*_{t-1} + \pi_1 \boldsymbol{d}_{t-1} + \pi_2 \bar{y} + \pi_3 \varepsilon_{t-1} \tag{12.5}$$

The next step is to solve for the undetermined coefficient 3 × 3 matrices, the π. The solutions are divided into two parts with respect to the coefficients of the policy variables and the shocks. One advantage of using the solution technique of undetermined coefficients is that, in this case, all the π do not have to be solved simultaneously. This piece-wise solution technique enables us to solve for the coefficients of the policy instruments without simultaneously solving for the coefficients of the stochastic elements.

The former, π_1, is presented below, followed by the solution of the coefficient of the vector of the shocks, π_3.

Substituting equations (12.3), (12.4), and (12.5) minus the stochastic element terms into (12.1) we obtain

$$\begin{aligned} A[\pi_0 \boldsymbol{p}^*_t + \pi_1 \boldsymbol{d}_t + \pi_2 \bar{y}] &= B[\pi_0 \, \psi^2 \boldsymbol{p}_{t-1} + \pi_1 \psi_d \boldsymbol{d}_{t-1} + \pi_2 \bar{y}] \\ &\quad + \lambda[\pi_0 \boldsymbol{p}^*_{t-1} + \pi_1 \boldsymbol{d}_{t-1} + \pi_2 \bar{y}] + c\bar{y} + d\boldsymbol{d}_{t-1} + e\boldsymbol{p}^*_{t-1} \end{aligned} \tag{12.6}$$

Rational expectations have been imposed here implicitly in the solution technique because equation (12.3), which is the 'guessed' solution, is in fact in the form of the guessed stochastic process governing p_t. The right-hand side of (12.3), $\pi_0 \boldsymbol{p}^*_t + \pi_1 \boldsymbol{d}_t + \pi_2 \bar{y} + \pi_3 \varepsilon_t$, is a probability distribution whose specific nature is yet to be determined. Expectations are based on this distribution, conditional on all available information. By solving for the parameters of the stochastic process in terms of the underlying structural parameters of the model, conditional expectations formed by agents will, on average, be correct.

Using equation (12.2) and the rule for domestic money creation, $d_t = \psi_d d_{t-1} + \varepsilon_t^m$, and equating coefficients of the vector of foreign variables, $\boldsymbol{p}^*_{t-1}$, we obtain

$$A\pi_0 = B\pi_0 + \lambda\pi_0(\psi^*)^{-1} + E$$

Simplifying:

$$\pi_0 = [A - B - \lambda(\psi^*)^{-1}]^{-1}E$$

Equating coefficients of the vector of policy instruments, d_{t-1},

$$A\pi_1\,\psi_d = B\pi_1\psi_d^2 + \lambda\pi_1 + D$$

Simplifying:

$$\pi_1 = [A\psi_d - B\psi_d^2 - \lambda]^{-1}D$$

and equating coefficients of the vector of constants, $\bar{y}$,

$$A\pi_2 = B\pi_2 + \pi_2\lambda + C$$

Simplifying:

$$\pi_2 = [A - B - \lambda]^{-1}C$$

The next step is to solve for each of the elements of the 3 × 3 matrix, π_1, where π_k^{ij} will be the element in row i and column j of the matrix k. The matrix system is represented in the following truncated form for computational simplicity:

$$\begin{bmatrix} a_0 & -a_1 & -a_2 \\ a_3 & a_4 & 0 \\ a_5 & a_6 & 0 \end{bmatrix} \begin{bmatrix} p_t \\ s_t \\ w_t \end{bmatrix} = \begin{bmatrix} b_0 & 0 & 0 \\ b_1 & b_2 & 0 \\ b_3 & b_4 & -b_5 \end{bmatrix} \begin{bmatrix} E_t p_{t+1} \\ E_t s_{t+1} \\ E_t w_{t+1} \end{bmatrix}$$

$$+ \begin{bmatrix} 0 & 0 & 0 \\ 0 & 0 & 0 \\ \lambda_0 & -\lambda_0 & \lambda_1 \end{bmatrix} \begin{bmatrix} p_{t-1} \\ s_{t-1} \\ w_{t-1} \end{bmatrix}$$

$$+ \begin{bmatrix} 0 & -d_0 & d_1 \\ d_2 & 0 & 0 \\ d_3 & -d_4 & d_5 \end{bmatrix} \begin{bmatrix} d_{t-1} \\ \tau \\ k_1 \end{bmatrix} + \begin{bmatrix} e_0 & e_1 & 0 \\ 0 & 0 & e_2 \\ e_3 & e_4 & e_5 \end{bmatrix} \begin{bmatrix} p^*_{t-1} \\ y^*_{t-1} \\ i^*_{t-1} \end{bmatrix} + \ldots \qquad (12.7)$$

The elements a_i, b_i, λ_i, d_i, and e_i ($0 \leqslant i \leqslant 6$) directly coincide with their corresponding elements in the detailed matrix system presented in appendix A.

The system then simplifies to

$$\begin{bmatrix} p_t \\ s_t \\ w_t \end{bmatrix} = \frac{1}{|D|}$$

$$\times \begin{bmatrix} 0 & a_i(b_5-\lambda_1)-a_2\lambda_0 & 0 \\ -(a_3\psi_d-b_1\psi_d^2)(b_5-\lambda_1) & i_0i_6+i_2i_4 & -a_2(a_3\psi_d)-b_1\psi_d^2 \\ (a_3\psi_d-b_1\psi_d^2)(\lambda_0) & (-1)(i_0i_5+i_1i_4) & i_1i_3 \end{bmatrix}$$

$$\times \begin{bmatrix} 0 & -d_0 & d_1 \\ d_2 & 0 & 0 \\ d_3 & -d_4 & d_5 \end{bmatrix} \begin{bmatrix} d_{t-1} \\ \tau \\ K_1 \end{bmatrix} + \ldots$$

where $|D|$ is the determinant of the inverted matrix

$$|D| = (a_3\psi_d - b_1\psi_d^2)\,[a_1(b_5 - \psi_d) - a_2\,\lambda_0]$$

The final solutions of the three domestic endogenous variables with respect to the policy instruments are

$$p_t = \left(\frac{1}{a_3 - b_1\psi_d}\right) d_{t-1} + \ldots \tag{12.8}$$

$$s_t = \left[\left(\frac{(a_0-b_0\psi_d)(b_5-\lambda_1)+a_2(a_5-b_3\psi_d)}{(a_3-b_1\psi_d)[a_1(b_5-\lambda_1)-a_2\lambda_0]}\right)\psi_d\right.$$

$$\left. - \frac{a_2d_3}{a_1(b_5-\lambda_1)-a_2\lambda_0}\right] d_{t-1} + \left(\frac{\beta_5(b_5-\lambda_1)+a_2d_4}{a_1(b_5-\lambda_1)-a_2d_0}\right)\tau$$

$$- \left(\frac{\beta_7(b_5-\lambda_1)+a_2d_5}{a_1(b_5-\lambda_1)-a_2\lambda_0}\right) K_1 + \ldots \tag{12.9}$$

$$w_t = \left(\frac{-\psi_d[(a_0\psi_d - b_0\psi_d^2)\lambda_0 + a_1 i_4]}{\psi_d(a_3 - b_1\psi_d)[a_1(b_5-\lambda_1) - a_2\lambda_0]} + \frac{a_1 d_3}{a_1(b_5-\lambda_1)-a_2\lambda_0} \right) d_{t-1} + \left(\frac{-1(\lambda_0\beta_5 + a_1 d_4}{[a_1(b_5-\lambda_1)-a_2\lambda_0]} \right) \tau + \left(\frac{\lambda_0\beta_7 + a_1 d_5}{[a_1(b_5-\lambda_1)-a_2\lambda_0]} \right) K_1 + \ldots \quad (12.10)$$

The solution of π_3, the coefficient of the 3 × 1 vector of the stochastic elements, is presented below. This vector ε_t in (12.3) is composed of three identical and independently distributed shocks with zero means and finite variances. The supply and demand shocks, ε_t^s and ε_t^d, are real, while the nominal shock stemming from the domestic money supply process is ε_t^m.

Substituting the guess, (12.3), into the vector representation of the matrix system, (12.1), and following the same procedure used to obtain the π_1 above, the coefficient of the vector of the stochastic elements is obtained. This coefficient π_3, obtained after equating the coefficients of ε_t, is

$$\pi_3 = (a)^{-1} [\pi_1 (b\psi_d - a) + f]$$

The next step is then to solve for each of the elements of the 3 × 3 matrix π_3, where π_3^{ij} is the coefficient in row i and column j of the matrix π_3.

The matrix $(b\psi_d - a)$ is

$$\begin{bmatrix} \gamma - a_0 & a_1 & a_2 \\ \gamma_5 - a_3 & 0 & 0 \\ \gamma_{15} - \gamma_{16} & 0 & (-\gamma_{12}/\gamma_{13})\,\psi_d \end{bmatrix}$$

Premultiplying this by π_1 gives

$$\begin{bmatrix} \pi_1^{11} & 0 & 0 \\ \pi_1^{21} & \pi_1^{22} & -\pi_1^{23} \\ -\pi_1^{31} & \pi_1^{32} & -\pi_1^{33} \end{bmatrix} \begin{bmatrix} \gamma - a_0 & a_1 & a_2 \\ \gamma_5 - a_3 & 0 & 0 \\ \gamma_{15} - \gamma_{16} & 0 & (-\gamma_{12}/\gamma_{13})\,\psi_d \end{bmatrix}$$

Simplifying, we obtain the following matrix for $\pi_1(b\psi_d - a) + f$:

$$\begin{bmatrix} \pi_1^{11}(\gamma-a_0)-1 & \pi_1^{11}a_1 + \dfrac{1}{1-a_2} & \pi_1^{11}a_2 \\ \pi_1^{21}(\gamma-a_0) + \pi_1^{22}(\gamma-a_3) - \pi_1^{23}(\gamma_{15}-\gamma_{16}) - \gamma_5 & \pi_1^{21}a_1 & (\pi_1^{21}a_2)\left(\pi_1^{23}\dfrac{\gamma_{12}}{\gamma_{13}}\psi_d\right)+1 \\ -\pi_1^{31}(\gamma-a_0) + \pi_1^{32}(\gamma_5-a_3) - \pi_1^{33}(\gamma_{15}-\gamma_{16}) + (\gamma_{15}-\gamma_{16}) & \pi_1^{31}a_1+f_3 & \pi_1^{31}a_2+\dfrac{\gamma_{12}}{\gamma_{13}}\psi_2\,\pi_1^{33} \end{bmatrix}$$

The next step is to obtain $(a)^{-1}[\pi_1(b\psi_d - \text{a}) + f]$. The determinant of (a), $|A|$, is $-a_2a_3a_6$ or $-\beta_2(1 + \gamma\gamma_5)(\gamma_{13} - \gamma_{11})$ and it is less than 0. The matrix $\pi_1(b\psi_d - a) + f$ is then premultiplied by the inverse of (a), $(a)^{-1}$, which is presented below:

$$\frac{1}{|A|}\begin{bmatrix} 0 & -a_2a_5 & a_2a_4 \\ 0 & a_2a_5 & -a_2a_3 \\ a_0a_6 - a_4a_5 & -(a_0a_6 + a_1a_5) & a_0a_4 + a_1a_3 \end{bmatrix}$$

This finally simplifies to the following solution of the domestic price level, p_t, with respect to the real and nominal shocks:

$$p_t = \frac{1}{|A|}(\pi_3^{11}\,\varepsilon_t^{s} - \pi_3^{12}\varepsilon_t^{d} - \pi_3^{13}\varepsilon_t^{m}) + \ldots \qquad (12.11)$$

where $|A| < 0$, and the coefficients π_3^{ij}, $i, j \leqslant 3$, are presented in detail in appendix C.

Similarly, the solutions of the nominal exchange rate and the domestic wealth balances with respect to the shocks are

$$s_t = \frac{1}{|A|}(-\pi_3^{21}\varepsilon_t^{s} + \pi_3^{22}\varepsilon_t^{d} - \pi_3^{23}\varepsilon_t^{m}) + \ldots \quad (12.12)$$

and

$$w_t = \frac{1}{|A|}(-\pi_3^{31}\varepsilon_t^{s} + \pi_3^{32}\varepsilon_t^{d} + \pi_3^{33}\varepsilon_t^{m}) + \ldots \quad (12.13)$$

The explicit solutions of each of the coefficients π_3^{ij} are derived from appendix A.

Solutions for case II

The system of equations for case II is reduced to a system of four equations in quasi-reduced form, with p_t, s_t, b_t^{d}, and w_t as the endogenous variables. This 4 × 4 matrix system is presented in appendix C.

Defining the following vectors:

$$\boldsymbol{p}_t = [p_t\ s_t\ b_t^{d}\ w_t] \qquad \boldsymbol{p}_t^* = [p_t^*\ y_t^*\ i_t^*]$$

$$\boldsymbol{g}_{t-1} = [g_{t-1}\ t_{t-1}] \qquad \varepsilon t = [\varepsilon_t^{s}\ \varepsilon_t^{d}\ \varepsilon_t^{m}]$$

The matrix system can then be represented in the quasi-reduced form:

$$A_2\boldsymbol{p}_t = B_2E_t\boldsymbol{p}_{t+1} + C_2\boldsymbol{p}_{t-1} + D_2\boldsymbol{g}_{t-1} + E_2\boldsymbol{p}_{t-1}^* + F_2\varepsilon_t + G_2\bar{y}$$

The vectors $\boldsymbol{p}_t$, $\boldsymbol{p}_t^*$ and $\boldsymbol{g}_{t-1}$ are the vectors of the domestic endogenous variables, foreign prices, and domestic policy instruments, respectively. The matrices A_2–G_2 are 4 × 4 matrices of structural parameters. The vector of foreign prices follows an exogenous process identical to (12.2) in case I. The vector $\bar{y}$ is a vector of the trend components.

Using a solution technique identical to that used earlier, we 'guess' a solution and then verify that the guess is in fact correct. This is, once again, the method of undetermined coefficients adapted to a matrix system.

A reasonable guess is

$$\boldsymbol{p}_t = \pi_0\boldsymbol{p}_t^* + \pi_1\boldsymbol{g}_{t-1} + \pi_2\varepsilon_t + \pi_3\bar{y}$$

Obtaining expressions for p_{t-1} and $E_t p_{t+1}$ by manipulating the above guess and using the Weiner–Kolmogrov procedure (appendix B) we get the solution for the 4 × 4 matrix π_1. This is the coefficient on the vector of policy instruments, $\boldsymbol{g}_{t-1}$, in the solution of the endogenous vector $\boldsymbol{p}_t$.

The solution of π_1 is

$$\pi_1 = [a - b\psi - c/\psi]^{-1}\,[d]$$

The inverted 4 × 4 matrix, $a - b\psi - c/\psi$, is

$$\begin{bmatrix} a_0 - b_0\psi_g & -a_1 & 0 & -a_2 \\ a_3 - b_1\psi_g + c_0/\psi_g & a_4(1-\psi_t) - \theta/\psi_t & 0 & 0 \\ -(a_5 + b_2\psi_g) & a_6 - b_3\psi_t & 0 & 0 \\ a_7 + b_3\psi_g - c_0/\psi_g & a_8(1-\psi_t) + \theta/\psi_t & a_9 & 0 \end{bmatrix}^{-1}$$

For the sake of computational simplicity, the above matrix is rewritten as

$$\begin{bmatrix} k_0 & -k_1 & 0 & -k_2 \\ k_3 & k_4 & 0 & 0 \\ -k_5 & k_6 & 0 & 0 \\ k_7 & k_8 & k_9 & 0 \end{bmatrix}^{-1}$$

where each of the k correspond to the symmetrically located element in the previous matrix, $a - b\psi - c/\psi$. This inverse is multiplied by the 4 × 4 matrix d:

$$\frac{1}{|J|}\begin{bmatrix} 0 & k_2k_6k_9 & -k_2k_4k_6 & 0 \\ 0 & k_2k_5k_9 & k_2k_3k_9 & 0 \\ 0 & -k_2(k_5k_8+k_6k_7) & -k_2(k_3k_8-k_4k_7) & k_2(k_3k_6+k_4k_5) \\ -k_2(k_3k_6-k_4k_5) & k_9(k_0k_6-k_1k_5) & -k_9(k_0k_4+k_1k_3) & 0 \end{bmatrix}$$

$$\times \begin{bmatrix} d_0 & -d_1 & 0 & 0 \\ -d_2 & d_3 & 0 & 0 \\ 0 & 0 & 0 & 0 \\ d_2 & -d_3 & 0 & 0 \end{bmatrix}$$

where $|J| = k_2k_9(k_3k_6 - k_4k_5) < 0$.

The solution of the domestic price level with respect to the policy instruments, obtained after performing the above computation, is

$$p_t = \left(\frac{-d_2k_6}{k_3k_6 + k_4k_5}\right) g_{t-1} + \left(\frac{d_3k_6}{k_3k_6 + k_4k_5}\right) t_{t-1} + \ldots \quad (12.14)$$

and the solution of the domestic nominal exchange rate with respect to the policy instruments is

$$s_t = \left(\frac{-d_2k_5}{k_3k_6 + k_4k_5}\right) g_{t-1} + \left(\frac{d_3k_5}{k_3k_6 + k_4k_5}\right) t_{t-1} + \ldots \quad (12.15)$$

Chapter thirteen

Sustainability under exogenous domestic money

This chapter is divided into three sections. In the first section, the solutions of case I for the three endogenous variables p_t, s_t, and w_t, with respect to the policy instruments, are analysed and interpreted, respectively. This section also includes the solutions of the vector of the stochastic elements and their effect on the volatility of prices and interest rates. The second section (p. 151) presents and analyses the case when real interest rates are introduced into the analysis. Both these sections pertain to the case of exogenous domestic money creation. The conclusions are summarised in the third section (p. 152).

Solutions with respect to the policy instruments: case I

Examining the solution of p_t, the domestic price level, we obtain our first result — budget deficits are non-inflationary in this economy. The solution for the domestic price level as a function of policy instruments resembles a standard quantity theory result. The price level is affected by the stock and growth rate of domestic money only, and is given by

$$p_t = \left(\frac{1}{a_3 - b_1\psi_d}\right) d_{t-1} + \ldots \qquad (13.1)$$

where d_{t-1} is last period's domestic money creation, given by $d_t = \psi_d d_{t-1}$ with $\psi_d > 1$, $a_3 = 1 + \gamma\gamma_5$, and $b_1 = \gamma_5$.

Result (13.1) states that the domestic price level, p_t, is completely unaffected, or *neutral* to, change in fiscal policy, i.e. neither K_1 nor τ influences the domestic price level. Furthermore, this implies that domestic output, y_t, is also neutral to changes in the government's share of current output or the tax rate. The intuition and interpretation of these results are provided after first examining the solutions of the nominal exchange rate and the interest rate, because these solutions shed further light on the neutrality results obtained above.

The solution of the nominal exchange rate as a function of the policy instruments is

$$s_t = \left[\left(\frac{(a_0 - b_0\psi_{\mathrm{d}})(b_5 - \lambda_1) + a_2(a_5 b_3 \psi_{\mathrm{d}})}{(a_3 - b_1\psi_{\mathrm{d}})[a_1(b_5 - \lambda_1) - a_2\psi_{\mathrm{d}}]} \right) \psi_{\mathrm{d}} - \frac{a_2 d_3}{a_1(b_5 - \lambda_1) - a_2\lambda_0} \right] d_{t-1}$$
$$+ \left(\frac{\beta_5(b_5 - \lambda_1) + a_2 d_4}{a_1(b_5 - \lambda_1) - a_2 d_0} \right) \tau - \left(\frac{\beta_7(b_5 - \lambda_1) + a_2 d_5}{a_1(b_5 - \lambda_1) - a_2\lambda_0} \right) K_1 + \ldots \quad (13.2)$$

The parameters $a_i - e_i$, $0 \leqslant i \leqslant 6$, have been defined in chapter 12 and appendix A.

By examining the solution of the nominal exchange rate, the following results are obtained.

1. Increases in either domestic money creation or the tax rate cause the domestic currency to depreciate – the dollar gets 'weaker'. An increase in either d_t or τ would mean that fewer discounted government bonds would have to be sold to finance the deficit. This decreased supply of government debt drives up bond prices. This in turn causes bond yields to fall, resulting in a lowering of domestic nominal interest rates. With stable prices, this means that the domestic and foreign real interest rate differential, $r_t - r_t^*$, would increase, resulting in a lower foreign demand for US government bonds. In a regime of floating exchange rates, this decrease in overseas demand for dollar-denominated assets and the consequent decrease in the demand for the US dollar in the foreign exchange markets cause the domestic currency to depreciate, or, the dollar gets weaker.
2. As the government increases its consumption share of current output, K_1, *ceteris paribus*, it causes the domestic currency to appreciate – the dollar gets 'stronger.' In this case, with domestic money held fixed, any increases in K_1, with the tax rate, τ, held constant, have to be financed with the issuance of larger numbers of bonds to domestic and foreign residents. This increased supply of government debt drives down bond prices and causes domestic and real interest rates to rise, resulting in a greater demand for dollar-denominated assets and hence an appreciation of the domestic currency. In this economy, both the nominal and real exchange rates, s_t and ρ_t,

appreciate. Conversely, a decrease in government spending would weaken the domestic currency.

We are now in a position to interpret the neutrality of the domestic price level, p_t, and the domestic output, y_t, with respect to increases in domestic budget deficits. More specifically, we examine why prices and output are neutral to changes in fiscal policy, *even when* individuals treat government deficits as permanent and incorporate the bonds which finance these deficits into their current wealth holdings.

The intuition behind this result is as follows. In this economy, the government can increase its consumption share of current output, K_1, only by issuing more bonds. As discussed earlier, this increased supply of bonds causes the domestic nominal and real interest rates to rise. Individuals do not discount future tax liabilities here, and they incorporate these bonds into their wealth holdings. But the reason why there are *no* aggregate demand or price effects stemming from changes in K_1 is that, with the incipient nominal and real appreciation of the domestic currency (explained earlier), domestic imports are 'cheaper' for the US residents, and the increase in domestic aggregate demand caused by the increased wealth holdings *literally overflows* into the foreign sector.[1] That is, the domestic country incurs a current account deficit due to the appreciation of the real exchange rate, ρ_t, and this is why the domestic aggregate demand effects manifest themselves in the form of stronger real exchange rates and a subsequent current account deficit *without* affecting domestic prices or output.

The solution for domestic real wealth is

$$w_t = \left(\frac{[a_0\psi_d - b_0\psi_d^2]\lambda_0 + a_1 i_4}{\psi_d(a_3 - b_1\psi_d)]a_1(b_5 - \lambda_1) - a_2\lambda_0} + \frac{a_1 d_3}{a_1(b_5 - \lambda_1) - a_2\lambda_0)} \right) d_{t-1}$$

$$+ \left(\frac{-1(\lambda_0\beta_5 + a_1 d_4)}{a_1(b_5 - \lambda_1) - a_2\lambda_0} \right) \tau + \left(\frac{\lambda_0\beta_7 + a_1 d_5}{a_1(b_5 - \lambda_1) - a_2\lambda_0} \right) K_1 + \ldots \quad (13.3)$$

where $i_4 = \psi_d(a_5 - b_3\psi_d) - \lambda_0$ and the rest of the parameters are as defined earlier:

$$[a_1(b_5 - \lambda_1) - a_2\lambda_0] < 0 \qquad i_4 < 0 \qquad \lambda_0 < 0$$

From the solution (13.3), domestic real wealth balances decrease with increases in the component of domestic money, d_t, or its rate of growth ψ_d. This is because increases in the domestic price level caused by increases in domestic money erode real wealth balances. From (13.3) it can also be seen that increases in the fraction of GNP the Treasury receives as tax revenues, τ, cause domestic real wealth balances to increase. These increases in τ cause the outstanding component of government debt to increase, thus freeing resources for the private sector. Furthermore, they cause the domestic currency to depreciate, as depicted in solution (13.2), by causing real and nominal rates to fall and by leading to a decrease in the real interest differential.

Therefore, there is a decreased demand for domestic government bonds from the foreign sector, and a larger percentage of the bonds outstanding are held by domestic residents. The 'mix' of government debt held by domestic and foreign residents has shifted, so that a greater debt load is borne by domestic residents as government bonds are now less attractive to foreigners.

The conclusion of the interpretation of the results of the three endogenous variables brings us to the issues of sustainability. Are debt-financed deficits sustainable in an economy when debt is continuously rolled over and domestic money creation is held fixed? The answer is, no: a debt-financing policy, such as the one discussed here, is non-sustainable because increases in the domestic deficit lead to *deterioration* of domestic real wealth balances. Increases in the Treasury's current consumption as a function of GNP, with taxes held fixed, cause *an outflow* of domestic real wealth. The incurrence of greater domestic deficits leads to higher domestic nominal and real interest rates. These, in turn, cause the domestic and foreign real interest rate differential to increase, resulting in an excess demand for US government bonds from the foreign sector which then accumulates ever-increasing shares of domestic debt. The percentage of US government bonds outstanding held by foreigners thus increases and that held by domestic residents decreases, thus leading to a deterioration of domestic real wealth balances.

In addition to discussing the issue of the sustainability of bond-financed deficits, this section offers an explanation for the causes of the volatility of prices and nominal exchange rates. This rational expectations open-economy model is particularly amenable to the analysis of price and exchange rate movements because the forward-looking expectations formation structure incorporated here is essential for a meaningful analysis of the fluctuations in prices and exchange rates.

The solutions of p_t and s_t with respect to the real and nominal shocks, ε_t^s, ε_t^d, and ε_t^m, are

$$p_t = \frac{1}{|A|} \left(\pi_3^{11}\varepsilon_t^{s} - \pi_3^{12}\varepsilon_t^{d} - \pi_3^{13}\varepsilon_t^{m} \right) + \ldots \tag{13.4}$$

$$s_t = \frac{1}{|A|} \left(-\pi_3^{21}\varepsilon_t^{s} + \pi_3^{22}\varepsilon_t^{d} - \pi_3^{23}\varepsilon_t^{m} \right) + \ldots \tag{13.5}$$

The unconditional variance of the price level is obtained from the fact that ε_t is a vector of iid shocks with zero mean and a finite variance. This is

$$\sigma_p^2 = \frac{1}{|A|^2} \left[(\pi_3^{11})^2 \, \sigma_{\varepsilon s}^2 + (\pi_3^{12})^2 \, \sigma_{\varepsilon d}^2 + (\pi_3^{13})^2 \, \sigma_{\varepsilon m}^2 \right]$$

and the unconditional variance of the nominal exchange rate is

$$\sigma_s^2 = \frac{1}{|A|^2} \left[(\pi_3^{21})^2 \sigma_{\varepsilon s}^2 + (\pi_3^{22})^2 \sigma_{\varepsilon d}^2 + (\pi_3^{23})^2 \sigma_{\varepsilon m}^2 \right]$$

The first result that is obtained from an analysis of the above variance is that the volatility of the domestic price level and the nominal exchange rate increases with an increase in the growth rate of domestic money, ψ_d. Both the coefficients π_3^{13} and π_3^{23} are functions of ψ_d, and as ψ_d increases, representing a 'looser' domestic monetary policy, both these coefficients increase, thereby resulting in an increase in the unconditional variance of prices and exchange rates.

The result has disturbing implications for domestic monetary policy. As demonstrated earlier in this section, the bond-financed deficits are non-sustainable, and the main ingredient of this non-sustainability is the fact that a deterioration of the current account balance is accompanied by an exodus of domestic real wealth. Any attempts by the monetary authority to rectify the situation by adopting a 'looser' money stance in an effort to reduce domestic real interest rates would only result in the greater volatility of domestic prices and nominal exchange rates. This result indicates that if the Fed. adopts, say, two different Friedman-like *x* per cent money growth rates, one with a higher rate of growth of domestic money than the other, then these rules will not be equivalent. The rule with the 'looser' domestic money growth will result in a greater volatility of prices and nominal exchange rates than the rule with 'tighter' domestic money, and hence the latter rule is clearly preferable. Therefore, in this economy, any attempts to shift from a 'tighter' money rule to a 'looser' one will prove detrimental.

The intuition behind this result is as follows. The Fed. increases the rate of growth of domestic money and holds it fixed at this new and higher rate of growth, with domestic money creation now being given by

$$d_t = \psi'_{\mathrm{d}}\, d_{t-1} + \varepsilon^{\mathrm{m}}_t$$

where ψ'_{d} is the new rate of growth of domestic money and $\psi'_{\mathrm{d}} - \psi_{\mathrm{d}} > 0$. Since current prices and exchange rates in this rational expectations economy are functions of future prices and exchange rates, it is imperative that expectations of future monetary policy, say *K* periods ahead, be formed in the present. Using the Weiner–Kolmogorov procedure outlined in appendix B, it can be shown that this expectation of future monetary policy, $E_t d_{t+k}$ can be represented by a moving average in terms of observed current and past nominal shocks. This turns out to be

$$E_t d_{t+k} = (\psi_{\mathrm{d}})^k\, d_t$$

Since $d_t = \psi_{\mathrm{d}} d_{t-1} + \varepsilon^{\mathrm{m}}_t$, and given that $|\psi_{\mathrm{d}}| < 1$, we implement the backward solution technique using lag operators (L) to obtain an expression for d_t in terms of current and past shocks:

$$d_t(1 - \psi_{\mathrm{d}} L) = \varepsilon^{\mathrm{m}}_t$$

therefore

$$d_t = \sum_{i=0}^{\infty} (\psi_{\mathrm{d}})^i\, \varepsilon^{\mathrm{m}}_{t-i} \qquad \text{or} \qquad d_t = \varepsilon^{\mathrm{m}}_t + \sum_{i=1}^{\infty} (\psi_{\mathrm{d}})^i\, \varepsilon^{\mathrm{m}}_{t-i}$$

Substituting this into the expression obtained for $E_t d_{t+k}$ we get

$$E_t d_{t+k} = (\psi_{\mathrm{d}})^k\, [\varepsilon^{\mathrm{m}}_t + \sum_{i=1}^{\infty} (\psi_{\mathrm{d}})^i\, \varepsilon^{\mathrm{m}}_{t-i}]$$

Therefore, current prices and exchange rates, which are functions of future prices and exchange rates and consequently of future paths of monetary policy, can be represented as functions of current and past nominal shocks weighted by the rate of growth of domestic money, $(\psi_{\mathrm{d}})^k$. Thus, it stands to reason that as a 'looser' domestic money policy is adopted and as ψ_{d} therefore increases, the coefficients of the money shocks (or the 'weights' attributed to these shocks) increase in magnitude, thereby resulting in greater unconditional variances of domestic prices and exchange rates.

Therefore, in an economy characterized by case I, any attempts to shift from a 'tighter' money rule to a 'looser' one, will prove detrimental.

Solutions incorporating the real interest rate: case I

In the preceding section, the sustainability results did not compromise those of Sargent and Wallace. However, the incorporation of the real interest rate long-term effects on the output supply does not replicate the above result of unambiguous non-sustainability.[2] Instead, the sustainability of bond-financed deficits is found to be crucially dependent on the responsiveness of aggregate supply to real interest rates.

When this responsiveness exceeds a certain threshold value, or when the elasticity of output supply to real rates is 'high', government bond issuances are found to be sustainable. In this case they tend to exert a dampening force on the domestic inflation rate while causing domestic real wealth holdings and capital inflows to increase. When the responsiveness is below the threshold value, bond-financed deficits are inflationary and not sustainable.

The same is true for the effects on the strength of the national currency. In the case where bond issuances are inflationary, domestic interest rates decrease, there is a decline in the demand for government bonds, and the nominal exchange rate depreciates with increases in bond issuances. This resembles the finding by Evans (1985) that increases in the deficit income rate might actually lower interest rates.

On the other hand, when the responsiveness of output to changes in the real rate is 'high', domestic currency appreciates (gets stronger) with increases in government bond sales. The intuition here is that in the case where bond-financed deficits are deflationary, increases in domestic real interest rates lead to an increase in the domestic and foreign demand for government bonds. This in turn leads to an appreciation of the domestic currency, or a decrease in the nominal exchange rate which is the domestic currency price of foreign currency.

Therefore, in this regime in which the Fed. maintains an exogenously fixed, or 'tight' money policy (case I), bond-financed deficits are sustainable when the elasticities of output supply are larger than their respective threshold values. When these elasticities are below the threshold values, increases in bond-financed deficits are inflationary, and they weaken the domestic currency, cause a deterioration of real wealth balances, and lead to an outflow of capital.

Summary of the results for case I

In the first section we found bond-financed deficits in an open-economy model, where money creation is held exogenously fixed, to be non-sustainable. This economy is characterized by output and price levels that are neutral with respect to increases in the domestic budget deficit, by an appreciation of the nominal exchange rates, and by an exodus of domestic real wealth. Even though government bonds are incorporated into individuals' real wealth holdings, the accompanying appreciation of the interest rate causes the incipient increase in domestic aggregate demand to manifest itself in the form of a current account deficit, thereby leaving the domestic price and output levels unaffected.

This scenario closely resembles the behaviour of the US economy in the early 1980s when the Fed. maintained a steady and curtailed rate of money growth to eradicate the inflation with which the country entered the decade. The resulting deterioration of the current account balance due to the strong dollar prompted a series of international agreements, or accords. These were all designed to manipulate national currencies and hence prevent the export sector of any particular nation from being adversely affected to an extent that might precipitate protectionist measures. These international exchange rate accords are discussed in the next chapter.

Increases in the tax rates, an idea that has been gaining momentum lately, have the same effect as a decrease in government spending – the domestic currency gets weaker. Therefore, policy makers intent on reducing the budget deficit must be prepared to accept the consequences of a weaker dollar when they contemplate further tax hikes or drastic cuts in government spending.

Lastly, any attempts to reduce the disparity between domestic and foreign real rates by adopting a looser path of money creation only serve to aggravate the volatility of the domestic price level and the nominal exchange rate. The arithmetic, it seems, remains unpleasant.

However, the incorporation of the long-term real interest rate effects on the output supply do produce different results regarding sustainability. Bond-financed deficits are now not universally non-sustainable. Instead, their sustainability is found to be contingent upon the magnitudes of the elasticities of output supply with respect to the real rate and real wealth balances relative to certain threshold values. When these elasticities exceed the threshold values, bond issuances are sustainable as domestic wealth holdings are found not to deteriorate, and the deficit-incurring country benefits from a capital inflow. On the contrary, when the deficits lie below the threshold values, bond-financed deficits are not sustainable as bond issuances are inflationary and there is a depletion of domestic real wealth balances and capital inflows.

The possible effects of bond-financed deficits on the domestic inflation rate and the nominal exchange rate are also examined here. While some recent studies have established fairly conclusive evidence of the inflationary effects of bond issuances, others have made strong cases for their neutrality with respect to aggregate demand effects. The research in this extension of case I reconciles these divergent findings with the result that bond-financed deficits could be either inflationary or deflationary, depending on the magnitudes of respective elasticities relative to the threshold values.

In conclusion, bond-financed deficits in case I, without including the real interest rate effects, are non-sustainable. The inclusion of the real interest rate effects on the output supply indicates that while the bond-financing arithmetic is not universally unpleasant, it is nevertheless ambiguous.

This does not mean that we are unable to determine the effects of bond-financed deficits in a regime where the domestic money creation is exogenously fixed. Clearly, economists could empirically determine the threshold values and the elasticities and verify the theoretical results obtained here. What these results do indicate is that in a regime where the monetary authority maintains a constant growth rate of money creation, bond-financed deficits cause the domestic currency to get stronger and the trade deficits to worsen and have no adverse effect on the domestic inflation rate in the short term. In the long term, when we incorporate the real interest rate effects on output, the results are ambiguous.

What are the implications of these results for the US bond-financed deficits? Since 1983, the Fed. has loosened the domestic money creation by monetizing more government debt. The double-digit inflation was a thing of the past, and the worsening current account deficit put tremendous pressure on the Fed. to depart from its tight money policies of the early 1980s and eventually try and spur US exports by weakening the dollar.

Case I, therefore, while ideally suited to analyse the economy of the US in the early 1980s, is not an appropriate monetary regime within which to analyse the effects of deficits in the current macroeconomic climate of the United States. Case II – the regime in which money creation is not fixed but endogenously determined – is the appropriate framework to analyse our present budget deficits, and the results are presented in chapter 15.

But first let us study the international consequences of the tight money policies of 1980–2. According to some economists and policymakers, the virtual elimination of inflation as an economic concern was achieved at great cost – the recession of 1981–2 and the deterioration of the US export sector. This has generated a strong protectionist sentiment and a call for the deliberate manipulation of the currencies of trading nations. In the next chapter we will see how and why protectionism and currency manipulation might not be in the best interests of the citizens of the deficit-incurring country.

Chapter fourteen

International policy co-ordination

In the previous chapter we found that increased government bond issuances in an economy characterized by 'tight' money on the part of the Federal Reserve resulted in high domestic real rates and a stronger US dollar. This currency appreciation aggravates the current account deficit by making exports more 'expensive' to foreigners and imports 'cheaper' to US residents.

This indeed was the case in the early 1980s. As the Federal Reserve embarked on a tight money policy to fight the double-digit inflation with which the United States entered the decade, government spending continued unabated. The large and progressively increasing deficits had to be bond-financed as the Federal Reserve had made it clear that it would rigidly adhere to its constant growth rate money policy and not relent and monetize some outstanding debt.

Case I replicated this macroeconomic scenario of the early 1980s, and we saw that the domestic nominal and real rates did appreciate. As the current account deficit worsened, there was increasing pressure from the export sector on the Federal Reserve to weaken the dollar somehow and stimulate US exports. The protectionist sentiment grew steadily till it had reached very dangerous Smoot–Hawley-like proportions. Lobby groups associated with the export sector rapidly propagated the trade deficit myths (chapter 10) to an unsuspecting public. These myths, inadvertently aided by a resurgent nationalist sentiment, called for draconian measures to stem the flood of imports.

Attempting to anticipate, and hence pre-empt these measures, policy makers of the industrialized countries decided to meet and co-ordinate their respective fiscal and monetary policies. Restrictions on international trade make trading partners in both countries worse off, and hence it was to their mutual advantage that this protectionist sentiment be nipped in the bud. The only group that benefits from trade restrictions such as tariffs and import quotas is the export sector of the country incurring the trade deficit; it benefits at the expense of the consumer who might now have fewer and more expensive choices of perhaps lower quality than those available with foreign competition.

Policymakers of Canada, France, Italy, Japan, West Germany, the USA, and the UK have met quite frequently since the dollar reached its zenith in 1985. They felt that it would be prudent to intervene directly in the international currency markets and co-ordinate their policies to ensure that the exchange rates remained manageable and did not completely eradicate the export sector of any particular country. Protectionist measures are detrimental to all parties in a macroeconomic sense, and these policy makers believed that this voluntary exchange rate manipulation would ward off the dangerously imminent protectionist backlash.

Let us now examine some of the forms of international policy co-ordination. It turns out that these are only marginally successful, and that too only in the short term. After this examination, we will see how and why the trend today is *away* from international policy co-ordination.

International policy rules

Policy co-ordination among countries may take different forms. At one extreme, we have agreements by countries to adhere to specific internationally agreed-upon policy rules. One example of these rules is the Bretton Woods international monetary system, in effect from 1944 to 1973. Under this rule, countries defined their own currency values in terms of the US dollar which, in turn, maintained the price of gold at $35 an ounce. This system thus pegged the world's monetary system to gold.[1]

As the United States maintained the price of gold, each of the other countries was expected automatically and voluntarily to intervene to bring its currency back into line should it depart from its fixed rate. Thus, for example, if the pound sterling were to move out of the exchange rate band, the Bank of England would intervene in the foreign exchange markets by exchanging either US dollars from its foreign exchange reserves for pounds, or vice versa. It would exchange dollars for pounds if the pound were to fall to the lower limit of the exchange rate band, and it would do the opposite if the pound were too strong with respect to the dollar.[2] The European monetary system (EMS) is a recent example of rule-based co-ordination of exchange rate management.

However, these rules, by definition, tended to limit policy

discretion on the part of individual countries, and the latter eventually 'bent' or broke these rules whenever they found it economically expedient to do so. The collapse of the Bretton Woods fixed exchange system was a symptom of the unwillingness of countries to exercise fiscal and monetary policy within the narrow bounds that would maintain their internationally agreed-upon fixed exchange rates.

For example, during the mid 1960s, when inflation was causing the US dollar to weaken relative to foreign currencies, the United States chose not to intervene but to let the dollar drop further in value. Abiding by the Bretton Woods accord would have meant domestic monetary tightening to shore up the falling dollar. This, of course, might have been accompanied by rising interest rates and subsequently greater unemployment, both of which were clearly undesirable during a period of economic stagnancy. Thus the United States, as had other countries before, gave precedence to domestic economic stability over the maintenance of the Bretton Woods accords and let the national currency fall with respect to its major trading partners.

International policy rules, which happen to be one extreme form of international policy co-ordination, finally sputtered to a halt in 1972. Countries simply did not, or could not, have the amount of policy discipline necessary to co-ordinate their activities and maintain their exchange rates.

At the other extreme, international policy co-ordination may take the form of *ad hoc* arrangements and agreements that deal with specific economic contingencies. These have been quite common following the demise of the Bretton Woods fixed exchange rate system, particularly in the 1980s.

The G-5 and G-7 meetings

On 22 September 1985, the so-called 'Group of Five' or G-5 countries – France, West Germany, Japan, the United Kingdom, and the United States – met informally in the New York Plaza Hotel to discuss sensitive international monetary problems. The focus was on resisting protectionism, improving the international co-ordination of macroeconomic policies, and, above all, on aspects involving central bank intervention to manipulate the strength of currencies.

All the five members supported a reduction in the foreign exchange value of the dollar. It is noteworthy that Japan, alarmed by all the flag-waving in the United States, decided to announce that the government of Japan would pursue a flexible monetary policy aimed at reducing the US trade deficit by making the dollar weaker with respect to the yen. While the dollar was already on a downward path, it continued to fall after the agreement.

In January 1986, the G-5 countries agreed that a lowering of interest rates was in order, and in March, the United States, West Germany, and Japan lowered their discount rates by half a percentage point. This was followed by another round of reductions in April by the Federal Reserve and the Bank of Japan. The Bundesbank, however, abstained from making a similar reduction for fear of renewed inflation.

In May 1986, the G-7 countries (G-5 plus Canada and Italy) agreed to attempt a more formal co-ordination of each others' policies by using a bunch of indicators such as output growth rates, inflation rates, interest rates, trade balances, and values of each country's currency.

The attempts with exchange rate manipulation were eventually met with some success; the dollar fell appreciably against the currencies of its trading partners – by as much as 30 per cent with respect to the yen. The steep dollar depreciation since February 1985 was at first hailed as a long-overdue exchange rate correction – a glowing tribute to the deft manipulations and swaps of national currencies. Protectionism, the international trade theorist's worst enemy, was finally vanquished, and the crisis was over.

Or so it seemed. Apparently the dollar depreciation had gone *too far*, and by 1987 the cheers had turned to worried frowns. Primarily because of declining exports caused by the foreign currencies' appreciation with respect to the dollar, America's trading partners found their economies foundering as their exports slowed down. Japan's output growth rate fell from 4.7 per cent in 1985 to 2.5 per cent in 1986.[3] Germany's stayed at a sluggish 2.5 per cent in both years. The average industrial growth for the industrial countries declined from 3 per cent in 1985 to 2.4 per cent in 1986 and declined further in 1987.

Rising inflationary pressures in the United States combined with the prospect of a global economic slow down prompted finance ministers and the central bank governors of the G-7 countries to hurry back for another meeting, this time in Paris in February 1987.

This meeting, known as the Louvre Accord, soon met its most severe test and its greatest (and maybe its last) trial. The G-7 countries had agreed in this meeting to limit exchange rate fluctuations by co-ordinating their fiscal and monetary policies. This was in February. By mid March the dollar, which seemed to have stabilized, began falling sharply again. Heavy and persistent intervention by the central banks proved to be useless.

To some, this fall (in retrospect) seems quite mysterious, a product of irrational inflationary expectations. I personally feel that this fall was primarily due to inflationary expectations generated by the increasingly large amounts of debt that had been monetized by the Federal Reserve since 1985. This monetization failed to show up as an increase in the domestic inflation rate because the effect was masked, or counterbalanced, by low oil prices. This dampening effect on inflation persisted till mid 1987 and then the inflationary pressure of past monetizations finally manifested itself. Individuals' inflationary expectations were, therefore, quite rational.

The sharp fall in the dollar, due to the deteriorating real interest rate differentials between the United States and the rest of the world was thus accompanied by sharp rises in long-term US interest rates. As the dollar fell further, interest rates rose too. Finally, on 4 September 1987, the Federal Reserve raised its discount rate from 5.5 to 6 per cent in a last desperate attempt to stop the seemingly free-falling dollar. Its efforts were to no avail. The stock market crashed on 19 October 1987. International policy co-ordination had failed. Some economists list the Louvre Accord as one of the causes for the crash. The last-minute bickering about interest rates between Treasury Secretary James Baker and the West Germans did nothing to soothe panicky investors. And once the dollar began to fall, no amount of intervention could stop it.

Why did the recent attempts at policy co-ordination, begun in 1985, eventually fail? And why is there a strong and growing sentiment among economists to put an end to international policy co-ordination? Martin Feldstein writes that the United States should 'in a clear but friendly way, end the international co-ordination of macroeconomic policy', and that it should continue to co-operate with other countries by exchanging information, yet recognizing that individual countries 'have the right to pursue monetary and fiscal policies that they believe are in their own best interests'.[4]

An end to policy co-ordination

Policy co-ordination by central bank intervention might have failed for two reasons. First, intervention in currency markets might be effective only in the short term. To understand why this is so, let us go back to the reason why the G-5 countries met in the first place.

In 1985, the dollar was incredibly strong with respect to the currencies of America's traders. This only worsened the American trade deficit, until it seemed that the protectionists would eventually have their way. The G-5 and G-7 countries met to weaken the dollar deliberately and make their goods more expensive to US residents and hence reverse, or at least stem, the burgeoning American trade deficits. But they *failed* to address the *cause* of the strong dollar – the budget deficits – which were putting a strain on the demand for loanable funds due to increased government borrowing. This increased demand for loanable funds was causing the US interest rates to be higher than those abroad, attracting foreign investors and hence making the dollar appreciate.

From the national savings identity

$$(G-T)=(S-I)+(M-X)$$

where $(G-T)$ is the domestic budget deficit, if $(G-T)>0$, $(S-I)$ is the excess of domestic savings over investment, and $(M-X)$ is the current account deficit, if $(M-X)>0$.

We can see that *as long* as the large deficit exists, it has to be financed by increased borrowing which in turn causes interest rates to rise. Swapping different currencies to raise or lower exchange rates will therefore be only a *temporary* measure so long as the deficit keeps guzzling loanable funds. Long-term movements in exchange rates are only determined by market fundamentals such as interest rate differentials caused by the interaction of the source and demand for real loanable funds.

Thus, the G-5 and G-7 accords were aimed at the *symptom* or the effect of the problem, and not the cause. In this sense they were eventually doomed to fail.

The second reason why international policy co-ordination failed is that different countries could not reconcile their various interests and views of the world. Some gave higher priority to fighting inflation, while others to lowering unemployment. The West German policy makers, for example, are more prone to inflation fears than their US counterparts.

Furthermore, in times of economic crises, these accords are often relegated to secondary status when individual nations have their own economic stability at stake. For example, following the stock-market crash on 19 October 1987, the Fed.'s response was quick and forceful. Chairman Greenspan assured the market of the Fed.'s determination to provide sufficient liquidity to 'support the economic and financial system'.[5] As reserves were generously provided, interest rates fell rapidly. The shift from equity to safer, and more liquid, assets caused interest rates to fall further. The dollar began another dive and between 26 October 1988 and the end of the year the trade-weighted dollar had fallen another 10 per cent. This is evidence that the Fed. was in no way going to let its commitment to the G-5 and G-7 accords get in the way when national economic stability was at stake.

Under the circumstances, we cannot expect any other central bank to do otherwise. International policy co-ordination once again fell victim to national economic contingencies. Since policy co-ordination can succeed only when it is consistent with the individual goals of the participating countries, and that too only in the short term due to the presence of the continuing American budget deficits, some policy makers now advocate that we abandon the whole idea.

Let us now turn to the determination of the sustainability of bond-financed deficits in an economy where the Fed. relents to external pressure and actively monetizes the debt. This case (case II, described in chapter 11) is designed to replicate the US economy since 1985 when increased pressure from the export lobby forced the Fed. to monetize outstanding debt and hopefully to weaken the dollar by lowering domestic interest rates.

Chapter fifteen

Sustainability with endogenous money creation: case II

Contrary to case I, money creation is endogenous here as the Federal Reserve monetizes a fraction of the outstanding principal and interest repayments. The results are presented in the first section below, a historical analogue is presented in the second section (p. 166), and a summary of the results of case II in the light of current US fiscal and monetary policy is in the third section (p. 167).

Solutions with respect to the policy instruments

From equation (12.14) we have that

$$p_t = \left(\frac{-d_2k_6}{k_3k_6 + k_4k_5}\right) g_{t-1} + \left(\frac{d_3k_6}{k_3k_6 + k_4k_5}\right) t_{t-1} + \ldots$$

The first important result is that in this case, where the amount of debt that is rolled over is fixed, the price level is *not neutral* with respect to changes in domestic fiscal policies. In contrast to the results in case I, increased domestic government spending causes domestic inflation. In this economy, deficits are inflationary.

As taxes remain 'fixed' into the indefinite future, any increase in government expenditures over revenues is financed by the issuance of government bonds, and the remainder is made up by the creation of domestic money. The traditional assumption, that government debt is temporary, therefore cannot be made here. In this case, the issuance of debt in lieu of current taxation does stimulate aggregate demand and is, therefore, inflationary. Here, debt issued today is not matched by additional savings because there are no foreseeable future taxes which might be imposed to retire the debt.

This tends to corroborate the findings of Cox (1985) that in the period 1950–84 federal government debt has not been temporary, i.e. backed by taxes. Government bonds have not been matched by future taxes and bond financing has contributed to the increase in the price level. He finds that over the period 1950–84, inflation in the United States was as closely related to the growth in outstanding government debt as to the growth in the monetary base.

The change in the domestic price level, in this model, is affected by two channels of influence. First, increased sales of bonds drive up the aggregate demand as discussed above. Second, increases in the deficit mean that the absolute amount of money creation for the retirement of last period's debt is larger, and this in turn exerts an upward force on the price level. Conversely, decreases in the deficit stemming from decreases in government spending, g_t, or increases in taxes, t_t, cause p_t to fall.

Now that it has been determined that the level of goverment spending does affect the price level, the next task is to determine how the *composition* of the government deficits affects p_t – or how θ_1, which is the fraction of principal payment that is bond financed, affects the domestic price level. This, after all, lies at the heart of the issue of the sustainability of domestic budget deficits.

From the non-singularity requirement for matrix $[A\psi_d - B\psi_d - \lambda]$, we get the following restriction which provides us with an expression for the maximum amount of debt that can be rolled over, before domestic money ceases to have any value:

$$\theta_1 < \frac{(a_5 - b_3\psi_t)(a_3 - b_1\psi_g) + [\beta_0 + (\gamma_{11} - \gamma\gamma_9)\psi_g]\,[a_4(1-\psi_t)]}{\psi_g[\beta_0 + (\gamma_{11} - \gamma\gamma_9)\psi_g] - \psi_t(\gamma_{15} - \gamma_{16})(a_6 - b_3\psi_t)} = \theta_c \quad (15.1)$$

According to this restriction, the amount of principal plus interest payments that are bond financed has to be less than the right-hand side, θ_c, or the 'critical value' of θ.

If $\theta_1 = \theta_c$, $p_t = \propto$, i.e. the sequence of domestic prices explodes. In this case, the rate of return on domestic bonds has exceeded the rate of growth of the domestic output leading to an explosive debt/income ratio. An upper bound on the number of bonds that can be absorbed is reached when the fraction of debt rolled over, θ_1, equals the amount denoted as θ_c. At this point the monetary authority is forced to purchase government debt directly – or monetize the debt. The θ_c expression involves parameters that correspond to coefficients of current and expected future price and nominal exchange rates. The latter are 'weighted' by the rates of growth of domestic government spending and tax revenues. The intuition behind the inequality (15.1) is that as increasingly larger amounts of government bonds are rolled over, or as θ_1 increases, p_t increases too ($dp_t/d\theta_1 > 0$), *but* when $\theta_1 = \theta_c$ an *upper limit* on the amount of bond financing is reached as individuals are loathe to hold everything denominated in worthless US dollars in their portfolios. Any bond financing at $\theta_1 = \theta_c$ produces an exploding price level and this is the 'critical amount' of debt that can be 'rolled over' in this economy. This result is similar to an aggregated version of the upper bound of debt that the 'rich' individuals are willing to hold in Sargent and Wallace's 'Some unpleasant monetarist arithmetic' (1981).

Furthermore, from (15.1) we obtain two interesting results regarding the effect the rates of growth of government spending and tax revenues have on this 'critical value' of θ_1. First, $d\theta_c/d\psi_g < 0$ and, second, $d\theta_c/d\psi_t > 0$. These are important results. In this economy, as the fiscal authority incurs bigger deficits by either increasing ψ_g or decreasing ψ_t, the 'critical' value or the upper limit of the amount of total debt that can be rolled over without causing the domestic price level to explode is *lowered.* The domestic price level would now explode at a lower value of θ_c, and hence the increase in the domestic deficit causes the upper limit on the amount of debt that can be financed, θ_c, to decrease. The intuition behind this result is that there is some absolute maximum amount of government debt that the world economy is willing to absorb, and therefore in an economy characterized by large and rapidly growing deficits, this absolute amount is reached *much sooner* than it would in one with a marginally increasing deficit.

From result (12.15)

$$s_t = \left[\frac{-d_2 k_5}{k_3 k_6 + k_4 k_5}\right] g_{t-1} + \left[\frac{d_3 k_5}{k_3 k_6 + k_4 k_5}\right] t_{t-1} + \ldots$$

The behaviour of domestic nominal exchange rates with respect to changes in g_t, t_t, and θ_1 can be determined. It is found that in this model the domestic nominal exchange rate, s_t, depreciates with either an increase in government spending or a decrease in tax revenues. The reason is that deficits are inflationary in this economy, and this causes the domestic and foreign real interest differential to diminish. This, in turn, leads to a decline in foreign residents' excess demand for US bonds, thereby causing the nominal exchange rate to depreciate. This result is in stark contrast to that obtained for s_t in case I where the exchange rate appreciated and the dollar grew 'stronger' as a result of the neutrality of the price level with respect to domestic deficits.

In (12.15), $ds_t/d\theta_1$ is positive and the dollar gets weaker as the amount of debt being rolled over as a proportion of total principal payments increases. When θ_1 equals θ_c, the domestic currency *collapses* ($s_t \rightarrow 0$) and the price level explodes, and this corresponds to the 'hard fall' of the dollar which has gained some attention lately.[1] Domestic currency rapidly ceases to be of any value and at this point bond-financed deficits are clearly 'strongly non-sustainable' as defined earlier.

The results $dp_t/d\theta_1$, $ds_t/d\theta_1 > 0$ are disconcerting for policy makers in that they make the arithmetic very unpleasant indeed. Any co-ordinated attempt by the fiscal and monetary authorities to 'tighten money today' by simply rolling over the last period's debt and thereby indulging in lesser amounts of monetary accommodation would *only serve* to exacerbate the domestic inflation further and cause the dollar to depreciate even more. In a sense these results corroborate the Sargent and Wallace result that 'tighter money today would mean more inflation today' in a rational expectations economy. Therefore, in this economy where the permanency of the deficit is ensured by the Bush administration's inflexibility on the tax issue, any attempt to prevent deficits from being inflationary, short of decreasing g_t, would prove futile. Furthermore, as larger amounts of bonds are retired by selling still more bonds, the domestic economy runs a greater risk of having its currency collapse and its price level explode, as θ_1 approaches θ_c – especially in an environment where run-away government spending causes this upper limit of bond financing, θ_c, to be *lower* due to the $d\theta_c/d\psi_g < 0$ result.

Let us now examine the mechanism causing this upper limit of debt financing to decrease with increases in the growth of domestic deficits.

In an economy characterized by persistent inflation due to increases in the deficit and in the amount of debt being rolled over, y_t decreases from trend. This is because (i) individual demanders substitute foreign goods for the higher-priced domestic goods, and (ii) suppliers of output, due to the intertemporal substitution of leisure incorporated into the aggregate supply equation, postpone supply indefinitely as the prices are always higher in the next period. Therefore, the perpetual postponement of output supply due to the continuous rise in the domestic price level caused by larger amounts of debt rolled over and the substitution of cheaper foreign goods for domestic goods cause a decline in national income, *and this in turn* causes the upper limit on debt holdings to be lowered.

Historical analogue to case II

The results obtained here resemble the Austrian, Hungarian, Polish, and German hyperinflations of the period 1919–24 quite closely. Immediately after the First World War, these countries, unlike the United States, were not on a gold standard. Under the gold standard, a government was obligated to convert into gold under certain specified conditions the demand notes and long-term debt that it issued. This imposed a certain discipline on the government because large bond-financed deficits could not be incurred as the government debt was 'backed' to some degree by its gold reserves and by its commitment to levy taxes in the future to service its outstanding debt. A country on the gold standard, therefore, had to honour its debts and could not engage in inflationary finance.

Since the four European countries in question were not on the gold standard, they had no such budgetary discipline imposed on them, and their currencies were unbacked or 'fiat'. This led the governments of those countries to resort to the printing of new unbacked money to finance their domestic budget deficits. The government debt (notes and treasury bills) could not be expected to be paid off by levying taxes in the future and tremendous amounts of debt were simply 'rolled over' by issuing yet more treasury bills, as in case II. Consequently, these countries experienced what we have defined as a 'strongly non-sustainable' deficit-financing policy characterized by domestic hyperinflation, a collapse of the currency, and a declining national output – all of which are results obtained in case II of this model.

Germany experienced the most severe case of debt non-sustainability. The German domestic inflation rate assumed immense proportions towards the end of 1923, as shown in figure 15.1. This was aggravated by an event that took place earlier in that year – the military occupation of the Ruhr by the French in January 1923 as a result of the inability of the Germans to make the staggering reparations payments. The German government, determined to fight this French occupation by a policy of 'passive resistance', made direct payments to striking workers which were financed by the issuance of discounted treasury bills to the public or the Reichsbank, i.e. by 'rolling over' the debt. Relevant plots pertaining to the German hyperinflation are in figures 15.1–15.4, and an examination of the plots of the price level, exchange rate, government debt outstanding, and domestic money creation, reveal a close similarity to the behaviour of these variables for the economy in case II.

Figure 15.1 German hyperinflation; 1918–23. Wholesale prices vs. time

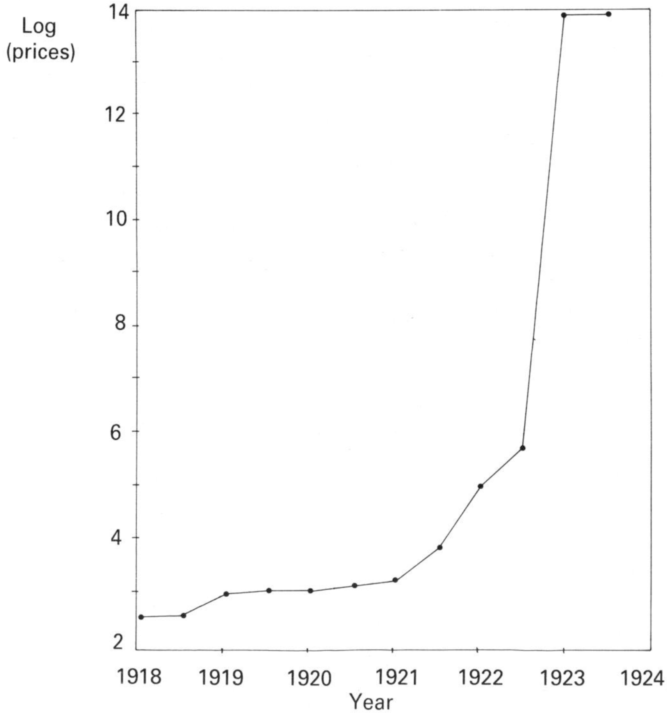

Sources: Young (1925), Sargent (1986)

Summary of the results: case II

When domestic money creation and government bond issuance are both endogenously determined, as in case II, we find that domestic deficits are inflationary. Here, a portion of government debt outstanding is monetized in every period and the *mix* of government bond issuance and domestic money creation is held exogenously fixed. As more bonds are rolled over, or as the mix of money and bonds changes so that a larger portion of the principal payment is now bond financed, we obtain an increase in the domestic inflation rate and a depreciation of the domestic currency, i.e. any attempt to put a restraint on domestic money creation only results in an exacerbation of the inflation rate and a weakening of the dollar.

Additionally, case II provides us with an upper limit on the amount of government debt that can be absorbed by the world

Figure 15.2 German hyperinflation: 1918–23. Exchange rates in cents per mark vs. time

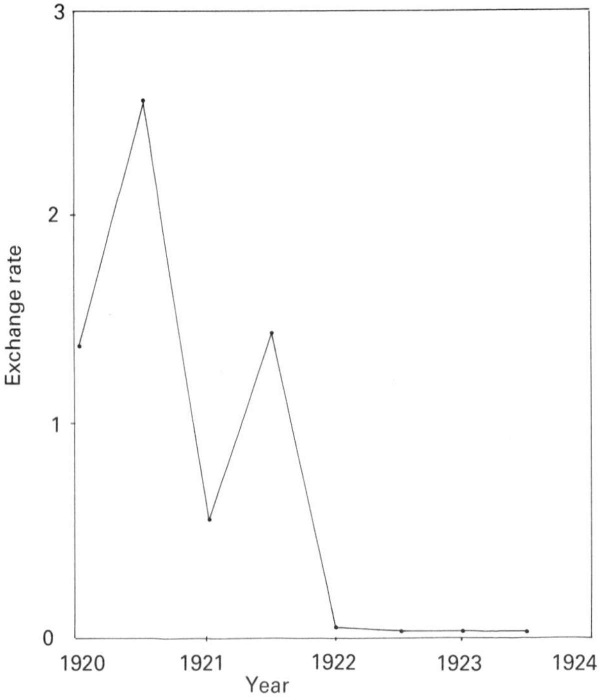

Sources: Young (1925), Sargent (1986)

economy. As larger fractions of principal repayments, θ_1, are financed by issuing yet more government bonds, an upper limit on the amount of debt that can be issued is reached when $\theta_1 = \theta_c$. Domestic and foreign residents are reluctant to absorb more government bonds in their portfolios and the monetary authority is therefore forced to monetize the deficit by directly purchasing these bonds from the Treasury. The economy at this stage is characterized by a rapidly escalating domestic price level and a collapsing national currency. Furthermore, this upper limit on the amount of debt that can be issued is found to bear an inverse relationship to the rate of growth of the domestic deficit, and this leads to the conclusion that there is some finite absolute amount of debt that can be absorbed by the world economy. The German hyperinflation of 1919–24 closely resembles that experienced by the economy in case II.

Figure 15.3 German hyperinflation: 1918–23. Discounted treasury bills vs. time

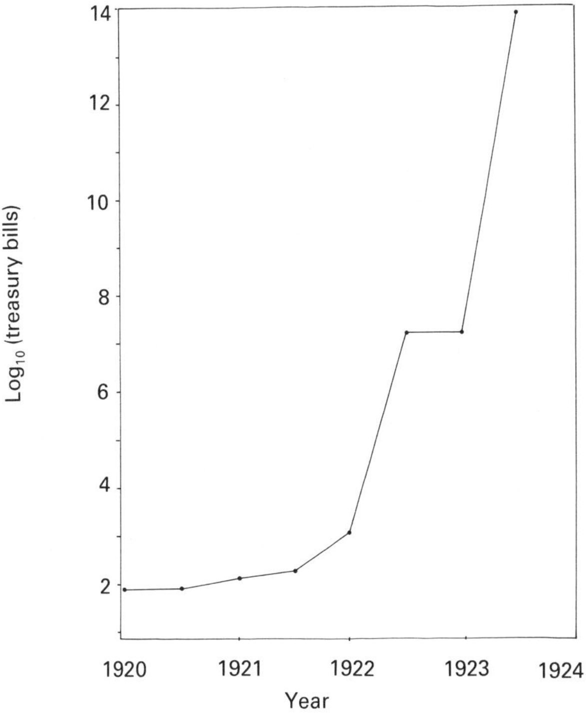

Sources: Young (1925), Sargent (1986)

In conclusion, large inflows of capital from abroad, stemming from burgeoning current account deficits, do not overturn the Sargent and Wallace proposition – bond-financed deficits are still non-sustainable in both cases of this open-economy rational expectations model.

This has some disconcerting and politically difficult implications for policy makers. Short of reducing the domestic deficit, tighter money policies and greater amounts of debt being rolled over would only serve to deplete domestic real wealth balances and deteriorate the export sector in case I, and to exacerbate the domestic inflation rate and drastically weaken the dollar in case II. In the theoretical cases discussed in this book, the arithmetic, it seems, is very unpleasant indeed.

Fortunately for the US economy, the future is not nearly as bleak as the above analysis in case II. Government spending and

Figure 15.4 German hyperinflation: 1918–23. Notes in circulation vs. time

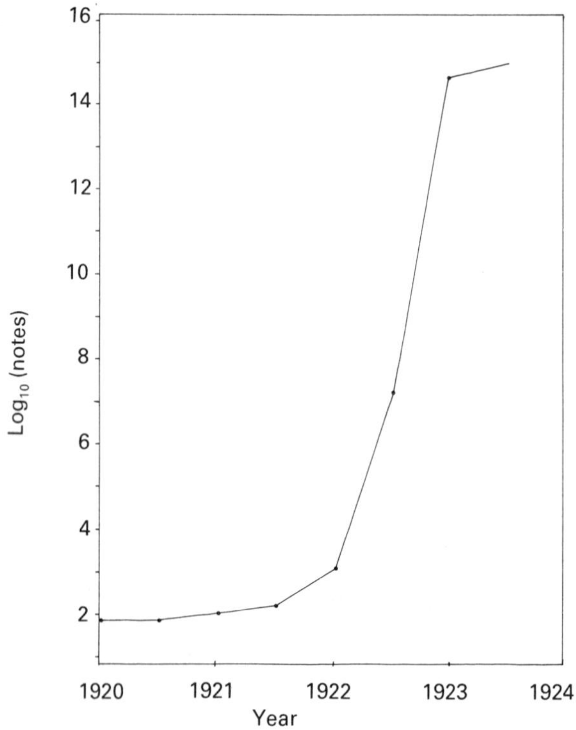

Sources: Young (1925), Sargent (1986)

deficits as percentages of GNP are declining. The Federal Reserve seems to be alert to the consequences of prolonged monetization. According to the research in case II, a finite fixed amount of monetization is consistent with a corresponding fixed rate of inflation. It is only the *increase* in the fraction of debt monetized, or rolled over, that worsens the inflation rate. Therefore, as long as the Treasury and the Federal Reserve are conscious of these implications, and as long as they attempt to curtail the amount of debt that is rolled over and implicitly monetized, bond-financed deficits will be associated with a steady inflation rate and a relatively stable domestic currency. But we know that even a steady and non-increasing primary deficit *will still generate larger debt issuances every period* by virtue of the accumulating interest expenses. This implies that for bond financing to be sustainable in the sense of stable domestic inflation and exchange rates, government spending and deficits will not only have to stop growing, but they will actually have to *decline* in order to negate the mounting interest expenses of the deficits incurred in the past.

At present the trends of deficits and government spending as percentages of GNP are moving in the right direction, and it is hoped that a fiscally responsible administration and Congress will have the strength, discipline, and moral turpitude necessary to maintain this trend into the future and prolong the present long-standing economic recovery.

Chapter sixteen

Some macroeconomic implications of the crash of 1987

The stock-market crash of October 1987 followed a historically rapid increase in US and world equity prices. The Dow–Jones industrial average (DJIA) increased about 200 per cent between January 1986 and the peak in August 1987. On 1 October 1986, the index was at 1782 and barely a year later at 2600. The price–earnings ratio for the Standard & Poor's 500 index averaged 22 in October, compared to the thirty-year average of 14.

This rise in equity prices was replicated in the world's exchanges as well. The Tokyo and Singapore exchanges experienced the most dramatic increases, with their share prices increasing by 220 and 250 per cent, respectively, from the beginning of 1986 till the peak in 1987. Other exchanges such as the London, Toronto, and Swiss exchanges experienced marginally less dramatic increases, with London's index increasing by 171 per cent; Toronto's by 148 per cent; and Switzerland's Swiss Bank Corp index by 136 per cent. None of the world's major exchanges experienced a downturn during the period discussed above.

It all started on Tuesday, 12 October 1987, when the DJIA declined by 10.5 per cent by the end of the week (figure 16.1). The individual day declines were large but not unprecedented. The weekend of 17–18 October was followed by a sharp decline in the DJIA by 23 per cent to 1738, on Monday, 19 October. This in turn was followed by sharp declines on all the other world exchanges, with the Australian and Singapore exchanges demonstrating the sharpest fall of nearly 50 per cent. The Japanese market, which had experts fearing the worst, did relatively better by declining by less than 15 per cent.

What caused the stock-market crash of 1987, and what are its implications for the future of the US economy? And what was the role, if any, played by the twin deficits in this dramatic collapse of world equity prices? Before we proceed with a discussion of these issues, it is imperative that we review the state of the US and world

Figure 16.1 Financial market indicators

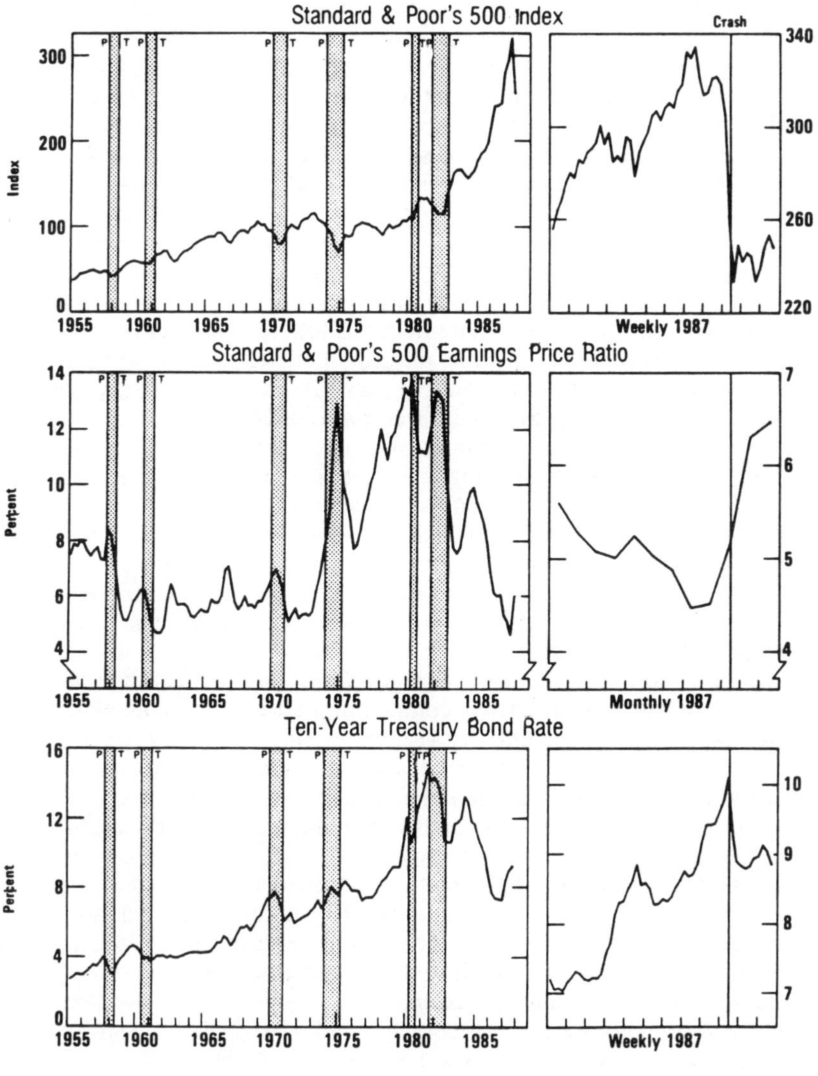

Sources: Congressional Budget Office; Standard & Poor's Corporation: Federal Reserve Board economies prior to the crash.

The stock-market crash occurred, paradoxically, at a time when the economy in general and all the real macroeconomic variables in particular were exhibiting a renewed robustness. Factories were humming with capacity utilization at over 80 per cent. Janet L. Norwood, commissioner of the Bureau of Labor Statistics, had just reported that 65,000 new factory jobs were added in October, bringing to 220,000 the number of new jobs since June 1987. In the furniture, rubber and plastics, and printing and publishing industries, employment had reached record levels. Third-quarter growth in the United States reached an annual rate of 3.8 per cent according to preliminary GNP estimates. This clearly dominated the consensus forecast of 2.6 per cent in June.

This economic performance was by no means restricted to the United States. Leading economic indicators for nine major industrial nations pointed upwards, and simultaneous growth was forecast for the Pacific basin, Europe, and America. In essence, the world economy was doing very well prior to the crash.

The crash itself was followed by a wave of recession fears, with Wall Street analysts making dire predictions of another Great Depression by pointing to superimpositions of the DJIAs of 1929 and 1987. Politicians rallied to this headline-making crisis by looking worried and emphasizing that 'something should be done' to avert the impending crisis, and in almost all cases they pointed to the scapegoats of the 1980s – the budget and trade deficits – as the cause of all the turmoil. As Professor Kristol points out in his scathing commentary in the *Wall Street Journal* (28 October 1987), Congressmen have a compelling desire to 'do something', for they believe that only by visibly reacting to a crisis can their reputations be made.[1] As we will soon see, this might not be a very good time for new policy experiments.

Let us now examine some of the possible causes for the crash.

1. There was a general feeling that the stock market was overdue for a 'correction' of about 20 per cent. This feeling was a result of a run-up of almost 400 per cent since 1982, and money managers had built up large cash reserves in anticipation of such correction.
2. Corrections are usually precipitated by exogenous events or announcements. Therefore, the forecast of higher inflation derived from the sharp rise in commodity prices, and the spectre of the inevitable monetary tightening and high interest rates, spooked an already nervous market.
3. The forecast of higher inflation stemmed from two sources:

(i) Money creation had been looser since 1983 as the Federal Reserve monetized larger amounts of government debt, as we discussed earlier. This had not manifested itself in a sharply rising inflation rate during 1983–7 due to the intermittent dampening influence exerted upon the inflation rate by sharply reduced oil prices. (ii) There was a growing sense that the economy had reached full employment and hence was about to 'overheat' as continually increasing aggregate demand placed strains on a fixed and maximum aggregate output. This, it was thought, would make goods and services more expensive and eventually lead to a fairly standard demand-side inflation. It seems ironic that the fears that might have triggered the stock-market crash stemmed from concerns that the economy was doing too well, rather than the opposite![2]

4. Recessions, in the past, have generally been preceded by monetary contractions, and the events of 1987, in terms of monetary policy, had convinced some individuals that a recession was indeed inevitable. It so happened that the Federal Reserve had responded to inflationary fears resulting from an overheated economy by actually sharply restricting money growth since the beginning of 1987. But the Fed. was in for some more responding – this time to stabilize the dollar.

The central banks of West Germany and Japan, monitoring their money supply figures and watching them rise even higher, decided to contract money growth and hence raise their interest rates substantially. Both these countries, West Germany in particular, have always been haunted by fears of a rapidly escalating price level, and they embarked on this monetary course despite no evidence of a resurgence of inflation. The Fed., fearing a flight from dollar-denominated assets to assets denominated in yen and marks, responded by raising short-term interest rates. We briefly discussed this when we studied the futility of international exchange rate co-ordination in chapter 14. This rise in short-term interest rates eventually pushed up longer-term rates too, and convinced nervous speculators that a recession was just around the corner.

5. Programmed trading, a feature thankfully absent in past stock-market corrections, might have been responsible for the magnitude, and not the cause, of the crash. There is general agreement among economists that programmed trading makes the market more volatile on both the upside and the downside. Therefore, what might have begun as a market correction based on inflation fears, and due to the contractionary actions of the Fed. and the prospect of higher interest rates, soon cascaded

into sharply and rapidly falling stock prices. And as the margin calls hit the market, the crash of 1987 was complete.

How do the US deficits figure in all this? Apart from the anxiety that they have generated, the deficits, contrary to popular belief, have had very little to do with the crash of 1987. If the deficits were involved, then a collapse of the dollar would have been experienced along with the stocks.

As we studied in case II, this would have happened if foreigners had finally reached the upper limit on US government debt that they had planned for their portfolios and had abstained from purchasing any more government bonds. The Fed. would have had to step in and purchase the bonds directly, or monetize the debt, thus causing the dollar to collapse along with the stock prices. There was no evidence of this following the crash. Furthermore, the crash was not only endemic to the US stock market, but also to the stock markets of Australia, France, West Germany, Hong Kong, Italy, Japan, the UK, and Singapore. Clearly there is a global factor at work, primarily the inflation and interest rate fears, and in this light it is quite meaningless to blame the US deficits for the happenings of October 1987.

Additionally, we have seen in earlier chapters that the budget and trade deficits are linked in a macroeconomic sense.[3] Some analysts have blamed the trade deficits for rocking financial markets. It is inconceivable, in this era of flexible exchange rates, and in the absence of a gold standard and an enacted trade bill, that the trade deficit of one of the countries (the United States) would cause a financial collapse in the trade-deficit-incurring country, *as well* as in a country with a trade surplus, such as Japan.

The dire prognosis of the US economy immediately following the crash has, thankfully, not come true. The crash has not been followed by a recession, and the outlook (in spite of rising inflation and a gradual economic slow-down in the US) is by no means bleak.

In fact, since the Second World War, only about half of the sharp declines in stock prices were followed by a recession.[4] And in almost *all* these cases the recession was caused by certain fiscal and monetary policies pursued *by the government and the Federal Reserve* following the decline in the stock prices, i.e. recessions that followed stock-market crashes were usually man-made. These often took the form of overly tight monetary policy, credit controls, discount rate increases, or currency manipulation.

For instance, the stock-market crash of 1929 was followed by a series of drastic policy measures, all of which served only to ensure that the crash would indeed have a profound and terrible effect on real variables. The stock market crashed on 24 October 1929 but the recession did not become the Great Depression till late 1930 and early 1931. The crash was followed by four major misguided policies: (i) Wage cuts were forbidden below a certain level, thereby worsening unemployment. (ii) The decline in output, and hence income, resulted in budget deficits, and the administration attempted to balance the budget in the middle of a recession by increasing taxes. This only caused output and income to fall even further. (iii) The money stock fell from 1929 to April 1933 as large banks failed, but Andrew Mellon, the deflationist, wanted prices to fall back to their pre-First World War levels, and hence he was against making liquidity available to the failing banks. (iv) The severe curtailment of international trade due to the Smoot–Hawley tariffs resulted in making all the trading partners worse off.

In the cases in which sharp stock-market declines have been blessed by the *absence* of drastic fiscal and monetary actions, the economy was able, with few exceptions, to adjust to the new and lower level of stock prices.

According to the Claremont Economics Institute: 'By themselves, lower stock prices are not likely to cause a recession.'[5] They go on to point out that: 'None of the eight recessions since 1947 have been caused by a drop in consumer spending triggered by the loss of wealth in the market', and they make the encouraging observation that the largest previous stock-market decline since 1947 – over 25 per cent in 1962 – produced only a one-month decline in personal consumption expenditures and a three-month decline in durables expenditures. They expect to see a similar temporary slowing down of economic activity this time around.

Another encouraging aspect is that the Fed. has performed admirably since the crash. The central bank correctly moved to supply liquidity after the market crash. Exchange rate co-ordination, doomed to fail anyway (chapter 14), was quickly abandoned in the face of this national contingency and $10 million was pumped into the economy in the two weeks following the crash. This injection of money had a two-fold purpose: it provided desperately needed liquidity and, simultaneously, the open-market purchase of bonds fuelled a bond-market rally. This, coupled with the fact that individuals were shifting from stocks to bonds immediately following the crash, helped to lower interest rates further. This sudden (and timely) injection of money did not, however, have inflationary consequences as the crash was itself deflationary.

The Federal Reserve's actions are in sharp contrast to its inactivity following the stock-market crash of 1929, where its inability to supply liquidity eventually resulted in the monetary contraction which was one major reason that the crash of 1929 deteriorated into the Great Depression.

The Federal Reserve signalled a tighter money stance in August 1988 by raising the discount rate from 6 to 6.5 per cent. This was partly to offset the sharp increase in the money supply since October 1987, and partly to act early and pre-empt any inflationary expectations. The discount rate hike came as a surprise to most economists as it took place when the economy was showing no real sign of overheating, but it did send a clear message that the Fed. would move quickly and decisively to nip any expectations of inflation in the bud. A replay of October 1987 would be a long time coming.

Therefore, it is safe to conclude that the stock-market crash, in the absence of any detrimental fiscal or monetary policies, will not manifest itself in the form of a serious recession. We have seen that those that do so have almost always been instigated by errant government policy. It seems that the Federal Reserve and the Administration have responded well to the crisis, and investor confidence in the economy is almost back to its old levels.

The alarmists and the preachers of doomsday scenarios have had a field day prognosticating another Great Depression. Others, who wrongly equate government budget and trade deficits with personal deficits, have jubilantly pointed to the crash as a vindication of all the wrong forecasts that they have made since 1983. I feel that their time and efforts as well as the time and efforts of their readers might be better served if they would understand the full theoretical economic framework, and interpret economic happenings within one consistent framework, such as that presented in this book.

Remember, ignorance breeds fear, and fear breeds drastic policy action. And this is no time to be afraid.

Appendix A

System of equations: case I

The system of equations for case I is reduced to a system of three equations in quasi-reduced form, with p_t, s_t, and w_t as the endogenous variables. In matrix form, these equations can be represented as:

$$\begin{bmatrix} \beta_1 & -\beta_3 & -\beta_2 \\ 1+\gamma\gamma_5 & \gamma_6 & 0 \\ a_5 & (\gamma_{13}-\gamma_{11}) & 0 \end{bmatrix} \begin{bmatrix} p_t \\ s_t \\ w_t \end{bmatrix} = \begin{bmatrix} \gamma & 0 & 0 \\ \gamma_5 & \gamma_6 & 0 \\ b_3 & (\gamma_{13}-\gamma_{11}) & -\gamma_{12}/\gamma_{20} \end{bmatrix} \begin{bmatrix} E_t p_{t+1} \\ E_t s_{t+1} \\ E_t w_{t+1} \end{bmatrix}$$

$$+ \begin{bmatrix} 0 & 0 & 0 \\ 0 & 0 & 0 \\ \lambda_0 & -\lambda_0 & \lambda_1 \end{bmatrix} \begin{bmatrix} p_{t-1} \\ s_{t-1} \\ w_{t-1} \end{bmatrix} + \begin{bmatrix} \beta_3\psi_p^* & \beta_6\psi_y^* & 0 \\ 0 & 0 & \gamma_6\psi_{\mathrm{i}}^* \\ e_3 & \gamma_{17}(\gamma_{15}-\gamma_{16})\gamma_4 & \gamma_{17}+\gamma_{13}\psi_{\mathrm{i}}^* \end{bmatrix} \begin{bmatrix} p_{t-1}^* \\ y_{t-1}^* \\ i_{t-1}^* \end{bmatrix}$$

$$+ \begin{bmatrix} 0 & -\beta_5 & \beta_7 \\ \psi_{\mathrm{d}} & 0 & 0 \\ d_3 & -q_0 & q_1 \end{bmatrix} \begin{bmatrix} d_{t-1} \\ \tau \\ K_1 \end{bmatrix} + \begin{bmatrix} \dfrac{1}{1-\gamma_2} & -1 & 0 & 0 \\ -\gamma_5 & & 1 & 0 \\ C_2 & & 0 & \gamma_{17} \end{bmatrix} \begin{bmatrix} \bar{y} \\ \bar{f} \\ \phi \end{bmatrix}$$

$$+ \begin{bmatrix} -1 & \dfrac{1}{1-\gamma_2} & 0 \\ -\gamma_5 & 0 & 1 \\ (\gamma_{15}-\gamma_{16}) & f_3 & 0 \end{bmatrix} \begin{bmatrix} \varepsilon_t^{\mathrm{s}} \\ \varepsilon_t^{\mathrm{d}} \\ \varepsilon_t^{\mathrm{m}} \end{bmatrix}$$

In this system the following substitutions have been made for notational simplicity:

$$a_5 = [\gamma_{11} - (1 + \gamma)(\gamma_{15} - \gamma_{16})]$$

$$b_3 = [\gamma_{11} - \gamma(\gamma_{15} - \gamma_{16})]$$

$$\lambda_0 = \gamma_{17}(\gamma_{15} - \gamma_{16}) \left(1 - \frac{\gamma_3}{1 - \gamma_2}\right)$$

$$\gamma_1 = \gamma_{17}(\gamma_{15} - \gamma_{16}) + \frac{\gamma_1}{1 - \gamma_2}$$

$$d_3 = \psi_d \left[\gamma_{15}\left(\frac{\gamma_{12}}{\gamma_{13}}\right) - 2\right] - \gamma_{17}$$

$$e_3 = \gamma_{17}(\gamma_{15} - \gamma_{16}) \frac{\gamma_3}{1 - \gamma_2} + \gamma_{11}(1 - \psi_p^*)\psi_p^*$$

$$q_0 = \gamma_{16} + \gamma_{17}(\gamma_{15} - \gamma_{16}) \frac{\gamma_0}{1 - \gamma_2} + \gamma_{15}\gamma_{17}$$

$$q_1 = \gamma_{15} + \gamma_{17}(\gamma_{15} - \gamma_{16}) \frac{\gamma_2}{1 - \gamma_2} + \gamma_{15}\gamma_{17}$$

$$c_2 = (\gamma_{15} - \gamma_{16}) \left(\frac{\gamma_{17}}{1 - \gamma_2} - 1\right)$$

$$f_3 = \gamma_{17} \frac{(\gamma_{15} - \gamma_{16})}{1 - \gamma_2}$$

Appendix B

Weiner–Kolmogorov procedure

The Weiner–Kolmogorov (W–K) k-step ahead, linear least-squares forecast is presented here.

Consider the first-order autoregressive process $(1-\rho L)y_t = \varepsilon_t$ where ε_t is white noise, $|\rho| < 1$. To obtain the expectation of y_t, k periods from now, based on all available information at time t, i.e. to obtain $E_t y_{t+k}$, we use the W–K prediction formula:

$$E_t y_{t+k} = \left[\frac{\rho(L)}{L^k}\right]_+ \varepsilon_t$$

Here $\rho(L)$ is $(1-\rho L)^{-1}$ and $[\ ]_+$ is the annihilator operator that ignores negative powers of L.

Substituting for the white noise from the given process:

$$E_t y_{t+k} = \left[\frac{\rho(L)}{L^k}\right]_+ \rho(L)^{-1} y_t$$

$$= \frac{\rho^k}{(1-\rho L)}(1-\rho L)y_t$$

Therefore, $E_t y_{t+k} = \rho^k y_t$ is the expectation of y_t in period $t+k$ based on all available information at time t.

Appendix C

System of equations: case II

The system of equations for case II can be reduced to the following four equations in quasi-reduced form:

$$\begin{bmatrix} (\gamma+\gamma_3) & -\gamma_3 & 0 & 0 \\ \beta_2 & \gamma_6 & 0 & 0 \\ -\beta_0 & (\gamma_8+\gamma_{10}-\gamma_{11}) & 0 & 0 \\ \beta_1 & (\gamma_{15}-\gamma_{11}) & \gamma_{12} & 0 \end{bmatrix} \begin{bmatrix} p_t \\ s_t \\ b_t^d \\ w_t \end{bmatrix} = \begin{bmatrix} \gamma & 0 & 0 & 0 \\ \gamma_5 & \gamma_6 & 0 & 0 \\ (\gamma_{11}-\gamma\gamma_9) & -\gamma_{11} & 0 & 0 \\ \gamma_{11} & (\gamma_{13}-\gamma_{11}) & 0 & 0 \end{bmatrix} \begin{bmatrix} E_t p_{t+1} \\ E_t s_{t+1} \\ E_t b_{t+1}^d \\ E_t w_{t+1} \end{bmatrix}$$

$$+ \begin{bmatrix} 0 & 0 & 0 & 0 \\ -\theta(\gamma_{15}-\gamma_{16}) & \theta & 0 & 0 \\ 0 & 0 & 0 & 0 \\ \theta(\gamma_{15}-\gamma_{16}) & -\theta & 0 & 0 \end{bmatrix} \begin{bmatrix} p_{t-1} \\ s_{t-1} \\ b_{t-1}^d \\ w_{t-1} \end{bmatrix}$$

$$+ \begin{bmatrix} \gamma_2\psi_g & -\gamma_0\psi_t & 0 & 0 \\ -\gamma_{15}(\theta+\alpha_1\psi_g) & \gamma_{16}(\theta+\alpha_1\psi t) & 0 & 0 \\ 0 & 0 & 0 & 0 \\ \gamma_{15}(\theta+\gamma_1\psi_g) & -\gamma_{16}(\theta+\gamma_1\psi_t) & 0 & 0 \end{bmatrix} \begin{bmatrix} g_{t-1} \\ t_{t-1} \\ \\ \\ \end{bmatrix}$$

$$+ \begin{bmatrix} -1 & 0 & 0 & 0 \\ -\gamma_5 & 1 & -\theta & 0 \\ \gamma_9 & 0 & 0 & -1 \\ 0 & 0 & \theta & 0 \end{bmatrix} \begin{bmatrix} \bar{y} \\ \bar{f} \\ \phi \\ k_n \end{bmatrix} + \begin{bmatrix} -1 & 1 & 0 & 0 \\ -\gamma_5 & 0 & 1 & 0 \\ \gamma_9 & 0 & 0 & 0 \\ 0 & 0 & 0 & 0 \end{bmatrix} \begin{bmatrix} \varepsilon_t^s \\ \varepsilon_t^d \\ \varepsilon_t^m \end{bmatrix}$$

Notes

Chapter 2 Interpreting budget deficits

1 The US unemployment rate fell to an all-time low of 5.6 per cent in June 1988. Some economists feel that the full-employment rate of 6 per cent is not time invariant, and that this basic rate of unemployment, or the 'natural' rate, rose in the 1970s and now has fallen.
2 See Baumol, W.J. and Blinder, A.S. (1985) *Economics, Principles and Policy*, Orlando, FL: Harcourt, Brace, Jovanovich, pp. 288–90, for a good discussion on this subject.
3 It is important to note that the standardized-employment deficit actually decreased in the final years of the Reagan administration. The dramatic increase from 1982 to 1986 was followed by a decline in 1987 and 1988, and this will be discussed in chapter 8.
4 For an excellent review chapter on the subject of budget deficit financing, see Dornbusch, R., and Fischer, S. (1987) *Macroeconomics*, New York: McGraw-Hill, pp. 581–623. We will be discussing deficit financing in detail in chapter 10.
5 Ibid., p. 597.

Chapter 3 Stabilization policies

1 See Lucas, R.E. (1977) 'Understanding business cycles', in *Carnegie–Rochester Series on Public Policy* 5: 7–29.
  It is worth mentioning that there is a relatively new body of literature on real business cycles, but the studies are few in number and the estimation methods are quite controversial.
2 Further discussion pertaining to time series analysis is relegated to chapter 11.
3 Mitchell, W.C. (1951) *What Happens During Business Cycles*, New York: National Bureau of Economic Research, and Gayer, A.D., Rostow, W.W., and Schwartz, A.J. (1953) *The Growth and Fluctuation of the British Economy, 1790–1850*, Oxford: Clarendon Press.
4 Lucas (1977) op. cit., pp. 7–10.

5 Lucas, R.E. (1973) 'Some international evidence on output–inflation tradeoffs', *American Economic Review* 63: 326–34, and Lucas (1977) op. cit., pp. 7–29.
6 Lucas (1977) op. cit., p. 10.
7 The natural unemployment rate of 6 per cent unemployment is evenly divided between frictional unemployment (workers voluntarily between jobs) and structural unemployment (workers with inadequate skills). This rate is determined by demographic factors such as the composition of the population, workers' tastes and preferences, and the level of technology. Hence the manipulation of the natural rate is not a macroeconomic policy objective.
8 I have included a very brief policy review of the classical and Keynesian frameworks in this chapter. A more detailed description can be found in any standard economics textbook.
9 Keynes, J.M. (1964) *The General Theory of Employment Interest and Money*, London: Harcourt, Brace, Jovanovich.
10 Carlson, K.M. (1987) 'Federal fiscal policy since the Employment Act of 1946', *The Federal Reserve Bank of St. Louis Review* 69: 14, has a good review and analysis of fiscal policy since 1947.

Chapter 4 A brief history of government expenditures and deficits from Truman to Reagan

1 See Parkin, M. (1984) *Macroeconomics*, Englewood Cliffs, NJ: Prentice-Hall, pp. 525–47, for a more detailed overview of US macroeconomic policy.
2 Ibid., p. 528.
3 The high-employment figures run from 1956 only, as that was when the Department of Commerce began revising these data.
4 With the exception of the Kennedy–Johnson administration.
5 The economic intuition and the framework for stagflation will be presented in chapter 5 when we discuss the demise of stabilization policies.

Chapter 5 Rational expectations and the demise of discretionary stabilization policies

1 Phelps, E.S. and Taylor, J.B. (1977) 'Stabilizing powers of monetary policy under rational expectations', *Journal of Political Economy* 85: 163–90. This paper falls in the class of models that comprise the new Keynesian theory of aggregate supply.
2 The points A and B on the labour supply and demand curves need not be in the same vertical line. They have been drawn this way in figure 5.1(c) to make the explanation a little simpler. In the real world, when points A and B might not be aligned, the equilibrium level of employment would be determined by point A, the new level of labour demand.

3 Adaptive expectations will be defined in greater detail later in this chapter.
4 This is a very intuitive introduction to a fairly technical concept. We will discuss rational expectations again later in this chapter and in chapter 6. In chapter 12 we will see how this concept is crucial in allowing us to solve for reduced-form solutions of some complex macroeconomic models.
5 These papers are, Taylor, J.B. (1979) 'Staggered wage setting in a macro model', *The American Economic Review* 69: 108–13, King, R.G. (1982) 'Monetary policy and the information content of prices', *Journal of Political Economy* 90: 247–90, and Gray, J.A. (1976) 'Wage indexation: a macroeconomic approach', *Journal of Monetary Economics* 2: 221–35.
6 Parkin, M. (1984) *Macroeconomics*, Englewood Cliffs, NJ: Prentice-Hall, p. 370.
7 Lucas, R.E. (1973) 'Some international evidence of output–inflation tradeoffs', *American Economic Review* 63: 326–34.

Chapter 6 Rational expectations: some common misconceptions

1 An expectation is said to be rational when the subjective expectation coincides with the conditional mathematical expectation based on all available information. This is from Muth, J.S. (1961) 'Rational expectations and the theory of price movements', *Econometrica* 29: 315–35. The second paper is Lucas, R.E. (1973) 'Some international evidence on output–inflation tradeoffs', *American Economic Review* 63: 326–34. Here he constructs his 'islands' model, and this paper was largely responsible for the surge in rational expectations research. We will discuss the other related research in chapter 11.
2 Lucas (1973) op. cit., pp. 328–30.
3 Lucas, R.E. (1974) 'Econometric policy evaluation: a critique', *Carnegie–Rochester Conference Series on Public Policy* 1: 19–46.
4 See Parkin, M. (1984) *Macroeconomics*, Englewood Cliffs, NJ: Prentice-Hall, pp. 448–51, for a superb introduction to macroeconomic policy under rational expectations.
5 This is the version presented by Douglas McTaggart, a Lucas student in the graduate macro class at the Virginia Polytechnic Institute and State University, in 1984.
6 Alternatively, this could be written as $y_t = g(x_{t-1}, y_{t-1}, u_{t-1})$.
7 See Lucas, R.E. and Sargent, T.J. (1979) 'After Keynesian macroeconomics', Federal Reserve Bank of Minneapolis *Quarterly Review* 3: 1–23, and Kydland, F.E. and Prescott, E.C. (1977) 'Rules rather than discretion: the inconsistency of optimal plans', *Journal of Political Economy* 85: 126–42.

Chapter 7 Supply-side economics

1 Feldstein, M. (1986) 'Some "supply-side" propositions', *American Economic Review* 76: 26.
2 See Henderson, D.R. (1988) 'Are we all supply-siders now?', Paper presented at the meeting of the Western Economic Association in Los Angeles, 2 July.
3 Parkin, M. (1984) *Macroeconomics*, Englewood Cliffs, NJ: Prentice-Hall, pp. 564–80, is strongly advocated for a discussion on the role of government intervention.
4 We are, however, seeing a change in the policies of the Soviet Union since the attempted reforms of Mr Gorbachev.
5 Work and leisure are both normal goods. As taxes increase, individuals 'consume' more work in the present period and substitute leisure to the future period. Implicit in this intertemporal substitution of leisure is the assumption that the tax increases are temporary in nature.
6 Henderson (1988) op. cit., p. 15. See also Laffer, A.B. (1981) 'Government exactions and revenue deficiencies', *Cato Journal* 1: 45–52, and Anderson, M. (1988) *Revolution*, New York: Harcourt, Brace, Jovanovich, pp. 152–6.
7 Fullerton, D. (1980) 'On the possibility of an inverse relationship between tax rates and government revenues', *National Bureau of Economic Research*, working paper no. 467, and Blinder, A.S. (1981) in *The Supply-Side Effects of Economic Policy*, Boston, MA: Kluwer–Nijhoff, pp. 81–92.
8 Secretary Mellon's speech is discussed in sufficient detail in Wanniski, J. (1978) *The Way the World Works*, New York: Touchstone, pp. 120–1.
9 Mirrlees, J.A. (1971) 'An exploration in the theory of optimum income taxation', *Review of Economic Studies* 31: 175–208.
10 Anderson (1988) op. cit., p. 12.

Chapter 8 'Reaganomics' and deficits: success, failure, or incomplete revolution?

1 See Wanniski, J. (1978) *The Way the World Works*, New York: Touchstone.
2 Perhaps the most vocal advocate of supply-side economics amongst the politicians was Congressman Jack Kemp.
3 An excellent review of Reaganomics in retrospect is Bartley, J. (1988) 'Whither voodoo economics?', *Wall Street Journal*, 19 August, p. 20, and Feldstein, M. (1986) 'Supply-side economics: old truths and new claims', *American Economic Review* 76: 20–30.
4 A good article by the arch-critic of Reaganomics is, Blinder, A.S. (1987) 'A handicapper's guide to macroeconomics', *Business Week*, 9 February, pp. 16–21.
5 Thurow, L. (1982) 'Supply-side economics', *New York Times Magazine* 17 October.

6 Blinder (1987) op. cit., pp. 16–20.
7 Ibid., p. 18.
8 Anderson, M. (1988) *Revolution*, New York: Harcourt, Brace, Jovanovich, pp. 152–6.
9 Lindsey, L.B. (1987) 'Individual taxpayer response to tax cuts: 1982–84: with implications for the revenue maximizing tax rate', *Journal of Public Economics* 33:203–16.
10 This quote appears in Bartley (1988) op. cit., p. 20.
11 Laffer, A.B. (1981) 'Government exactions and revenue deficiencies', *Cato Journal* 1: 45–52.
12 Cox, W.M. (1984) 'What is the rule for financing government debt', Federal Reserve Bank of Dallas *Economic Review* September, pp. 25–31, is an interesting paper where it is shown that all the interest payments since 1977 have been bond financed, or the interest payments have simply been rolled over.

Chapter 9 Another view of the 1980s deficits

1 Charles Schultze's comment appears in Baumol, W.J. and Blinder, A.S. (1985) *Economics, Principles and Policy*, New York: Harcourt, Brace, Jovanovich, p. 211.
2 Ibid., p. 212.
3 The mechanics of budget deficit financing as well as the dynamics of the intertemporal government budget constraint will be discussed in detail in chapter 11.
4 Sustainability, both strong and weak, is defined in chapter 11.

Chapter 10 Financing budget deficits

1 According to Sargent, T.J. (1986) 'Interpreting the Reagan deficits', Federal Reserve Bank of San Francisco *Economic Review* No. 4: 5–12, Wallace advanced his ideas orally, which in turn led to a spate of papers later.
2 See Cook, T.Q. and Summers, B.J. (1981) *Instruments of the Money Market*, Richmond, VA: Federal Reserve Bank of Richmond, pp. 1–30, for a thorough review of the money market and T-bills.
3 The model, and the macroeconomic implications of my results, are presented in chapters 11–13.
4 Sargent (1984) op. cit., p. 10.
5 Ibid., p. 10.
6 Baumol, W.S. and Blinder, A.S. (1985) *Macroeconomics, Principles and Policy*, New York: Harcourt, Brace, Jovanovich, p. 291.
7 For a more complete history of capital inflows, see Glick, R. (1987) 'Foreign capital inflows', Federal Reserve Bank of San Francisco *Weekly Letter* 30 October.
8 These figures were compiled by Ohmae, K. (1987) in 'Deficit myths', *Japan Times* 12 October.

9 Cox, W.M. (1984) 'What is the rule for financing government debt?', Federal Reserve Bank of Dallas *Economic Review* September, pp. 25–31.
10 Sargent, T.J. and Wallace, N. (1981) 'Some unpleasant monetarist arithmetic', Federal Reserve Bank of Minneapolis *Quarterly Review* pp. 1–17.
11 This example is along the lines of the simple example provided by Parkin, M. (1984) in *Macroeconomics*, Englewood Cliffs, NJ: Prentice-Hall, pp. 459–60.

Chapter 11 The sustainability of deficits: model description

1 This approach is related to that presented in Dornbusch, R. and Fischer, S. (1984) *Macroeconomics: Update*, New York: McGraw-Hill, pp. 1–25.
2 It should be noted here that the model in this book incorporates a flexible exchange rate regime.
3 Stability is viewed in the context of the increase in the size of the budget deficit over time, along the lines of the simple Dornbusch model discussed earlier.
4 S.J. Turnovsky discusses this in greater detail in his book (1977) *Macroeconomic Analysis and Stabilization Policy*, Cambridge, Cambridge University Press.
5 This expression is obtained from the standard national income accounting identity.
6 See McTaggart (1985, 1988) for a neat discussion of these mechanisms.
7 The significance of the imperfect substitutability of domestic and foreign goods comes into play in preventing real interest parity and thus creating a mechanism that allows domestic real rates to differ from foreign real rates.
8 We assume that the log of an expected value is equal to the expected value of the log of the variable, i.e. $\ln (E_t X_{t+1}) = E_t X_{t+1}$.
9 This is a fairly standard short-term rational expectations aggregate supply function. The systematic supply term is assumed to be independent of changes in fiscal policy, i.e. the marginal product of labour is not a function of changes in fiscal policy and the aggregate supply is therefore not directly affected by increases in government spending. Furthermore, equation (11.6) abstracts from the effect of capital accumulation on the trend rate of growth of the domestic output.
10 Turnovsky (1977) op. cit., emphasizes the importance of incorporating beginning period wealth in the analysis of government policies.

Chapter 13 Sustainability under exogenous domestic money

1 The reason why the increase in domestic aggregate demand manifests itself in a 100 per cent complete overflow is the following. There are

two goods (or two composite goods) in this economy, and these are domestic and foreign goods. They are similar but not identical to each other. Individuals therefore behave in a rational manner and choose the goods with a lower price, i.e. they choose either the domestic or the foreign goods and not a combination of both. This is why the overflow is 'complete'.

2 This is a summary of my paper (1988) 'Real interest rates, inflation, and the sustainability of bond-financed deficits: an open economy perspective', presented at the meeting of the Western Economics Association in Los Angeles, June 1988.

Chapter 14 International policy co-ordination

1 See Glick, R. (1986) 'International policy coordination', Federal Reserve Bank of San Francisco *Weekly Letter*, 13 June.
2 Exact nominal exchange rates were very difficult to maintain, so a range, or a 'band', of acceptable exchange rate values was adopted.
3 Cheng, H.S. (1988) 'Monetary policy 1987', Federal Reserve Bank of San Francisco *Weekly Letter*, 12 February, is a good review of this subject.
4 Feldstein, M. (1987) 'The end of policy coordination', *Wall Street Journal* 9 November, p. 16.
5 A. Greenspan was cited in (1987) *Wall Street Journal*, 20 October, p. 1.

Chapter 15 Sustainability with endogenous money creation: case II

1 Research pertaining to the 'hard-fall' versus the 'soft fall' of the dollar gained momentum in 1984–7 as the dollar reached new heights. The proponents of the 'hard fall' scenario argue that since the domestic and foreign real interest rate differential is negligible, the strength of the dollar can only be attributed to a speculative bubble. This bubble, based on short-term irrational forecasts, is by definition not supported by market fundamentals, and will therefore eventually burst, resulting in the 'hard fall' of the dollar.

Proponents of the 'soft fall' believe that continuous debt monetization on the part of the Federal Reserve will gradually erode the US and foreign real interest rate differential, with the dollar decreasing steadily with increasing domestic inflation. See Krugman (1985) for an excellent discussion of this subject.

Chapter 16 Some macroeconomic implications of the crash of 1987

1 See Kristol, M. (1987) 'Look at 1962, not 1929', *Wall Street Journal* 28 October.

2 Another way to interpret the points made here is by using the speculative bubble literature. A speculative bubble is a movement in the price of an asset that is not driven by fundamentals. Some economists have argued that speculative bubbles can exist even in markets that are otherwise 'efficient'. The bubble explanation, which is quite controversial, reconciles the magnitude of the decline in stock prices with the relatively small changes in market fundamentals.

See Pozdena, R.J. (1988) 'October postmortem', Federal Reserve Bank of San Francisco *Weekly Letter* 29 April for an excellent little summary of the events of 19 October 1987.

3 We studied this link when we did the national savings identity.

4 Two useful articles are Melloan, G. (1987) 'How much will the crash effect the real sector?', *Wall Street Journal* 17 November, p. 39, and Higgins, B. (1988) 'Is a recession inevitable this year?' Federal Reserve Bank of Kansas City *Economic Review* January, pp. 3–16.

5 Melloan (1987) op. cit., p. 39.

Bibliography

Anderson, M. (1988) *Revolution*, New York: Harcourt, Brace, Jovanovich, pp. 152–6.

Aoki, B. and Canzoneri, M. (1979) 'Reduced forms of rational expectations models', *Quarterly Journal of Economics* February, pp. 59–71.

Barro, R.J. (1976) 'Rational expectations and the role of monetary policy', *Journal of Monetary Economics* 11: 1–32.

—— (1980) 'Federal debt policy and the effects of public debt shocks', *Journal of Money, Credit and Banking* November pp. 747–52.

—— (1980) 'A capital market in an equilibrium business cycle model', *Econometrica* 48: 1393–417.

Bartley, J. (1988) 'Whither voodoo economics?', *Wall Street Journal* 19 August, p. 20.

Baumol, W.S. and Blinder, A.S. (1985) *Macroeconomics, Principles and Policy*, New York: Harcourt, Brace, Jovanovich.

Blinder, A.S. (1981) *The Supply-Side Effects of Economic Policy*, Boston, MA: Kluwer–Nijhoff.

—— (1987) 'A handicapper's guide to macroeconomics', *Business Week* 9 February, pp. 16–21.

Blinder, A.S. and Solow, R.M. (1973) 'Does fiscal policy matter?' *Journal of Public Economics* 2: 319–38.

Branson, W.H. (1977) 'Asset markets and relative prices in exchange-rate determination'. Sozialwissenschaftliche Analen, 1: 69–89.

—— (1985) 'The dynamic interaction of exchange rates and trade flows', *National Bureau of Economic Research*, paper no. 1780, December.

Branson, W. and Frenkel, J. (1985) 'Causes of appreciation and volatility of the dollar', *National Bureau of Economic Research*, working paper no. 1777, December.

Burdekin, R.C.K. (1988) 'Interaction between central bank behaviour and fiscal policy: the US case', *Applied Economics* 20: February.

Burdekin, R.C.K. and Wohar, M. (1988) 'Deficit monetization, output and inflation in the United States, 1923–1982', Paper presented at the June 1988 meeting of the Western Economic Association in Los Angeles.

Carlson, K.M. (1987) 'Federal fiscal policy since the Employment Act of 1946', *The Federal Reserve Bank of St. Louis Review* 69: 14.
Cheng, H.S. (1988) 'Monetary policy 1987', Federal Reserve Bank of San Francisco *Weekly Letter* 12 February.
Cook, T.Q. and Summers, B.J. (1980) *Instruments of the Money Market*, Richmond, VA: Federal Reserve Bank of Richmond.
Cox, W.M. (1984) 'What is the rule for financing government debt?', Federal Reserve Bank of Dallas *Economic Review* September, pp. 25–31.
—— (1985) 'Inflation and permanent government debt', Federal Reserve Bank of Dallas *Economic Review* May, pp. 12–26.
Dornbusch, R. (1976) 'Expectations and exchange rate dynamics', *Journal of Political Economy* LXXXIV: 1161–76.
Dornbusch, R. and Fischer, S. (1985) 'The open economy: implications for monetary and fiscal policy', *National Bureau of Economic Research* working paper no. 1422, August.
—— (1987) *Macroeconomics*, New York: McGraw-Hill.
Driskill, R. and McCafferty, S. (1980) 'Exchange-rate variability, real and monetary shocks, and the degree of capital mobility under rational expectations', *Quarterly Journal of Economics* XCV November: 577–86.
Dwyer, G.P. (1982) 'Inflation and government deficits', *Economic Inquiry* 20: 315–29.
Evans, P. (1985) 'Do large deficits produce high interest rates?' *American Economic Review* 75: 68–87.
Feldstein, M. (1986) 'Some "supply-side" propositions', *American Economic Review* 76: 26.
—— (1986) 'Supply-side economics: old truths and new claims', *American Economic Review* 76: 20–30.
—— (1987) 'The end of policy coordination', *Wall Street Journal* 9 November, p. 16.
Fleming, J.M. (1962) 'Domestic financial policies under fixed and under floating exchange rates', *IMF Staff Papers* 9: 369–72.
Floyd, J. (1969) 'Monetary and fiscal policies in a world of capital mobility', *Review of Economic Studies* 36: 503–18.
Frenkel, J.A. and Razin, A. (1984) 'Federal policies, debt and international economic interdependence', *National Bureau of Economic Research* working paper no. 1266, January.
—— (1984) 'The international transmission of fiscal expenditures and budget deficits in the world economy', *National Bureau of Economic Research* working paper no. 1527, December.
—— (1986) 'Deficits with distortionary taxes: international dimensions', *National Bureau of Economic Research* working paper no. 2080, November.
Fullerton, D. (1980) 'On the possibility of an inverse relationship between tax rates and government revenues', *National Bureau of Economic Research* working paper no. 467, March.
Gayer, A.D., Rostov, W.W., and Schwartz, A.J. (1953) *The Growth and*

Fluctuation of the British Economy, 1790–1850, Oxford: Clarendon Press.
Glick, R. (1987) 'Foreign capital inflows', Federal Reserve Bank of San Francisco *Weekly Letter* 30 October.
Gray, J.A. (1976) 'Wage indexation: a macroeconomic approach', *Journal of Monetary Economics* 2: 221–35.
Helliwell, J.F. (1969) 'Monetary and fiscal policy for an open economy', *Oxford Economic Papers* 21: 31–55.
Henderson, D.R. (1988) 'Are we all supply-siders now?' Paper presented at the meeting of the Western Economic Association in Los Angeles, 2 July.
Higgins, B. (1988) 'Is a recession inevitable this year?', Federal Reserve Bank of Kansas City *Economic Review* January, pp. 3–16.
Hirschhorn, E. (1984) 'Rational expectations and the effects of government debt', *Journal of Monetary Economics* 14: 55–70.
Hoelscher, G. (1986) 'New evidence on deficits and interest rates', *Journal of Money, Credit and Banking* 18: 1–17.
Keynes, J.M. (reprinted 1964) *The General Theory of Employment, Interest and Money*, London: Harcourt, Brace, Jovanovich.
Kimbrough, K.P. (1983) 'Price, output, and exchange rate movements in the open economy', *Journal of Monetary Economics* 11: 24–44.
King, R.G. (1982) 'Monetary policy and the information content of prices', *Journal of Political Economy* 90: 247–90.
King, R.G., Wallace, N., and Weber, W. (1987) 'Nonfundamental uncertainty and exchange rates', Federal Reserve Bank of Minneapolis working paper, July.
Kristol, M. (1987) 'Look at 1962, not 1929', *Wall Street Journal* 28 October.
Krugman, P.R. (1985) 'Is the strong dollar sustainable?' *National Bureau of Economic Research* working paper no. 1644, June.
Kydland, F.E. and Prescott, E.C. (1977) 'Rules rather than discretion: the inconsistency of optimal plans', *Journal of Political Economy* 85: 126–42.
Laffer, A.B. (1981) 'Government exactions and revenue deficiencies', *Cato Journal* 1: 45–52.
Langdana, F. (1987) 'The sustainability of bond-financed deficits under different monetary regimes: an open economy perspective', Doctoral Dissertation, Virginia Polytechnic Institute and State University, May.
Lindsey, L.B. (1987) 'Individual taxpayer response to tax cuts: 1982–84: with implications for the revenue maximizing tax rate', *Journal of Public Economics* 33: 203–11.
Lucas, R.E. and Sargent, T.J. (1979) 'After Keynesian macroeconomics', tradeoffs', *American Economic Review* 63: 326–34.
—— (1974) 'Econometric policy evaluation: a critique', *Carnegie–Rochester Conference Series on Public Policy* 1: 19–46.
—— (1977) 'Understanding business cycles', *Carnegie–Rochester Series on Public Policy* 5: 7–29.

—— (1984) *Studies in Business-Cycle Theory*, Cambridge, MA: MIT Press.
Lucas, R.E. and Sargent, T.J. (1979) 'After Keynesian macroeconomics', Federal Reserve Bank of Minneapolis *Quarterly Review* 3: 1–23.
McCallum, B.T. (1984) 'Are bond-financed deficits inflationary? A Ricardian analysis', *Journal of Political Economy* 92: 123–5.
—— (1988) 'Theoretical analysis of the demand for money', Federal Reserve Bank of Richmond *Economic Review* 74/1: January/February.
McKinnon, R.I. (1969) 'Portfolio balance and international payments' in R.A. Mundell and A. Swoboda (eds) *Monetary Problems of the International Economy*, Chicago: University of Chicago Press.
McTaggart, D. (1985) 'Commercial policy and output stabilization', Virginia Polytechnic Institute working paper no. 126, Virginia Polytechnic Institute and State University, June.
—— (1988) 'An approach to modeling macroeconomic linkages in trade models with an application to agriculture', Virginia Polytechnic Institute working paper no. 287, Virginia Polytechnic Institute, December 1986, revised 1988.
Melloan, G. (1987) 'How much will the crash affect the real sector?', *Wall Street Journal* 17 November, p. 39.
Mirrlees, J.A. (1971) 'An exploration in the theory of optimum income taxation', *Review of Economic Studies* 31: 175–208.
Mitchell, W.C. (1951) *What Happens During Business Cycles?* New York: National Bureau of Economic Research.
Mundell, R.A. (1962) 'The appropriate use of monetary and fiscal policy for internal and external stability', *IMF Staff Papers* 9: 70–77.
—— (1968) *International Economics*, New York: Macmillan.
Muth, J.S. (1961) 'Rational expectations and the theory of price movements', *Econometrica* 29: 315–53.
Nguyen, D. and Turnovsky, S.J. (1983) 'The dynamic effects of fiscal and monetary policies under bond financing', *Journal of Monetary Economics* 11: 45–71.
Oates, W.E. (1966) 'Budget balance and equilibrium income: a comment on the efficiency of fiscal and monetary policy in an open economy', *Journal of Finance* 21: 489–98.
Ohmae, K. (1987) 'Deficit myths', *Japan Times*, 12 October 1987.
Parkin, M. (1984) *Macroeconomics*, Englewood Cliffs, NJ: Prentice-Hall.
Phelps, E.S. and Taylor, J.B. (1977) 'Stabilizing powers of monetary policy under rational expectations', *Journal of Political Economy* 85: 163–90.
Pozdena, R.J. (1988) 'October postmortem', Federal Reserve Bank of San Francisco *Weekly Letter* 29 April.
Sargent, T.J. (1979) *Macroeconomic Theory*, New York: Academic Press.
—— (1986) *Rational Expectations and Inflation*, New York: Harper & Row.
—— (1986) 'Interpreting the Reagan deficits', Federal Reserve Bank of San Francisco *Economic Review* no. 4.

—— (1987) *Dynamic Macroeconomic Theory,* Cambridge, MA: Harvard University Press.

Sargent, T.J. and Wallace, N. (1985, 1985) 'Some unpleasant monetarist arithmetic', Federal Research Bank of Minneapolis *Quarterly Review* fall 1981, pp. 1–17. Reprinted winter 1985.

Scarth, W.M. (1987) 'Can economic growth make monetarist arithmetic pleasant?', *Southern Economic Journal* 53: 1028–36.

Takayama, A. (1969) 'The effects of fiscal and monetary policies under flexible and fixed exchange rates', *Canadian Journal of Economics* 2: 190–209.

Taylor, J.B. (1979) 'Staggered wage setting in a macro model', *The American Economic Review* 12: 108–13.

Thurow, L. (1982) 'Supply-side economics', *New York Times Magazine* 17 October.

Tower, L. (1972) 'The short-run effects of monetary and fiscal policy under fixed and flexible exchange rates', *Economic Record* 48: 411–23.

Turnovsky, S.J. (1976) 'The relative stability of alternative exchange rate systems in the presence of random disturbances', *Journal of Money Credit and Banking* 3: 29–50.

—— (1977) *Macroeconomic Analysis and Stabilization Policy,* Cambridge, Cambridge University Press.

—— (1983) 'Wage indexation and exchange market intervention in a small open economy', *Canadian Journal of Economics,* 16: November, 574–92.

—— (1986) 'The dynamics of fiscal policy in an open economy', *Journal of International Economics* 6: 111–42.

—— (1986) 'The relative stability of alternative exchange rate systems in the presence of random disturbances', *Journal of Money, Credit and Banking* February, pp. 29–50.

Turnovsky, S.J. and Wohar, M.E. (1987) 'Alternative modes of deficit financing and endogenous monetary and fiscal policy 1932–1982', *Journal of Applied Economics* January.

Wanniski, J. (1978) *The Way the World Works,* New York: Touchstone.

Young, J.P. (1925) *European Currency and Finance,* Washington, DC: Government Printing Office.

Zahid, K.H. (1988) 'Government budget deficits and interest rates: the evidence since 1971, using alternative deficit measures', *Southern Economic Journal* 54: 725–31.

Index